# Cafe Wisconsin Cookbook

# Cafe
# WISCONSIN
~ ~ ~
# Cookbook

*Joanne Raetz Stuttgen and Terese Allen*

**THE UNIVERSITY OF WISCONSIN PRESS**

The University of Wisconsin Press
1930 Monroe Street
Madison, Wisconsin 53711

www.wisc.edu/wisconsinpress/

3 Henrietta Street
London WC2E 8LU, England

Designed by Jane Tenenbaum

5   4   3   2   1

Printed in the United States of America

Library of Congress Cataloging-in-Publication Data

Stuttgen, Joanne Raetz, 1961–
Cafe Wisconsin cookbook / Joanne Raetz Stuttgen and Terese Allen.
p. cm.
Includes index.
ISBN 0-299-22274-8 (pbk. : alk. paper)
1. Cookery, American—Midwestern style. 2. Cookery—Wisconsin.
3. Restaurants—Wisconsin. I. Allen, Terese. II. Title.
TX715.2.M53S78        2007
641.5'9775—dc22        2006031774

# Contents

# Preface

Crispy corned beef hash. Roast beef and a mound of mashed potatoes smothered in homemade gravy. Puckery-sweet lemon pie with a crown of foamy meringue.

Sound good to you? We thought so. Welcome to *Cafe Wisconsin Cookbook*.

*Cafe Wisconsin Cookbook* is a spin-off from the second edition of *Cafe Wisconsin* (2004), the guide to Wisconsin's down-home cafes first written by Joanne Raetz Stuttgen in 1993. She traveled more than twelve thousand miles in six months, visiting old business districts and main streets in search of the ultimate cafe, the perfect slice of homemade pie, and the meaning of life in diners across the state.

In aptly named eateries like the Coffee Cup, Main Street, and Chatterbox, cafe owners and customers come together over plates of traditional midwestern farm food: meat and potatoes, vegetables, and baked goods, especially pie. They forge bonds of community and friendship and strengthen collective and individual identity with dishes like traditional Bohemian kolaches and Grandma's butterscotch pie. Occasionally, they create an entirely new and unique identity with idiosyncratic yet delicious inventions of their own, such as the multitiered Bob Burger. Whether as pervasive as Friday night fish fry or as one-of-a-kind as chicken enchilada soup, cafe fare is a traveler's solace, a region's treasure, an adventure eater's delight. Now you can savor it anew, by creating cafe favorites in your own kitchen. Think of it as going out to eat by eating in.

The genesis of this book—or at least its early possibility—occurred when we two authors first met, not long after the first edition of *Cafe Wisconsin* was released. It was a "had to happen" encounter. Terese Allen, a former-chef-turned-cookbook-author and Wisconsin-ophile, had just completed her own statewide exploration of farmers' markets and was about to embark on another journey investigating butcher shops, cheese factories, and other specialty shops. Knowing that a guide to homey, good-eatin' establishments would help her avoid the heartless fare of fast-food joints during her travels, Terese was quick to buy a copy of *Cafe Wisconsin*. Reading it, she discovered that Joanne was as happily obsessed with regional foods as she was. When Joanne appeared at a Madison bookstore to promote her book, Terese came calling and introduced herself.

That's when our food talk began. For several years it was a mere appetizer, an occasional and largely long-distance dialogue carried out through e-mail that covered everything from cafes (of course) and bakeries to church suppers and food festivals. These are topics that lie at the intersection of our shared passions. Joanne is a material culture folklorist with a thing for foodways. Terese is a "foodist"—a passionate food writer who aims a folkloric "lens" on her subjects. We'd been content with nibbling our way through common interests until Joanne proposed a good idea to the good folks at the University of Wisconsin Press. Their enthusiasm put our talk to work. And the work became *Cafe Wisconsin Cookbook.*

We started with a fairly straightforward goal: to bring the cafe experience home by sharing delicious recipes from top cafes and by telling great cafe stories (which, despite two story-filled editions of *Cafe Wisconsin,* never seem to come to an end). We wanted home cooks to be able to prepare what has become, more and more in recent decades, the nearly exclusive culinary niche of cafe and family restaurant cooks: classic pot roasts, country-style pies, long-simmered soups, heritage specialties—the whole, soul-satisfying spectrum of Wisconsin cafe fare.

So we invited each of the owners of the 133 cafes featured in *Cafe Wisconsin* to contribute recipes, with many asked to submit specific dishes that Joanne had encountered on her statewide food foray. A handful of owners responded quickly and eagerly, returning handwritten recipes for everything from side dishes and soups to daily plate specials and desserts. Others had to be gently prodded with follow-up letters, and then less gently pushed with direct phone calls. Should we admit it? There were times we resorted to downright begging.

For several reasons, it wasn't easy collecting the number and variety of recipes we wanted. Cafe owners are very busy people, often working an average of twelve to fourteen hours a day, juggling everything from cooking and baking to ordering supplies, managing the help, and dealing with unexpected crises like the breakdown of equipment. It is difficult to catch an owner over the phone at a time when he or she is available to talk, so we often had to schedule a time to call back and collect recipes over the phone. Some cafe owners were hesitant to divulge secret recipes, fearing that people would stop coming in if they could make their favorite dishes at home. Others took the opposite position and reasoned that if people liked what they made at home, they'd be more likely to come in to see what else the cafe had to offer.

Perhaps the most significant handicap to collecting recipes is that written recipes often do not exist. Many cafe owners or their cooks told us that they cooked by "memory" rather than from written instructions. In a sidebar in chapter 6, Terese explores cooking by "rhythm"—a kind of sixth sense a cook is born with or develops with years of experience. This intuition or gift is seen in cooks who can look at a photograph of a dish and re-create it; who can decipher a dish by merely tasting it; or who can look in the pantry and create a winning daily plate or soup special with what's on hand. For cooks like these, writing down a recipe often meant setting aside time to put ingredients and rote methods into words. This occasionally led to errors in measurements, glosses in instructions, and overlooked ingredients.

Terese tested the recipes in her home kitchen. Most presented no trouble, but others required several calls to cafe owners or cooks, and some recipes required multiple testings before she was confident that they would be successful for a home cook. While Joanne collected recipes from cafe owners, she envied Terese for having all the fun. Terese got to eat. Joanne was left salivating over words that were full of promise but completely lacking in flavor.

Terese is quick to point out, however, that testing over 150 recipes has issues of its own. One is how to consume all of the food. Terese's husband, JB, and friends willingly participated in dinner parties and taste-testings, and she took food to potlucks, meetings, and other gatherings. Then there is the challenge of reducing a recipe for a forty-pound roast that might last a few days in a cafe to one that will feed a family of four for Sunday dinner, or of finding the right words to transform a "simple" technique like crimping a pie crust into readily understood written instructions. Other trials include finding appropriate substitutes for commercial products unavailable for home use, converting instructions for commercial equipment such as convection ovens and malt mixers to those for home kitchen appliances, and dealing with recipes that contradict instinct and experience—like the pie crust recipe that calls not for ice-cold but boiling water. (Terese notes that in this case, you try it, it works well, and you move on.)

Throughout the collecting and testing process, we constantly monitored the recipes coming in against those we still needed. We had determined early on that we wanted *Cafe Wisconsin Cookbook* to be organized like a menu, with each chapter representing a type of meal or a type of food. As recipes were received, we noted which chapters remained scant. Joanne then began asking specifically for soups or baked goods. In this way, the cookbook began to fill up and chapters began to balance out. We find it intriguing and also highly indicative of Wisconsinites' fondness for sweets that the last chapter—Pies and Other Desserts—has more recipes than any other. When given the choice as to what recipes to contribute, many cafe owners opted for pie. (Rather sheepishly, Joanne also admits to personally requesting a disproportionate number of recipes for pie.)

Our growing collection of recipes, accompanied by stories, comments, and instructions of cafe owners and cooks, inspired many ideas for sidebars and essays. Terese's commentary focuses on culinary asides and tips—a kind of chef's tour of *Cafe Wisconsin*. Joanne's sidebars include excerpts from *Cafe Wisconsin,* personal narratives, and what Terese describes as "folkloric ruminations" on food history and traditions. When an idea for a sidebar struck, we conferred with each other and then sat down at our own keyboards and put it into words.

As an actual cookbook emerged out of our initial conception and plan, some exciting things began to happen. We recognized and wrote about our occasional divergence in preferences of taste—as in the case of real whipped cream and nondairy whipped topping. We also discovered the differences in our culinary knowledge and experience. Our sidebars developed into a sometimes spirited dialogue in which one writer's opinions were tempered by the other's perspective.

Occasionally, Terese offered solutions to Joanne's trials in the kitchen, as in "Cream Pie Woes" on page 157. In addition, Joanne's tendency to ask "Why?" about common culinary methods and techniques led Terese to address similar unspoken questions by home cooks who would use the cookbook.

Clearly our food talk had been kicked up a notch!

As a recurrent theme in *Cafe Wisconsin Cookbook,* the meeting and mediation of differences also play out in the cross-cultural examination of Wisconsin food and food traditions. What is cooked and eaten in Wisconsin's small town cafes identifies us as Wisconsinites but also connects us to people in other places. For example, the Cornish pasties prepared by Helena Lawinger at the Red Rooster Cafe in Mineral Point are important symbols of the community's heritage shared by others in Michigan's Upper Peninsula, and the recipe for Amish cream pie from M & M Cafe in Monticello is a variation of an Indiana specialty.

We are happy that you have picked up the *Cafe Wisconsin Cookbook* and invite you to join us on our journey through Cafe Wisconsin. Come on. Let's go out to eat by eating in.

# Acknowledgments

Too many cooks may spoil the soup, but there's no such thing as too many recipe testers. Each one's approach is different and therefore helpful when a cookbook author is trying to "put pan to paper." I'm grateful to the kind cooks who buttressed my kitchen tests with their own: Lucia Allen-Voreis, Punky Egan, Paul Lyne, and Emil Sattler. I also appreciate the friends, neighbors, and colleagues who were "taste-testers," and those who kept my refrigerator from exploding—and my weight gain lower—by taking leftovers home. A special salute to Karen Faster, Janie Capito, Virginia Evangelist, and Jennifer Buxton, who listened and gave primo advice (and only when asked). A tip of the hat to Madison's *Isthmus* newspaper, for which I pen the "Local Flavor" column and from which I adapted a few of the sidebars herein. Here's to Joanne Raetz Stuttgen, for the opportunity of this book, to staff at the University of Wisconsin Press, for their fine work publishing it, and to the incredibly hard-working, magic-making cafe folks featured in it. Finally, a ba-jillion thank you's to my husband, Jim Block: go-to guy, hot beef connoisseur, love of my life.

I dedicate this book to my cousin and oldest friend, Susie Regan, whom I cherish more than mashed potatoes and gravy.—T. A.

A special thank you to Cathy Weiss, Joanne Flemming, Mark and Peter Stuttgen, and the staff at University of Wisconsin Press, especially Carla Aspelmeier, Rick Marolt, Diana Cook, Raphael Kadushin, and Adam Mehring.—J. S.

## CAFE OWNERS/CONTRIBUTORS

Perry Andropolis and Ann Andropolis, Perry's Cherry Diner, Sturgeon Bay; Jerry Bechard, Norske Nook, Osseo; Brenda Beise, Brenda's Village Cafe, Exeland; Jenell and Ralph Britton, Main Dish Family Restaurant, Luck; Pam and Byrdie Chamberlin, Curve-In Cafe, Redgranite; Deb and Bob Chonos (former owners), Old Store Cafe and Deli, Dale; Mark and Laura Chrest, Country Cafe, Black River Falls; Rosemary and Kevin Clarke, Rudy's Diner, Brillion; Sheri and Jim Coldwell, Village Haus, Fall Creek; Cecelia Cruse, Sand Creek Cafe, Sand Creek; Mike and Mary Davis, M & M Cafe, Monticello; Sherri Dessart, Country Cafe, Babcock; Mark and Becky Dittel, Crystal Cafe, Phillips; Connie and Jim Farrell, Clinton Kitchen, Clinton; Owen and Joan Farrell, OJ's

Midtown Restaurant, Gillett; Denise J. Fischer, Denise's Cafe, Randolph; John and Dana Glaubitz, Brick House Cafe, Barronett; Diane Gray, Diane's Restaurant (formerly Gus and Ann's), Wittenberg; Beth Groom and Corliss "Corky" Mead, Hayseed Cafe, Wauzeka; Kendall and Trish Gulseth, Koffee Kup, Stoughton; Diane Hess and Nicole Jackson, Country Gals Cafe, Wonewoc; Faye and Dale Hillner, Faye's Dinky Diner, Eagle River; Wendy and Terry Holman, Wendy's Place, Minong; Chris and Gary Jacobs, Village Kitchen, Casco; Paula and Ed Jenneman, Stacker Cafe, Cornell; Bob and Nance Klapper and June Klapper Otto, Wolf River Diner, Fremont; Larry and Carol Van Lankvelt (former owners), Tucker's Inn, Little Chute; Joe and Kathy Lass, Wolf Pack Cafe, St. Germain; Helena Lawinger and Patti McKinley, Red Rooster Cafe, Mineral Point; Mike and Jan LeBrocq, Birchwood Cafe, Birchwood; Doyle and Nancy Lewis and Annette Wagner, Unique Cafe, Boscobel; Mary and James "Mac" McBrair, Ideal Cafe, Iron River; Lin McConnell and Missy Ramsdell, Little Babe's Cafe, Mukwonago; Marshall and Janette Maxwell, Daddy Maxwell's Arctic Circle Diner, Williams Bay; Elly and Jerry Mocello, Four Seasons Cafe and Deli, Eagle River; Shelley Moon, Bonnie's Diner, Phillips; Diane Moulai and Santo Pulvino (former owners), Oak Street Cafe, Juneau; Joan Nehls, Joan's Country Cookin', Hustisford; Lisa O'Brien, O'Brien's Restaurant (now the Rusty Rooster owned by Nancy Zorn), Pardeeville; Linda Orvis, Linda's Wilmot Cafe, Wilmot; Gary Ourada and Sue Ourada Stanton, Dixie Lunch, Antigo; Susan and Larry Palubicki, Log Cabin Cafe, Crandon; Jill and Larry Petit, Lakewood Cafe, Winter; Kate Platson-Phalin, Kate's Cafe, Glenwood City; Sherry and John Rawson, CJ's Cafe, Blair; Ernesto and Linda Rodriguez, former owners of Greenwood Family Restaurant, Greenwood; Conny Roy, Main Street Cafe, Siren; Debbie and Jeff Saueressig, Knotty Pine Restaurant, Oostburg; Rick and Helen Scott, Skipper's Family Restaurant and Outdoor Cafe, Merrill; Teri Scott (former owner), Teri's Restaurant, Baraboo; Mark and Colleen "Cow" Stanis, Cowmark Cafe, Trevor; Diane Stroik, Amherst Cafe, Amherst; Terry and Kim Tassi, Outpost Cafe, Presque Isle; Larry and Sherrie Wilson, Wilson's Cafe, Pound.

# Cafe Wisconsin Cookbook

# ONE

~ ~ ~

# Breakfast

# Chef Carl Brach's French Toast

## OUTPOST CAFE, PRESQUE ISLE
*Terry and Kim Tassi*

When Presque Isle's little Mill Pond restaurant burned to the ground, the Tassis bought the lot and went into the restaurant business themselves. Their Outpost Cafe is heir to much of the former restaurant's success, including this recipe developed by its founder and trained chef, Carl Brach. Eventually, he moved on to bigger and better things, becoming a personal chef touring with recording artist Sting. Word has it that Carl's french toast was a favorite of Sting's. One succulent bite tells you why.

"This is a special recipe that is thick and delicious," Kim promises. "Each slice of our french toast is one-fifth of a loaf of homemade bread. It is a very popular item on our regular breakfast menu and served through the breakfast and lunch hours. It's offered in one-, two-, or three-slice portions."

> 3  **eggs**
> ¼  **cup milk**
> ½  **teaspoon vanilla extract**
> ¼  **teaspoon cinnamon**
> ¼  **teaspoon nutmeg**
> 3  **pieces homemade bread (1½–2 inches thick),**
>      **cut in half diagonally**
>    **butter**
>    **warm maple syrup**

Whisk eggs, milk, vanilla, cinnamon, and nutmeg. Heat a griddle or cast-iron skillet over medium-high flame until hot. Immerse bread in batter to cover all sides and soak into the bread. Add a little butter to hot griddle; swirl to coat the cooking surface. Grill bread until golden brown on both sides. Serve immediately with butter and warm syrup. Makes 3 servings.

# Banana Stuffed French Toast

## BIRCHWOOD CAFE, BIRCHWOOD
### *Mike and Jan LeBrocq*

Once you try Mike's stuffed french toast, you'll never look back. Sweet and luscious, this deluxe version is easy to assemble. Do it the night before for a family brunch, or just before you start a special dinner for a warm and very different kind of dessert.

*Batter*
- 4 **eggs, lightly beaten**
- 1/2 **cup milk**
- 1/2 **teaspoon vanilla extract**
- 1/4 **cup sugar**

*Filling*
- 1 **package (8 ounces) cream cheese, softened**
- 1/4 **cup brown sugar**
- 1/2 **teaspoon vanilla extract**
- 1 **cup mashed bananas (about 2 large ripe bananas)**
- 1/4 **cup chopped walnuts**
   **dash of ground cinnamon**
- 1–2 **tablespoons orange juice concentrate, rum, brandy, orange liqueur, or other liqueur (optional)**

*Also*
- 8 **regular slices white bread (or substitute equal amount of whole wheat, sourdough, etc.)**
- 1–2 **tablespoons butter**
   **topping choices: powdered sugar, maple syrup, whipped cream, or ice cream**

Mix batter ingredients in large bowl. Cover and refrigerate. (Alternatively, if you're not cooking the french toast until the following day, make the batter then, if desired.) Use a separate bowl to mix the cream cheese, brown sugar, and vanilla until smooth. Fold in mashed bananas, walnuts, cinnamon, and optional orange juice concentrate or liqueur. Spread filling generously on four slices of the bread. Top each slice with another one, place sandwiches on large plate or tray, cover with plastic wrap, and chill until filling is firm, one hour or up to overnight.

Heat griddle or large, heavy (preferably cast-iron) skillet over

## VARIATIONS ON A THEME

The former Old Store Cafe and Deli in Dale was well known for its own version of stuffed french toast made with cherry pie filling instead of bananas. Just about any fruit, in fact, can be used to vary the dish. Try sliced strawberries, raspberries, blueberries, diced melon, diced pineapple, partially cooked diced pears or apples, and pumpkin or other pie filling. Frozen fruit works well, too, but it must be thawed and well drained before tucking it between the slices of bread. If playing with food is your game, experiment with flavorings such as rum, brandy, orange liqueur, or other liqueurs. And with all the artisanal breads on the market today, why limit yourself to white? Try whole wheat, sourdough, cinnamon raisin—whatever sounds good to you. Go for broke on the toppings, too. How about sweetened cocoa, maple syrup, yogurt, whipped cream, even ice cream?
—T. A.

medium-low flame until hot. Add butter and swirl to coat the cooking surface. Dip french toast sandwiches in batter to cover both sides and place on griddle. Cook slowly until golden brown on one side, then flip sandwiches and cook until the other side is golden brown and the filling is warm and creamy throughout. Serve immediately with toppings of your choice. If you're making this for dessert, cut the sandwiches with a serrated knife into quarters just before serving. Makes 4 large brunch servings or 6–8 dessert servings.

### BREAKFAST IS BIG IN WISCONSIN

At home, away from Cafe Wisconsin, breakfast for me is a protein shake and fresh fruit with a quick read of the daily newspaper. I'm generally in a rush to get the day started and unwilling to spend time cooking or washing dirty dishes. This is in part why, during my second sweep through Wisconsin's cafes, I was struck by how breakfast is such a big—make that BIG—deal, especially with local men and summer people.

It was not so on my first Wisconsin food foray. But ten years later, owners repeatedly told me that breakfast is their busiest meal of the day—both in terms of a morning meal and in breakfast-type foods ordered any time of day. They identified Saturday as the busiest day of the week due in most part to the heavy breakfast traffic.

During the workweek, breakfast is a male social ritual that begins early— often before a cafe officially opens—and runs through the morning, with shifts of men coming and going from the community table as schedules allow. Frequently, they pluck a cup off a rack or wall shelf and pour their own coffee. It's at breakfast that a town's movers and shakers discuss improvements to the town park, the Fourth of July fireworks display, the need to hire another fireman. It's also where local contractors line up the day's work on cell phones, retired gents solve the problems of the world, and farmers discuss their progress in the fields and the price of corn. The atmosphere is chummy and clubby, not unlike the fellowship at the Legion hall or VFW post.

Whether they're heading off to work or spending another day of retirement around the house or on the golf course or lake, men stick pretty close to a reasonable diet during the workweek—say, a fried egg or two with a side of toast, potatoes, and bacon washed down with bottomless cups of coffee. On Saturdays, however, caution is thrown to the wind. That's when orders for impressive pileups of hash browns, eggs, biscuits and gravy, and meat—sausage, bacon, ham, pork chops, steaks, fish, bratwurst patties, corned beef hash—go to and fro between the dining room and kitchen at a breakneck pace. Unlike Sunday mornings occupied with churchgoing, Saturdays are relatively unstructured and freeflowing, allowing time to splurge on eats and linger in conversation with community members.

To summer people—tourists, cabin dwellers, full-time seasonal residents—breakfast is a decadent splurge, a languorous elongation of the morning with family and friends. Vacation time is suspended and weightless, with no difference at all between Wednesday and Saturday. Any day—and any time of day—is perfect for omelets, hash browns or American fries, cinnamon rolls, fried doughnuts, plate-sized pancakes, and stuffed french toast eaten in sizeable portions. As Cindy Starke, owner of Cindy's Country Cafe in Three Lakes, notes, "We're mainly a breakfast place now. The emphasis on breakfast has definitely increased. I think it's because it's a cheaper meal, and you can afford to take out the whole family where you can't always for dinner. It's really popular with tourists because they can come in, fill up, then head out on the boat for the day. They'll take a picnic with them and then be able to afford going out to dinner."

In comparison with both local men and tourists, local women tend to be nibblers. An order of toast with tea, a pancake with a single egg over easy, a doughnut with coffee is about all they need to start their day. It's quite rare for a woman to breakfast alone (I was an oddity as both a lone woman and a stranger), slightly more common for a pair to breakfast together, more common yet for a husband and wife. Groups of women, such as church members, school bus drivers, Red Hatters, and walkers and other exercise groups commonly meet at cafes for breakfast. "It's a good way to network with people from the town," Carole Anderson told me over raisin toast at the Home Plate Diner in Mishicot, featured in the first edition of *Cafe Wisconsin*. "For us, it's "a support group where we can discuss the good and bad about exercising. Some mornings it's really hard to get up and get going, but just knowing the other gals are waiting on you helps a lot.

"We'll come in here after exercising and we might be in a good mood or we might not. Julie, our regular waitress, . . . has our coffee and toast waiting for us when we come in. That kind of pampers us and makes us feel special. That's the kind of thing you can only get in a small town restaurant, don't you think? That little extra love from people who know you and care."

Carole and her chums may have preferred toast, but you can expand your own breakfast repertoire with these additional favorites from cafes across the state. For recipes, see the next chapter featuring Baked Goods.

- Badger State Muffins
- Cinnamon Rolls with Buttermilk Icing
- Grandma's Old-Fashioned Doughnuts
- Kolaches
- Baking Powder Biscuits
- Jim Donuts
- Fry Cakes

—J. S.

**PANCAKE OPTIONS**

On pancakes nothing can top real butter and 100 percent pure Wisconsin maple syrup. But man does not live by butter and syrup alone. Cafe menus often tempt with a list of add-ons, giving customers the chance to create their own breakfast special. At Bonnie's Diner in Phillips, for example, options include diced apples, pecans, and chocolate chips. "People can add whatever they want, or mix and match," says owner Shelley Moon.

The Dixie Lunch in Antigo may have more mouth-watering pancake possibilities than any other cafe in the state. How can you choose from blueberry, cinnamon spice, strawberry delight, peanut butter, and banana? Sizes range from silver dollar cakes to manhole cover.

Bonnie's Diner also has Mickey Mouse pancakes for kids, with one large pancake for the head and two smaller ones for the ears. Mickey's eyes are made of sliced sausage links, his mouth is a slice of bacon, and his nose is

*(continued on facing page)*

# German Apple Pancake

## LINDA'S WILMOT CAFE, WILMOT
### *Linda Orvis*

Former owner Russell Badtke brought this *apfelpfannkuchen,* or "Dutch baby," with him from Walker Brothers Pancake House when he bought the Wilmot Cafe in 1976. Blessedly, the recipe has in turn been passed on to current owner Linda Orvis. It is not a flapjack-style pancake as we know it; instead, sautéed, sugar-glazed apples are cooked in an eggy batter, then baked to a tender, golden finish in the oven. It's the kind of dish you have to wait for, as the menu warns, but one that is so very worth the wait.

Our home version of the cafe recipe serves four or more from one skillet, but if you have smaller skillets and want to make two large individual pancakes, do. If you're serving this as a dessert, use the larger amount of apples. Linda specifies Granny Smith because they remain firm when cooked.

*Batter*
2    **cups flour**
2    **teaspoons sugar**
¾    **teaspoon baking powder**
2    **cups heavy cream**
4    **eggs, beaten**
2    **tablespoons vegetable oil**

*Filling*
1–2  **Granny Smith apples**
2    **tablespoons butter**
2    **teaspoons sugar**
1    **teaspoon cinnamon**

*Also*
**powdered sugar**

Heat oven to 375 degrees. To prepare batter, combine flour, sugar, and baking powder in a bowl. Stir in heavy cream, eggs, and vegetable oil.

To make the pancake, peel and slice the apples. Melt butter in a 9-inch cast-iron (or other ovenproof) skillet over medium-low flame. Add apple slices and cook, turning to coat the slices. Combine sugar and cinnamon and sprinkle over apples. Continue cooking a minute or two. Pour pancake batter over apples and cook until set, about 10 minutes. Transfer skillet to the hot oven and bake until firm and brown, 25–35 minutes. Loosen the sides and bottom with a metal spatula. You can serve the pancake right from the skillet, slide it onto a plate, or invert it so that the apples end up on top. Serve it hot or warm, sprinkled with powdered sugar. Makes 4–6 servings.

## For the Love of Pancakes

I grew up with pancakes made from the contents of a box—Aunt Jemima, mostly, I think—and they were good enough for a kid who didn't know anything else. Later, when I was a high school student hooked on summer episodes of the soap opera *All My Children,* I watched with considerable surprise as giddy newlyweds Cliff and Nina Warner playfully measured buttermilk, flour, and eggs into a glass mixing bowl. Until that moment, it had never occurred to me that pancake batter could be made from scratch!

Real buttermilk makes a flavorful cake that's tender and light. I especially like my cakes with an outer edge that's golden brown, crispy with butter or other subtle, flavorful oils from the grill (bacon is nice), and a surface laced with tiny popped bubbles. Prepared mixes too often make cakes that are dry and leaden, with a tough outer skin or crust. When I encounter a pancake like this, I try to salvage it by poking holes in it with my fork so that melted butter and syrup can soak in. I've stubbornly persisted in believing a pancake can be saved with more butter, more syrup, but the truth is, it's not a syrup-soaked sponge I'm interested in. I crave pancakes like Cliff and Nina's: genuine and true, made with love and filled with promise.

It will come as no surprise, then, that I am not partial to butter substitutes like margarine, butter-margarine blends, or, worst of all, yellow-tinted grease scooped into a little mound and served in a paper cup. What exactly is that stuff? Donnie Stoik, owner of the Main Street Cafe in Bloomer, says, "The woman at the milk marketing board told me that out-of-state tourists know Wisconsin as the Dairy State, and they have this image of Wisconsin restaurants serving only real milk, pots of cream on the table, real butter, things like that." Wisconsinites expect nothing less. I say, give me the real thing or give me nothing at all.

I'm a lot easier to please when it comes to syrup. I'm not particularly partial to authentic maple syrup, which I find too powerfully sweet for pancakes. A good quality corn syrup with artificial maple flavoring suits me fine, but I'll reject every time the generic brands that tend to be thin and watery. I often give blueberry, blackberry, and other fruit-flavored syrups a chance by dribbling a dot on a fork-sized bit of pancake. But I'm pretty much partial to maple. Call me a purist.—J. S.

*(continued from facing page)*

a maraschino cherry. In Black Earth, at the Lunch Bucket Cafe, every pancake that leaves Barb Paar's grill wears a smiley face—except for the Christmas trees during the holidays, the hearts for Valentine's Day, and the bunnies at Easter. You can customize your own pancakes the way Barb does. Fill a mustard or other dispenser bottle with thinned batter, then "draw" a design on the hot griddle. When it's set and brown, spoon pancake batter over it. When bubbles appear on the edges, flip the pancake over to reveal your artwork.—T. A.

**MORE PANCAKE
PICK-ME-UPS**

🦌 apples sautéed in
   butter with sugar
   and cinnamon

🦌 dried cherries or
   cranberries

🦌 blueberry or raspberry
   syrup

🦌 yogurt mixed with
   maple syrup

🦌 cherry pie filling and
   whipped cream

🦌 vanilla yogurt and
   granola

🦌 softened butter
   whipped with grated
   orange zest

🦌 cranberries pureed with
   a seedless orange and
   superfine sugar

🦌 brown sugar and
   toasted pecans

—T. A.

# *Buttermilk Pancakes*

## DENISE'S CAFE, RANDOLPH
### *Denise J. Fischer*

Denise serves pancakes so large that even a very hungry person usually can eat only one. Of course, some people take that as a challenge and boldly order two. Take care not to overmix the batter, or you'll be downing one tough pancake.

> 4  **cups flour**
> 1  **rounded tablespoon baking powder**
> 1  **teaspoon baking soda**
> 1  **teaspoon salt**
> 4  **large eggs**
> 5  **cups buttermilk**
>    **oil**

Whisk flour, baking powder, baking soda, and salt in large bowl until well combined. Beat eggs in another bowl; whisk in buttermilk until well combined. Stir the liquid mixture into the dry mixture until barely combined. Batter should be lumpy and thick, but if it's really sludgy, add more buttermilk and stir very briefly.

   Heat a stove-top griddle or large cast-iron skillet over medium flame for several minutes. Generously brush oil on hot surface and continue to heat for another moment. Make large pancakes, using about 2 good-sized ladles per pancake. (Make two at a time if you're using a griddle, one at a time if using a skillet.) Spread the batter into a circle and cook until top is covered with bubbles. The first side should be golden brown; if not, adjust heat up or down. Flip and cook on other side until just done. It's okay to nick the pancake and check it; when it looks dry and fluffy on the inside, it's done. Serve immediately with your favorite toppings or hold in a warm oven while you cook the rest. Makes 8–10 big pancakes.

# Classic Hash Browns

## Sand Creek Cafe, Sand Creek
### *Cecelia Cruse*

Cecelia "Cece" Cruse serves archetypal hash browns, made from scratch with fresh, raw potatoes and real butter, and dressed with nothing more than seasoned salt. Add grilled onions, if you like.

Cece says, "Our mom, Christine Hagen, made hash browns like this. The butter gives a nice brown color and enhances the potato flavor. We started out using the deep-fried hash brown potatoes that we bought through our food distributor. Then we tried what they called the fresh hash browns, which were better but didn't have the flavor and good color. Mom's style were a hit with all our customers. We use bakers—the Kitchen Klean brand. They're not as mealy as other bakers. Margarine is never used."

> **potatoes ("bakers")**
> **butter**
> **seasoned salt**
> **diced onions (optional)**

Cece's instructions: "Wash and boil potatoes with the skin on until center is soft. Drain and cool. Heat griddle or fry pan over medium to medium-high until the butter will sizzle when you add it. Grate potatoes, with skin on, on top of the butter. Grater should have at least ¼-inch slots—we use ½-inch slots. (Onions should be put on now, too, if they're wanted.) Add some seasoned salt. When potatoes are brown, turn them and allow the other side to get at least half as brown. Serve with browner side up." Makes any number of servings.

# Bluegill Hash Browns

## BIRCHWOOD CAFE, BIRCHWOOD
### *Mike and Jan LeBrocq*

"I started doing our specialty hash browns a few years ago and was experimenting with a lot of combinations, trying to utilize the products we already purchase," says Mike. He features Denver, Spanish, and veggie hash browns on the menu, plus this monster-sized version blanketed with sausage, onions, and peppers and smothered with cheese. There's no fish, so what's with the name?

"Birchwood is the Bluegill Capital of Wisconsin," Mike explains. He advises, "If you're cooking this for a larger group, heat the oven to 375 degrees, cook up the hash browns, put them on a sheet pan, top with the sausage mix and cheese, and put it in the oven until the cheese melts."

- 2–3 **tablespoons oil or butter**
- 10 **ounces packaged hash brown–style potatoes**
  **salt and pepper**
- ¼ **cup diced onion**
- ¼ **cup diced sweet peppers**
- 3 **ounces cooked breakfast sausage (about ½ cup ground sausage, sliced links, or chopped patty)**
- 3 **ounces shredded cheese (cheddar, swiss, mozzarella, or American)**

Heat a cast-iron griddle or heavy skillet over medium flame until hot. Add some of the oil or butter, heat briefly, then lay down the hash browns to form a rectangle. Season to taste with salt and pepper. Cook to golden brown on both sides, about 10 minutes per side. You may need to add more oil or butter to the griddle when you turn the potatoes. Meanwhile, heat a little more oil or butter on the other end of the griddle or in a separate pan. Add the onion and sweet peppers and cook, stirring often, until tender, 5–10 minutes. Stir in cooked sausage and heat through. Mound this mixture over the cooked hash browns. Top with cheese of your choice. Cover hash browns with a deep lid and cook until the cheese melts. Serve immediately. Makes 1 large serving.

## HASH BROWN HEAVEN

Potatoes are the people's food. They are as comfortable, affordable, and versatile as food gets. It's a toss-up whether the most popular potato dish in cafes is french fries, mashed, or hashed, but the last may lend itself best to variation and personal preference. There's onions versus no onions versus grilled onions. Cheese or no cheese, margarine versus oil versus butter. But first and foremost is the potato itself in all its varieties: red, white, or yellow, waxy, mealy, or all purpose.

Kendall Gulseth, of the Koffee Kup in Stoughton, prefers large, one-pound Idahos for hash browns. He boils them until tender, then drains, cools, and refrigerates them. (Chilling the cooked potatoes firms them up and makes them easy to work with.) The next day they're peeled and shredded and scattered onto the hot flat-top. "It's a lot of work," admits Kendall. He has experimented with frozen and dehydrated hash browns—what he calls the "predone" kind—but his customers let him know what they prefer.

Hash browns can be as simple as the butter-and-salt-seasoned ones made at the Sand Creek Cafe (see page 9), or they can be one-skillet meals piled high with meat, veggies, cheese, eggs, even sausage gravy. Specialty hash browns are born when a cook gets creative with leftovers or bored with the menu. Sometimes a customer's hunger for a family favorite or for something just a little bit different evolves into a menu item. Or inspiration might derive from a town's ethnic heritage or someone's recent vacation.

Here are some heavenly hash browns from Wisconsin cafes:

**Celtic**—Corned beef, cheddar cheese, mushrooms, onions, and eggs (Faye's Dinky Diner, Eagle River)

**Farmer Skillet**—Diced ham, green peppers, onions, mild cheddar, and eggs (Crystal Cafe, Phillips)

**Kitchen Nest**—Diced ham, sautéed peppers, onions, and mushrooms topped with two eggs, more hash browns, and sliced American cheese, all slid under the broiler to melt the cheese. Everything but the kitchen sink. (Village Kitchen, Casco)

**Meat Skillet**—Crumbled pork sausage, bacon, canned mushroom pieces, and eggs (Crystal Cafe, Phillips)

**Mexican Skillet**—Taco meat, sour cream, shredded cheese, and salsa, topped with two eggs any style (Main Dish Family Restaurant, Luck)

**New England**—Cheddar cheese, onions, mushrooms, pork sausage, and eggs (Faye's Dinky Diner, Eagle River)

**Rosie's Favorite Irish Potatoes**—Hash browns scrambled with egg and chopped onion (Kate's Cafe, Glenwood City)

—T. A.

## Omelet Encore

Like hash browns, omelets lend themselves to endless variation.

**Cajun Omelet**—Mild andouille sausage, mushrooms, and green onions (Koffee Kup, Stoughton)

**Everything Omelet**—Ham, onion, mushrooms, and cooked hash browns (Main Street Cafe, Siren). Owner Conny Roy says this is served on the weekend, "when the city people come."

**Farmer's Omelet**—Browned hash browns, sausage, ham, bacon, gyro meat, onions, tomatoes, and peppers (Greenwood Family Restaurant, Greenwood)

**Fiesta Omelet**—Seasoned taco meat, sweet peppers, onions, and tomatoes topped with cheddar cheese sauce and served with salsa and sour cream (Village Kitchen, Casco)

*(continued on facing page)*

# Portobello Mushroom Omelet

## Skipper's Family Restaurant and Outdoor Cafe, Merrill
*Rick and Helen Scott*

Rick started serving this savory omelet in 2003; since then he's had to double his purchase of portobello mushroom caps. If you don't have a griddle large enough to cover two burners, use two cast-iron skillets instead. Nonstick pans are okay, too, if that's what you have, but you'll get truer diner flavor with cast iron. Or, you could use one pan, cooking the mushroom mixture first and keeping it warm while you make the omelet.

3–4 tablespoons olive oil
  1 portobello mushroom cap, chopped
  $\frac{1}{4}$ cup chopped fresh tomato
  $\frac{1}{4}$ cup chopped onion
  1 tablespoon minced garlic
  3 extra-large eggs
    salt and pepper
  $\frac{1}{4}$ cup shredded mozzarella cheese

Heat a large cast-iron griddle over two burners, with one burner on high and the other on medium. When the half on high is hot enough that a drop of water sizzles when sprinkled onto it, drizzle about half the olive oil over that area. Add chopped mushroom, tomato, onion, and garlic. Sauté the vegetables, stirring often, until mushrooms are tender. Meanwhile, beat eggs in a bowl and add a little salt and pepper. When mushrooms are done, drizzle the remaining olive oil over the "cooler" side of the griddle. Let it heat briefly, then pour on the egg mixture to make an oval pattern. Cook briefly to set the bottom, then flip to cook the other side. Add the cooked vegetables lengthwise down the center of the omelet. Sprinkle cheese over the vegetables, then fold the omelet in half. (Alternatively, you may roll it into a cylinder.) Serve immediately. Makes 1 large omelet.

## A MONSTER OF AN OMELET

For Mark and Colleen "Cow" Stanis of the Cowmark Cafe in Trevor, the proverbial golden goose doesn't lay eggs. It lays omelets. Mark has gained notoriety around these parts with his self-titled Mark Omelet filled with ham, sausage, bacon, hash browns, American, swiss, and cheddar cheese. But if you think that sounds like a platter full, loosen your belt a notch. Heck, take it off altogether! Prepare yourself for the Monster Omelet, a behemoth made with a half dozen eggs and fifteen different fillings awash in homemade sausage gravy. "There's no specific order to the fillings," Cow says. "We just mix them all in together."

Here they are in random order: mushrooms, onion, green pepper, tomato. Okay so far. Ham, bacon, sausage. Still within the normal range. Corned beef hash. Huh? Hash browns and American fries. ("Of course, there's also potatoes in the hash," Cow reminds us.) American, cheddar, and swiss cheese. Urp. Jalapeños. Gasp. Sausage gravy over the top. Now that's really over the top!

"I can't say just how it got started," Mark shrugs. "I was looking for a gimmick."

Weighing in at six pounds, the Monster measures five inches thick and fourteen inches across. Mark hands me a serving platter to give me a feel for its size. "It hangs over the edge about this much," Cow adds, holding apart her thumb and forefinger the width of a dollar bill. It's monstrous all right, and if you eat it all, Mark will pick up the tab. "I have one or two people every weekend who try it," he says. "Most can't eat the whole thing."

Out of the more than five hundred Monster Omelets Mark has prepared, only nine people have succeeded in eating the whole thing. Only one has achieved the gut-busting feat in the past two years.—J. S.

*(continued from facing page)*

**Garbage Omelet**— Bacon, ham, sausage, mushrooms, green peppers, onions, tomatoes, swiss cheese, and American cheese topped with homemade chili (Koffee Kup, Stoughton)

**Greek Omelet**— Spinach, mushrooms, and feta cheese (Koffee Kup, Stoughton)

**Killer Omelet**—Bacon, ham, mushrooms, green pepper, onions, tomatoes, and choice of cheese (Koffee Kup, Stoughton)

**Super Deluxe Omelet**— Four eggs, onions, mushrooms, tomatoes, green pepper, ham, bacon, and sausage (Faye's Dinky Diner, Eagle River)

—T. A.

# *Tenderloin Tip Omelet*

## WOLF PACK CAFE, ST. GERMAIN

*Joe and Kathy Lass*

Out of doggy bags can come great meals, and the proof is this omelet created by Joe and Kathy. "Before buying the restaurant, Joe and I would go out for dinner on Saturday nights and order steak and lobster," explains Kathy. "Leftovers were made into an omelet on Sunday morning. When we bought the cafe and made it there, Joe had to leave out the lobster due to cost."

The Lasses first ran it as a breakfast special, but it proved so popular they added it to the regular menu. When an out-of-town customer requested the recipe via a newspaper columnist, Joe and Kathy shared it with the *Milwaukee Journal Sentinel*.

> 2–3  **tablespoons butter, divided**
> 8  **ounces beef tenderloin tips**
> ¼  **cup diced onion**
> ¼  **cup sliced mushrooms**
>     **McCormick brand garlic and herb seasoning**
>       **to taste**
> 6  **eggs, beaten**
> 2  **tablespoons milk**
>     **salt and pepper to taste**
> 2  **slices swiss cheese**

Melt 1 or 2 tablespoons butter in a pan over medium-high flame. When butter is sizzling but not brown, add the beef tips, onion, mushrooms, and seasoning. Cook, stirring often, until onions and mushrooms are tender and meat is cooked through, 5–8 minutes. Drain off excess liquid. (Alternatively, you may transfer meat to a bowl with a slotted spoon, then raise heat to high and reduce liquid to a glaze. Stir glaze into meat. This will give added flavor.)

Keep beef warm while you melt the remaining butter in a nonstick 12-inch pan over medium-high flame. Mix eggs, milk, salt, and pepper in a bowl. Pour into hot pan and cook until nearly done, then flip over. Place cheese slices on one side of omelet and spread beef tips over the other side. Fold omelet over, leave it on the flame briefly to melt the cheese, then serve immediately. Makes 2 servings.

## UNSCRAMBLING THE EGG

Nothing is as basic as eggs for breakfast. But nothing is so deceptively simple either, as I inadvertently found out the first time I ordered a fried egg, in a narrow old Main Street cafe in southwestern Wisconsin's coulee country. As the only out-of-towner perched at the counter at eight o'clock in the morning, I was as out of place as a lone dove on a power line filled with blackbirds.

"How'd you like that?" the waitress asked.

How indeed? Just how many ways could an egg be fried?

I described what I wanted: an egg with the white firm and tight, with no uncooked skim on top. Yolk set but not cooked through so I could use my toast to mop up what would flow onto the plate after I broke the quivery globe with my fork.

"You want it sunny side up," she said.

By the end of four months on the road, I had eaten eggs cooked just about every way possible. Here is a report of my investigation:

**Sunny side up, basted**: a fried egg whose yolk is cooked by spooning hot fat (preferably bacon drippings or butter) over it.

**Sunny side up, steamed**: a fried egg that is finished off by adding a little water to the grill before covering the egg with a saucepan lid. The steam sets the yolk.

**Over easy/medium/hard**: a fried egg that is carefully flipped over so the yolk cooks. Specify easy, medium, or hard, depending on how runny or firm you like the yolk.

**Poached**: an egg broken into and cooked in barely simmering water. Not a favorite of most cafe cooks because of the extra care and time it requires. A poached egg on toast is known as "man on a raft." Two eggs are "Adam and Eve on a raft."

**Bird's nest**: a slice of bread, buttered on both sides, with a hole the size of a silver dollar torn out of the middle. An egg is broken into the hole and the whole thing is fried on a grill, then flipped carefully to cook the other side.

**Scrambled**: eggs whisked with a bit of milk or water or nothing so that the yolk and white intermingle, and cooked on a grill. Variety comes with any number of add-ins, including shredded cheese, ham, corned beef hash, veggies, hash browns, you name it, to make what is known as a skillet, scramble, or haystack.

**Omelet**: a thin skin of scrambled eggs folded and filled with an assortment of goodies usually combined to convey a certain theme. There are cheese omelets, meat omelets, cheese and meat omelets, Greek and Mexican omelets, and so on.

**Soft and hard boiled**: I never encountered soft-boiled eggs in their shells served for breakfast. Their hard-boiled siblings are reserved for side dishes like salads and deviled eggs, although once I saw them chopped and served in cream sauce over toast.

Eggs are rarely served without toast and jelly—grape, strawberry, mixed fruit, apple, and, if you're lucky, orange marmalade, in those little, foil-topped plastic tubs. If you're very, very lucky, you'll be served homemade jam. At Rudy's Diner in Brillion, Rosemary Clarke makes jelly from Door County cherries and other fresh seasonal fruit. Her most popular jam is cherry-pineapple.

An egg's best friend on the plate includes bacon, sausage, ham, steak, pork chops, and fish, as well as corned beef hash. I have not yet found a better bacon than the thick, meaty, applewood-smoked variety made by Nueske's of Wittenberg. It's "the beluga of bacon, the Rolls-Royce of rashers," wrote R. W. Apple Jr. in a 1999 *New York Times* article. That's right. The *Times!*

But back to eggs. Eggs can also come smothered with sausage gravy and layered into ham and sausage sandwiches made with biscuits, bagels, and English muffins. Spruced up with Canadian bacon and hollandaise—a rich sauce of butter, lemon juice, and more eggs—they become fancy-schmancy eggs Benedict. On the other end of the sauce continuum is eggs with ketchup, especially popular when stirred together with hash browns or American fries.

The humble egg is so versatile that it shows up in even the most unlikely of places, like sandwiched between bacon and lettuce in the Bob Burger, the quirkiest burger in all of Wisconsin. See page 124 for instructions on how to make your own.—J. S.

# Biscuits and Gravy

## LOG CABIN CAFE, CRANDON
*Susan and Larry Palubicki*

The Palubickis' customers clamor for biscuits and gravy, made fresh every Friday at the Log Cabin Cafe. "They eat this at breakfast and will eat it anytime. They'll eat it all day long!" says Susan. "We have two locals who eat it every Friday, and if they don't come in, we save 'em some. They'll eat it the next day. One guy on the rescue squad— if he doesn't come in for breakfast, he forgets the Friday fish and has it for dinner."

Susan uses packaged biscuits. You might prefer homemade baking powder biscuits like those made at the Koffee Kup in Stoughton; see page 23 for the recipe.

  1 **pound Jimmy Dean's brand pork sausage**
  4 **tablespoons butter**
2½ **tablespoons flour**
1½–2 **cups milk**
   **salt and pepper to taste**
  4 **baking powder biscuits, split in half horizontally**

Heat a skillet over medium-high flame. Add the pork sausage and break it up with a spoon or spatula as it browns and cooks. When all the pink is gone, reduce heat to low and drain off about three-quarters of the fat from the pan. Transfer sausage and remaining fat in pan to a bowl; set aside. Return skillet to the heat and add the butter. When it has melted, stir in the flour. Cook, stirring often, 3–4 minutes. Gradually whisk in most of the milk. Raise heat to medium and simmer gravy until it thickens. Stir in pork-fat mixture. Add milk to reach desired thickness. Season to taste with salt and pepper. Serve over biscuits. Makes 4 servings.

### Kentucky Foodways in Northern Wisconsin

When the original *Cafe Wisconsin* came out in 1993, Larry and Susan Palubicki's Log Cabin Cafe in Crandon was nearly the only cafe in Wisconsin serving biscuits and gravy, a breakfast staple in the South. Today you'll find it everywhere, as popular as fireworks on the Fourth of July.

Back then, I was surprised to find it so far up north. Its presence in Crandon isn't a mystery, however. It was brought to the Northwoods by Kentucky migrants who came to work in the logging industry around 1900. Enticed by the misleading promise of good farmland in Wisconsin's cutover lands, Appalachian folk cashed in all they could for one-way train tickets north, convinced that they'd be much better off with virgin land in an unfamiliar place than with the hardscrabble, mountainside farms they were leaving behind.

As it was one hundred years ago, biscuits and gravy—affectionately known as B&G—is popular with today's loggers, who, Larry reports, "want a lot of stick-to-the-ribs stuff." In the years since I first met the Palubickis, B&G has become standard fare across the state, equally popular with lazy tourists and hard-working woodsmen. Ironically, however, it no longer has a permanent place on the Log Cabin's menu. "We serve it as a Friday breakfast special," Susan explains. "If we didn't have it as a treat, you couldn't get in here, it's so popular."

Another Log Cabin favorite with deep Appalachian roots is the bean soup found on page 58.—J. S.

# Corned Beef Hash

## LOG CABIN CAFE, CRANDON
*Larry and Susan Palubicki*

Lunch customers can tell quickly if a cafe is top-caliber by asking if the pie crusts are rolled by hand or the soups are made from scratch. At breakfast, corned beef hash is the indicator of quality. A cafe that simmers corned beef brisket and boils fresh potatoes instead of scraping hash from a can is a jewel indeed.

The Log Cabin Cafe's version is straightforward and oh-so-satisfying. According to Susan, it's less popular with women than men, who really consume it in quantity during deer hunting season.

|   |   |
|---|---|
| 1 | **package (about 3 pounds) corned beef brisket, with spice packet** |
| 2 | **bay leaves** |
| 2–3 | **pounds russet potatoes** |
|   | **vegetable oil** |
|   | **butter** |
|   | **diced onion** |
|   | **salt and pepper** |
|   | **eggs** |

To cook brisket and potatoes, place meat, contents of spice packet, and bay leaves in dutch oven or large pot. Cover with cold water. Bring to simmer over medium flame, skimming surface as needed to remove foam that forms. If necessary, weight the brisket with a plate to keep it below the surface of the liquid. Partially cover the pot, reduce heat to low, and slowly simmer brisket until very tender, 3–4 hours. It's done when a meat fork inserted in the thickest part releases easily from the flesh. Cool it in the liquid or remove it to a bowl to cool down. Chill it all day or overnight in the refrigerator. Meanwhile, peel the potatoes and boil them in water until barely tender. Cool and chill.

To prepare hash two, three, or four servings at a time, thickly slice some of the brisket and then dice it or cut it into small chunks, whichever size you prefer. Cut the potatoes similarly. Heat a griddle or large cast-iron pan over medium flame until it's good and hot. (A nonstick pan works well, too, but heat it with the oil and butter added.) Add a little oil and butter and some diced onion. Cook the onion a moment or two before adding corned beef and potatoes in a ratio you like. Let it fry until the bottom browns, then toss and cook

## CORNED BEEF CUES

Beef brisket is a tough but super-flavorful cut that needs to simmer a long time to reach the requisite fork-tenderness. Cook the meat the day before you plan to serve the hash and let it chill overnight; it will, as Susan Palubicki says, "chunk up real easily then." (You can also cook the potatoes the day before.) One of the secrets to great corned beef is to get the griddle very hot before adding the fat, so the ingredients will brown better without sticking to the pan. For a bright touch on the finished dish, sprinkle chopped fresh parsley on top. And of course, don't forget ketchup on the side.—T. A.

to brown the jumble all over, adding a bit more oil or butter as needed. Season with salt and pepper as it cooks. Meanwhile, fry some eggs in another pan. Serve the hash as a loose jumble with eggs on top. Makes 10–12 servings.

## HASHING IT OVER

My mom made corned beef occasionally when I was a kid but never often enough for it to become ingrained in my culinary repertoire. I'd watch her remove the brisket from its plastic bag and place it in a large roaster before adding the contents of the pickling packet. A few hours later, she'd set the roast—an unlikely hue of subdued magenta—on the dining room table. Corned beef was never a weekday affair, so it was privileged to bypass the mundane kitchen dinette set in favor of the large walnut table in the next room. We ate there only on holidays or when someone was coming for dinner.

Oftentimes sided with stewed red cabbage and boiled potatoes, corned beef was a special treat. If there were any slices left after the family feast, they'd more likely than not be reserved for thick Reuben sandwiches made with swiss cheese and sauerkraut on pungent pumpernickel rye.

It was not until I began work on *Cafe Wisconsin* that I had my first taste of corned beef hash, and even though I was a neophyte, I knew without a doubt that it had come out of a can. It had that potted taste reminiscent of the smell of canned cat food, and the potatoes had the cookie-cutter sameness and grainy texture of processed hash browns. I ate one forkful and pushed the plate aside. It was weeks before I found corned beef hash truly worth eating, hash that reverses the cultural biases that cloud my consideration.

In *American Taste,* James Villas laments the relegation of hash—what he terms an important part of America's culinary evolution—in the popular imagination to dirty truck stops, military rations, and low-brow "hash houses." This is precisely where I am still stuck. I pride myself on not having my nose in the air, but I pity hash as a rather sorry conglomeration of scraps left over from the night before—probably because I have had more sorry hash than not.

Terese, on the other hand, adores homemade corned beef hash. "If a cafe makes it, I'll order it before anything else. Making something out of 'nothing' is an age-old means of creating wonderful food. And it doesn't get more wonderful to me than a crisp-edged, onion-y, egg-topped mess of real hash."

If you must satisfy your cravings for corned beef hash, you'd do well to navigate to Crandon's Log Cabin Cafe, where Susan Palubicki makes it the old-fashioned way, one forty-pound roast at a time.—J. S.

# TWO

~ ~ ~

# Baked Goods

# Badger State Muffins

## M & M Cafe, Monticello
*Mike and Mary Davis*

When *Midwest Living* magazine came calling for an article on favorite recipes from small town cafes, the Davises happily shared this gem, which appeared in the April 2003 issue. These muffins feature two of Wisconsin's signature fruits.

  1  **cup shredded apples (cored but unpeeled)**
⅔  **cup sugar**
½  **cup chopped cranberries**
½  **cup shredded carrots**
½  **cup chopped walnuts or pecans**
1¼  **cups flour**
1½  **teaspoons baking powder**
  1  **teaspoon baking soda**
  1  **teaspoon cinnamon**
  1  **teaspoon ground coriander**
¼  **teaspoon salt**
  1  **egg**
¼  **cup cooking oil**

Heat oven to 375 degrees. Oil ten to twelve 2½-inch muffin cups or line them with paper muffin liners. Combine apples, sugar, cranberries, carrots, and nuts in a large bowl. Using a second bowl, combine flour, baking powder, baking soda, cinnamon, coriander, and salt. Whisk until well blended. Stir flour mixture into fruit mixture. Beat egg and oil in the second bowl. Add to batter and stir to barely combine (do not overmix). Fill muffin cups three-quarters full. Bake until a toothpick inserted near center of a muffin comes out clean, 20–25 minutes. Let muffins cool in the pan for 5 minutes, then remove. Serve warm. Makes 10–12 muffins.

# *Baking Powder Biscuits*

## KOFFEE KUP, STOUGHTON
### *Kendall and Trish Gulseth*

Biscuits are a southern-born specialty, but in recent years they've become almost as revered in the North. In Wisconsin diners, they are a big part of the allure of such specials as biscuits and sausage gravy, chicken à la king, and biscuit-topped pot pie. With a tablespoon of sugar added to the flour mixture, they can be used as the base for strawberry shortcake, too. Versatility is a key to successful cafe cooking.

> **about 2 cups flour**
> 2½ **teaspoons baking powder**
> ½ **teaspoon salt**
> 4 **tablespoons cold butter, margarine, or shortening,**
> **cut into small pieces**
> **scant ¾ cup milk**

Heat oven to 425 degrees. Sift flour and measure out 2 cups. Add baking powder and salt and sift again into a medium bowl. Use a pastry cutter to cut the butter into the flour until butter pieces are about the size of hulled sunflower seeds. Add milk and stir briefly—just until mixture comes together. Dough should be only a little moist, and it should not be smooth.

Turn dough onto a very lightly floured surface and knead it for no more than four or five turns. Use a lightly floured rolling pin or floured fingers to roll or pat the dough out to a circle that is about ¾-inch thick. Cut round biscuits with a 3-inch biscuit cutter, pushing it straight down into the dough and pulling it straight back out without twisting. (Alternatively, you can make triangular biscuits by cutting the dough into wedges with a sharp knife.) Gather and reroll scraps and cut remaining biscuits. Place 1 inch apart on ungreased baking pan. Bake until golden brown, about 15 minutes. Serve as soon as possible. Makes 6–8 biscuits.

## SHARING THE WEALTH

When we approached Kendall Gulseth about contributing recipes, he was happy to comply. Like most people who are passionate about cooking, he gets deep satisfaction from sharing not just what he makes but what he knows. As we polished off lunch in one of the Koffee Kup's booths, Kendall handed us a well-stained family collection called Mother's Recipes and said, "Use whatever you like." We were thrilled. There were some holes in our recipe lineup, and we couldn't think of a more capable cook to fill them.

The generous man said yes to each of our requests. Then he cheerfully walked us through each recipe and patiently answered every question to make sure we got it all right. When food is seasoned with this kind of generosity, it's no wonder it tastes so good.—T. A.

# Cinnamon Rolls with Buttermilk Icing

## Koffee Kup, Stoughton
*Kendall and Trish Gulseth*

Make a batch of Kendall's oh-my-god-good cinnamon rolls and give half of them away. They will yield you friends for life. As for the rest, they're all yours.

### Dough
- 5 teaspoons quick-rise dry yeast
- ¼ cup warm water
- ¼ cup sugar
- ¼ cup warm (not hot) melted butter
- 1 egg
- 1 cup warm (not hot) milk
- 4 cups flour
- 1 teaspoon salt
  additional flour as required

### Filling
- ½ cup melted butter
- 1 cup firmly packed brown sugar
- 1½ teaspoons cinnamon

### Icing
- 2 cups powdered sugar
- 1 teaspoon vanilla extract
- 2 tablespoons butter, softened
  buttermilk

To make the dough, dissolve the yeast in ¼ cup warm water in a small bowl. Mix sugar, melted butter, egg, and milk in large bowl until smooth. Stir in dissolved yeast mixture. Combine flour with salt and stir into wet mixture; it will be somewhat loose and sticky. Flour a work surface and scrape dough onto it. Knead dough 2–3 minutes with floured fingers, adding additional flour judiciously as needed. Form dough into a ball. Oil or butter the dough bowl, place dough in it, cover it with plastic wrap, and let it rise in a warm place until doubled in bulk, 1–1½ hours.

To make the filling, combine ingredients in a small bowl.

To make icing, combine icing ingredients, stirring in buttermilk 1 tablespoon at a time until icing reaches a spreadable consistency. (Note: It will thicken somewhat as it stands; just stir it again when you're ready to use it.)

To form and bake the rolls, heat oven to 375 degrees. Grease two or three large baking pans. Transfer dough to floured work surface and knead it briefly. Roll it out with a floured rolling pin into a rectangle ⅜- to ½-inch thick. Spread filling evenly over the surface. Starting at a long end, roll the dough into a cylinder; it should take about four "turns" of the dough. Use a sharp knife to cut rolls crosswise, 2 inches thick for large pastries and about 1 inch for small ones. Pinch the open ends of rolls to seal them and place them 2 inches apart on baking pans. Bake until lightly colored, 15–20 minutes, depending on size.

You can frost and serve these while they're still warm from the oven, but frost only those that will be eaten right away. To enjoy a cinnamon roll later on, frost it first, then reheat it in the microwave for 15–20 seconds and serve immediately. Makes 12 or more cinnamon rolls.

## RAISE AND SHINE

I relied on favorite "test" foods in my search for good home cooking in Wisconsin's small town cafes. Baked goods, especially bread, buns, dinner rolls, and sweet rolls, ranked near the top among menu items that verified truth and authenticity. I learned fairly quickly that if a cafe owner spent the extra time to mix dough, proof it, and shape it into loaves or breakfast sweets, he or she wasn't likely to be taking short cuts in other areas of the menu. So I ate—or rather, sampled—a lot of cinnamon rolls, caramel rolls, and other sweet rolls. These were frequently ordered sight unseen, so I was never sure if I'd be brought a cellophane-wrapped Danish or muffin delivered by a bakery truck or a golden cinnamon roll still warm from the oven.

If uncertainty was a bane of my adventure eating, a well-stocked bakery case was even more so. In a quick glance I could see without the slightest waver of doubt that everything inside was made from scratch, by hand, and with a passion for doing things honest and right. Clearly, there was no need to taste, but was there ever a desire! A beautiful cinnamon roll the likes of those made at the Koffee Kup demanded to be ordered. And I did. Again and again.

Upon learning that I have eaten my way through Wisconsin not once but twice, people generally ask two questions: "How much weight did you gain?"

## DOUGHNUT DOS AND DON'TS

Cake doughnut dough is soft and "loose," more like a thick batter than a dough. Handle it gently and don't overwork it.

Use floured fingers or a floured rolling pin to pat or roll out the dough. I think $1/3$-inch-thick makes the best ratio of surface crust to inner, tender flesh, but if you're really into a crusty outside, roll it a bit thinner.

Use a 3-inch doughnut cutter for standard-size doughnuts. (You can also make them smaller or larger, depending on what you like.) Don't twist the cutter in the dough, just cut straight down with a firm hand. If you don't have a doughnut cutter, use a cookie cutter, or even a cup and a sharp knife. Then, cut out the holes with a sharp-edged bottle top.

Which is better for frying doughnuts, oil or lard? That depends in part on whether you're trying to

*(continued on facing page)*

(To this I answer fifteen pounds, or enough that the pants I brought from home grew so uncomfortably snug that I went to Goodwill and bought a pair of bib overalls.) And "Where is the best—?"

To this I judiciously provide no answer. It is impossible for me to identify a single best anything. This should cheer us all because it means that Wisconsin's small town cafes are chock full of inspired cooking and even better eating. This said, however, I am often pressed for my opinion on the top two, five, or ten of this or that. When it comes to cinnamon rolls, the buttermilk-iced beauties at the Koffee Kup rank near the top. Soft yeast dough is coiled with a thick cinnamon and sugar mixture, baked to the color of August wheat, and then spread with a clever buttermilk icing. So pretty. So good. So distinct among all the cinnamon rolls I encountered that the memory of them lingers and makes me pine for a taste even now.—J. S.

# *Fry Cakes*

### KOFFEE KUP, STOUGHTON
*Kendall and Trish Gulseth*

This classic Norwegian fry cake recipe makes several dozen cake doughnuts. You can fry them all in one session for a crowd or keep the raw doughnuts for a day or two in the refrigerator. Then you can "fry to order" just as Kendall does at the Koffee Kup.

They're perfection straight out of the fryer, unadulterated with frosting or sugar. Crunchy on the outside, crumbly on the inside, warming with spice. Are you a dunker? Would you like some coffee or cold milk with your order?

> 3  **eggs**
> $1\frac{1}{2}$  **cups sugar**
> 4  **tablespoons butter, melted and cooled a little**
> $1\frac{1}{2}$  **teaspoons baking soda**
> $1\frac{1}{2}$  **cups buttermilk**
> $5\frac{1}{2}$  **cups flour, divided**
> 3  **teaspoons baking powder**
> $1\frac{1}{2}$  **teaspoons cinnamon**
> 1  **teaspoon nutmeg**
> 1  **teaspoon allspice**
> 1  **teaspoon salt**
>    **additional flour as needed**
>    **canola oil for deep-frying**

Crack eggs into large bowl of electric mixer. Beat on medium speed until smooth and frothy. Continue beating as you gradually add the sugar. The mixture will become thickened and light in color. Beat in melted butter until just combined. Mix baking soda into buttermilk; beat this into the sugar mixture until just combined. Using a separate bowl, whisk 2½ cups of the flour with baking powder, cinnamon, nutmeg, allspice, and salt. Add to wet mixture and beat no more than 2 minutes while occasionally scraping the sides of bowl. Reduce speed to low, add another 3 cups flour, and continue beating and scraping for 1 more minute.

Dough will be loose and sticky, more like a very thick batter than a dough. It will be soft but easy to work with. Generously flour a work surface. Line several trays with waxed paper. Working with a portion of the dough at a time, turn dough out onto work surface and, using floured hands, pat it out to a ¼- to ⅓-inch thickness. Cut doughnut shapes with a 3-inch doughnut cutter. Carefully transfer doughnuts and holes to lined trays and chill at least 1 hour, or until you're ready to fry them. (Cover them with plastic wrap or more waxed paper if you're going to store them for longer than a couple of hours.) Repeat with remaining dough and dough scraps.

To fry doughnuts, place enough oil in a heavy pot or deep-fat fryer to come at least 2 inches up the sides of the pot. Heat over medium flame to 370 degrees, about 10–15 minutes. If you don't have a thermometer to check the temperature, you can tell when the fat is hot enough by dropping a doughnut hole into it. The ball should begin to "boil" and rise to the surface almost immediately. Or, fry one test doughnut; it should take about 1½ minutes to become golden brown on the bottom. Flip it with tongs and fry the other side; the doughnut will be fully colored and splitting open somewhat when done. Break it open to check for doneness. Adjust heat up or down as needed. Fry doughnuts in small batches, without crowding the pot. Drain each batch on paper towels. Let the fat return to 370 degrees between each batch. Serve warm. Makes about 4 dozen doughnuts.

*(continued from facing page)*

limit trans-fats or cholesterol. In a doughnut taste-testing session with several friends, lard won the most votes for flavor. (The lard-cooked doughnuts also seemed to keep their "surface crunch" longer.) But then again, some folks couldn't tell the difference. The upshot? It's up to you.

How do you know the exact moment to flip a frying doughnut? Kendall says the doughnuts themselves tell you. After about a minute and a half on the first side, when the bottom is golden brown, nudge the doughnuts with tongs or a long fork. "They'll flip when they're ready. It's just like they want to," says Kendall.

The holes are the best part, and the fry cook should have dibs.—T. A.

# Grandma's Old-Fashioned Doughnuts

## CLINTON KITCHEN, CLINTON
*Connie and Jim Farrell*

The older guys at the Clinton Kitchen call these cake doughnuts "sinkers" or "fry cakes," says Connie. "We make a batch every day, Monday through Friday. Some people dip them in sugar, some dunk them in their coffee."

Connie doesn't say what type of fat to deep-fry the doughnuts in, but these are dynamite whether cooked in oil or lard. Either way, they may make your nutritionist cringe, but depending on how you choose to spend your discretionary calories, it's your decision.

The orange juice gives this recipe a little zip, a little unusualness. The doughnuts can be formed one day and cooked the next, if desired.

> 1 **extra-large egg**
> ⅔ **cup sugar**
> 1 **teaspoon vanilla extract**
> 4 **tablespoons (¼ cup) margarine, melted and cooled**
> ⅔ **cup buttermilk**
> ⅓ **cup orange juice**
> 2½ **cups flour, divided**
> 2 **teaspoons baking powder**
> 1 **teaspoon baking soda**
> 1 **teaspoon nutmeg**
> 1 **teaspoon salt**
> **additional flour**
> **vegetable oil or lard for deep-frying**
> **sugar (optional)**

Line a large tray with waxed paper. Mix egg, sugar, and vanilla extract with a wire whisk until smooth. Whisk in margarine, buttermilk, and orange juice. Sift 1 cup of the flour with baking powder, baking soda, nutmeg, and salt. Stir into wet mixture until well combined. Stir in another 1½ cups flour. Dough will be loose and sticky, more like a very thick batter than a dough. It will be soft but easy to work with. Generously flour a work surface. Turn dough out onto it and, using floured hands, pat it out to a ¼- to ⅓-inch thickness. Cut doughnut shapes with a 3-inch doughnut cutter. Gather scraps of dough, press together, and cut additional doughnuts. Carefully transfer doughnuts and holes to lined tray and chill until you're ready to fry them. (You can store them overnight, too, if you cover them with more waxed paper.)

To fry doughnuts, place enough vegetable oil or lard in a heavy pot or deep-fat fryer to come at least 2 inches up the sides of the pot. Heat over medium flame to 370 degrees, about 10–15 minutes. If you don't have a thermometer to check the temperature, you can tell when the fat is hot enough by dropping a doughnut hole into it; it should begin to "boil" and rise to the surface almost immediately. Or, fry one test doughnut; it should take about 1½ minutes to become golden brown on the bottom. Flip it with tongs and fry the other side; the doughnut will be fully colored and splitting open a bit when done. Break it open to check for doneness. Adjust heat up or down as needed. Fry doughnuts in small batches, without crowding the pot. Drain each batch on paper towels. Let the fat return to 370 degrees between each batch.

If you like, dip the doughnuts in sugar while they're still warm. Makes 20–24 doughnuts.

## WHO'S COUNTING?

Call them fry cakes, doughnuts, or donuts. If I had my way, this cookbook would have almost as many recipes as Homer Price had doughnuts from his uncle's newfangled, malfunctioning doughnut machine. Written by Robert McCloskey, the story of Homer and the dough-nut machine is one of my childhood favorites. I remember it as fondly as I do the sour cream fry cakes at Irma's Kitchen in Argyle, the golden fry cakes served with their hole at the Hixton Cafe, the orange juice–spiked gems made at the Clinton Kitchen, the chocolate iced beauties at the Sand Creek Cafe, and the subtly spiced Norwegian cakes at the Koffee Kup in Stoughton.

But Terese said, "Stop! That is too many doughnut recipes." We finally agreed that three is just right.

Food historians believe that fry cakes—the preferred Wisconsin term— are of Northern European origin. Dutch *oilekoeken,* or "oily cakes," were brought to America by the Pilgrims, but it may have been the Pennsylvania Dutch who added the hole. Another doughnut story I remember from child-hood attributes the hole to a sea captain who put his wife's oilekoeken on the spokes of his ship's wheel. Doughnut cutters with corers to make the hole appeared in mail-order catalogs by 1870 and were standard issue by 1900. Another significant change to doughnuts was the formulation of baking pow-der in 1859; it substituted for yeast as a leavening agent and made doughnuts more like cake than bread. This may well be the origin of the term fry cake, which refers to cake doughnuts and not raised or yeast doughnuts.

As enamored as I am of exceptional fry cakes, I am not the only one in search of them, as it turns out. Kendall Gulseth, owner of the Koffee Kup in Stoughton, shares this story: "A guy from Janesville came in for fry cakes. He said he learned about us in a trivia quiz based on *Cafe Wisconsin* that ran in the Wisconsin Rapids paper. He'd been looking for years for fry cakes like his mother used to make. He came right back into the kitchen and watched me make them. 'Those are them!' he said. 'Soft inside. Crispy outside.' He bought a dozen and took them home."

It was White Castle that coined the slogan "Buy 'em by the sack," but it applies to the Koffee Kup just as well.—J. S.

# Jim Donuts

## SAND CREEK CAFE, SAND CREEK
*Cecelia "Cece" Cruse*

Following a bad skiing accident, Jim Nelson came to work and recover in the kitchen of the Sand Creek Cafe, gradually taking over Cece's share of the baking and cleaning. He adapted this recipe for chocolate doughnuts from a church cookbook.

Jim now lends a hand at the cafe about two or three times a month. "Since 1995, my locals don't let Jim leave unless the showcase is stocked with 'Jim Donuts,'" says Cece. "They are very popular, velvety, fry cake–style doughnuts, and Jim knows just how to handle the raw dough so they will be tender. We make these at least twice a month.

"Before 1995, I always made the regular white fry cakes, but now I just don't bother with them. Taste buds change . . . younger generations want chocolate. Jim has tried to teach me how to make them, but I know that if I learn how, I will find him out front visiting with customers and I'll be in the kitchen with the apron on making doughnuts. I'm smarter than that!"

     2 eggs
 1¼ cups sugar
     4 tablespoons (¼ cup) melted butter
 ⅓ cup chocolate syrup
     1 cup buttermilk
 1½ teaspoons vanilla extract

**5–5½ cups flour, divided**
**1 teaspoon baking soda**
**1 teaspoon cinnamon**
**¼ teaspoon salt**
**lard for deep-fat frying**
**chocolate frosting on page 41 or page 191, or**
**a favorite recipe of your own**

Line two trays with waxed paper. Beat eggs in a large bowl with electric mixer until well blended. Jim uses a KitchenAid mixer, but it can also be done by hand. Gradually beat in the sugar. Beat in butter. Stir or mix in chocolate syrup, buttermilk, and vanilla. Sift 4½ cups of the flour, the baking soda, cinnamon, and salt into a second bowl. Stir or mix flour mixture into wet mixture until combined.

Dough will be loose and sticky, more like a thick batter than a dough. Generously flour a work surface. Turn dough out onto it and knead additional flour into it—just enough to form a very soft dough. Use a floured rolling pin to roll it out to a ½-inch thickness. Cut doughnut shapes with a floured 3-inch doughnut cutter and carefully transfer doughnuts to lined trays. Gather scraps of dough, press together, and cut additional doughnuts. Chill doughnuts thoroughly.

Place enough lard in a heavy pot or deep-fat fryer to come at least 3 inches up the sides of the pot when melted. Heat lard over medium flame to 365–375 degrees, about 10–15 minutes. If you don't have a thermometer to check the temperature, you can tell when the fat is hot enough by dropping a doughnut hole into it; it should begin to "boil" and rise to the surface almost immediately.

Fry the doughnuts a few at a time, without crowding the pot. (Jim stretches out the raw, chilled doughnuts a little so that the hole is larger and won't close up during the frying.) As soon as each doughnut floats to the surface, flip it over, then turn it twice more as each side gets done. Drain each batch on paper towels. Let the fat return to 365–375 degrees between each batch.

Cool the doughnuts. Frost them with chocolate frosting. Makes 20–24 doughnuts.

# *Kolaches*

## DIXIE LUNCH, ANTIGO

*Gary "Gus" Ourada and Sue Ourada Stanton*

Using a family recipe, Gus and Sue's mother, Georgian, makes about ten dozen Bohemian *kolaches* early every Friday and Saturday morning. By the time the lights are turned off, they're long gone.

        2 **egg yolks**
        1 **whole egg**
    ¹⁄₂ **cup sugar**
        1 **teaspoon salt**
        1 **cup evaporated milk**
        1 **cup boiling water**
        2 **packages (each ¹⁄₄ ounce) quick-rising dry yeast**
4–4¹⁄₂ **cups flour, divided**
    ¹⁄₂ **cup oil**
        **melted butter**
        **filling options: stewed prunes, canned poppy seed**
            **filling, apricot or raspberry jam, apple or cherry**
            **pie filling, sweetened cream cheese**

Beat egg yolks and egg until smooth. Stir in sugar, salt, and evaporated milk. Stir in the boiling water. When mixture has cooled to warm room temperature, stir in the yeast and about 3 cups flour. Beat until well blended. Slowly add the oil, stirring well. Transfer dough to a floured surface and knead in additional flour, a little at a time, until dough is smooth and shiny, about 10 minutes. Lightly oil the bowl, place dough in it, cover and let rise in a warm place until doubled in bulk, about 1 hour and 15 minutes. Punch the dough to deflate it; form it into a ball again, cover and let rise again for 30 minutes.

Oil some baking pans or line them with parchment paper. To form the kolaches, roll the dough out on a floured surface to a thickness of about ¹⁄₄ inch. Use a round 3- to 4-inch cookie cutter or the bottom of a glass and a sharp knife to cut out kolaches. Place on baking pans and brush each one with melted butter. Cover lightly and let rise until double in bulk, 20–30 minutes.

Heat oven to 375 degrees. Make an indentation with your fingers in center of each kolache. Fill center with fillings of your choice. Bake until light golden brown, 12–15 minutes. Cool to room temperature. Makes 2–3 dozen pastries.

## STRANGE AND FAMILIAR

"If security could ever have a smell, it would be the fragrance of a warm *kolache*," wrote the novelist Willa Cather. Considered the national pastry of Czechoslovakia, kolaches are soft, dense pillows of yeast dough filled with poppy seed, cheese, or fruit fillings. Eaten primarily for breakfast or with coffee or tea, kolaches are edible emblems of Slavic culture brought to Wisconsin by immigrants like the Ourada family, which continues to identify its ethnic origin as Bohemian rather than Czech.

Given a choice between two ethnic Bohemian foods, kolache and *jaternice*, a pork sausage made with snouts, hearts, and tongue, who wouldn't play it cautious and choose the pastry? After all, a sweet roll is a sweet roll in any culture. As the authors of *The Minnesota Ethnic Food Book* note in general about ethnic foods offered for public consumption, "[Kolaches] are 'exotic' or distinctive enough to convey an ethnic image, yet they are tame enough to appeal to the uninitiated." The same can't be said about hog innards stuffed into a casing.

Other ethnic foods found in Wisconsin's small town cafes strike the same balance between exotic and tame, squeamish and safe. On the safe side are those featured in recipes in this book: kolaches; Cornish pasties—hearty meat and potato pies; Norwegian creamed cod; and Mexican rice and beans, salsa, pico de gallo, and other specialties. On the exotic side and more appealing to the initiated than to novices is Norwegian *lutefisk*—dried and reconstituted cod—served at the Norske Nook in Osseo (as well as the Nooks in Rice Lake and Hayward) twice during the months of October and November. Don't misconstrue "twice" as meaning that lutefisk isn't popular. Each time it's served, it quickly sells out. It's the difficulty in getting lutefisk from his St. Paul supplier that prevents owner Jerry Bechard from satisfying customer demand.

Foods become ethnic only through cross-cultural interaction; differences become apparent and symbolic only in comparison to what others in the same social context are cooking and eating. Traditional ethnic foods passed out of the everyday as immigrants in America shed or altered their ethnic traditions out of a desire to cast off the old world and embrace the new. Other contributing factors included a lack of familiar foodstuffs (for example, cod for lutefisk and poppy seeds and apricots for kolache fillings), adaptation to different cooking equipment such as cookstoves, and fear of political repercussions, especially between the two world wars. Reappearances of ethnic foods today are largely ritual, reserved for holidays and other festive family gatherings, as well as community festivals that honor local history and heritage. A good example is *Cesky Den,* or "Czech Day," a festival of Czech heritage held every June in Hillsboro, featuring pork with potato dumplings and sauerkraut, kolache, and jaternice (for those interested in not playing it completely safe). In Price County, the town of Phillips also offers traditional pastries and food, including blood dumplings, along with music, crafts, costumes, and dancing, during Czechoslovakian Days.

As with festivals, ethnic foods prepared and served in cafes identify and promote a community as special or unique. They also serve to celebrate and honor the family heritage and cultural traditions of individual owners—the Bohemian heritage of the Ourada family in Antigo, for example, or the Mexican heritage of Ernesto Rodriguez in Greenwood. By sharing kolaches or pico de gallo with the larger public, cafe owners act as "ritual specialists" expressing their own and their community's cultural identity through culinary capsules of heritage.—J. S.

# *Dinner Rolls*

## Ideal Cafe, Iron River
### *Mary and James "Mac" McBrair*

They're called dinner rolls, but what if you want to serve them for lunch? On busy cafe mornings when Mary battles the onslaught of breakfast orders, there's no time to prepare a yeast-raised dough. Instead, she prepares the first part of this recipe the night before and lets the dough rest in the refrigerator overnight. The rolls are shaped early in the day and set aside to rise all morning. Baked just before the lunch rush, they come to the table hot and golden, as welcome as snow at Christmas.

Mary received this recipe from the wife of a coworker many years ago. "I'd always had some trouble making yeast doughs, and then about five years ago I decided to try making my own bread. I saw a recipe for dinner rolls in the newspaper that a fourth-grade teacher used to have her students make. Well, I tried it and flunked fourth grade! But it spurred me on to get better at bread making. Now I make homemade rolls or bread for two or three lunch specials a week."

The recipe yields enough rolls to keep up with the demand when lunch special orders are coming in fast and furious—and enough for a home cook to freeze some for a future meal.

½  **cup sugar**
2  **tablespoons shortening**
1  **scant tablespoon salt**
2¼  **cups boiling water**
2  **packages (each ¼ ounce) dry yeast**
2  **eggs, beaten**
6½–7  **cups bread flour, divided**
   **melted butter or milk (optional)**

Place sugar, shortening, and salt in large bowl. Stir in the boiling water until shortening is melted. Cool mixture to lukewarm, 10–15 minutes. Stir in yeast. Add eggs and mix well. Add 4 cups of the flour and beat well. Stir in more flour, a half a cup at a time, until you've added 2 more cups. Turn dough out onto floured surface and knead briefly until dough is smooth and elastic. Return dough to the bowl, cover it tightly, and refrigerate it overnight.

Remove dough from refrigerator. Grease baking sheets or line them with parchment paper. For a simple shape, divide the dough into 24–36 pieces. Roll each piece on an unfloured surface into a ball (you can also elongate the balls into oblong rolls) and place them 2 inches apart on the prepared baking sheets.

For cloverleaf shapes, divide dough into 24 pieces and roll each piece into a ball. Cover the balls loosely with a cloth and let rest 10 minutes. Grease muffin tins. Divide each ball into 3 pieces and roll each piece into a small ball. Tuck 3 balls close to each other into the bottom of each of the greased muffin cups.

Place rolls in a warm location, cover with a light cloth or oiled plastic wrap, and let rise until doubled in bulk, approximately 3 hours.

To bake rolls, heat oven to 425 degrees. Lightly brush rolls with melted butter or milk, if desired. This will help them brown beautifully. Bake until golden brown, 10–15 minutes. Makes about 2–3 dozen rolls.

# Cream Puffs

## KATE'S CAFE, GLENWOOD CITY
### *Kate Platson-Phalin*

Kate was born a baker. As a girl she'd wait until her mother left the house, then hit the kitchen to concoct kid-favorite treats out of this and that. Her talent matured as she worked alongside her mother, grandmother, and Aunt Phyllis in the kitchen. "Baking was a growing up thing," she explains.

What could be more Wisconsin than Kate's versatile cream puffs, popular for dessert, teas, business meetings, and whenever anyone needs a treat? "I use real everything—cream, butter, fresh eggs," she says. Thank you, Kate.

You can fill these with plain whipped cream (see page 154) but Kate relies on her grandmother's recipe for vanilla cream filling to which she adds various flavorings. "Grandma also used it for fillings between layer cakes," she notes. The puff recipe itself came from Kate's cousin, Jan, who pleased her guests with savory fillings like tuna, ham, and chicken salad.

Kate puts the puff dough to work in coffee cakes, too. "I layer cherries, fillings, apples, anything. The cream puffs and the coffee cake look impressive but are very easy."

*Puffs*

1   cup water
½   cup (8 tablespoons) butter
1   cup all-purpose white flour
⅛   teaspoon salt
3   eggs

*Vanilla Cream Filling*

½   cup sugar
2½  tablespoons flour
¼   teaspoon salt
1½  cups heavy cream
1   teaspoon vanilla extract
¼   teaspoon almond extract
    optional flavoring ingredient: 1 cup mashed bananas
        or shredded coconut, 1 teaspoon instant coffee, etc.

*Savory Fillings*
**tuna salad, ham salad, chicken salad, smoked
fish spread, etc.**

To make puffs, heat oven to 375 degrees. Lightly grease a baking sheet. Place 1 cup water and the butter in a 2-quart sauce pan. Bring it to a boil. Add the flour and salt all at once and stir quickly. (For savory puffs, Kate suggests using ¼–⅓ cup rye or whole wheat flour and white flour for the remaining amount, to make 1 cup total.) It will form a ball almost immediately. Remove from heat and place in a mixing bowl. Then add the eggs one at a time, beating on low speed until mixture is smooth before adding the next egg. After the third egg has been incorporated, scrape the beaters down using a rubber spatula.

Use the same rubber spatula to place 6 large or 12 small, high mounds on baking sheet. Bake 45 minutes. Do not open the door as they bake or they will fall. "Once they fall, you can't use them for anything," says Kate. "They're hard and leaden and have to be thrown away. So don't open the door!" Remove from oven and leave puffs on sheet to cool completely. Don't puncture or disturb them while they are cooling or they will deflate.

To make vanilla cream filling, sift sugar, flour, and salt into a bowl. Place heavy cream in a 2-quart sauce pan and heat slowly until it scalds (that is, comes to a boil). Measure ½ cup of the hot cream and stir it into the sugar mixture. Mix this into the cream remaining in the pan and cook it slowly, stirring constantly, until thickened, about 10 minutes. Stir in the vanilla and almond extracts and optional flavoring ingredient of your choice. Chill filling thoroughly.

To finish the puffs, cut off tops of puffs and fill bottoms with sweet or savory filling. Cap and serve. Makes 6 jumbo or 12 small puffs.

# Beer Bread

## IDEAL CAFE, IRON RIVER
*Mary and James "Mac" McBrair*

Mary McBrair makes her own breads from scratch, but when she's in a pinch for time, she turns to this "Ideal" recipe.

> 3  **cups self-rising flour**
> 2  **tablespoons sugar**
> 1  **can or bottle (12 ounces) beer, at room temperature**

Heat oven to 350 degrees. Oil a large loaf pan. Mix flour and sugar in a bowl. Stir in beer. Spread batter in pan. Bake 45 minutes. Cool. Makes 1 loaf.

### HAVE YOUR BEER AND EAT IT, TOO

Beer can improve recipes in many ways. When a fermented malt beverage is heated, most of the alcohol is steamed away. Left behind is bountiful bouquet and flavor that soften strong flavors or highlight subtle ones. Beer lends its rich essence to long-simmered soups and stews. As a marinade, it tenderizes and adds a zesty tang to meats and fish without the bite that vinegar or lemon juice adds. It also makes baked goods moist and batters crispy and tender.

Wisconsin, of course, abounds in local brews. Beer comes in numerous forms and flavors—dark, light, sweet, bitter, heavy, delicate, fruity, spicy, fizzy, flat—and you can choose anything from mild pilsners and pale ales to malty bocks and smoky stouts. Just as you would with wine, consider the taste, color, and body of the dish you're making and select a beer to complement it.

Beef stew, for example, calls for a deep, dark brew like Sprecher Black Bavarian or Gray's Oatmeal Stout. For simmering brats, many cooks choose a lighter, less expensive choice, like Regal Brau from Huber. Even dessert can benefit from a splash of ale. Try substituting the milk in a fudge recipe with fruity Belgian Red from New Glarus Brewing Company.

For more about having your beer and eating it too, see page 129.—T. A.

# Sugar Cookies

## KATE'S CAFE, GLENWOOD CITY
*Kate Platson-Phalin*

Back in the late 1960s in Janesville, where Kate used to live, the Rolling Pin Bakery made sugar cookies that Kate has never forgotten. "These cookies are the closest in flavor and texture as I could come to their sugar cookies," she explains. "The recipe is from a good friend, Rita Monroe, of Janesville. She is my son's godmother."

The cookies are very popular at Kate's Cafe. "I keep these cookies in glass jars on the bakery counter. If I don't have them, I hear about it."

The dough is fairly versatile, Kate says. "You can use the dough for cut-out cookies, or I also roll it into balls and flatten them for giant cookies. I start with three ounces in weight and flatten them with the back of my hand to six inches in diameter. I sprinkle them with sugar after I flatten them. But the cut-outs are especially popular at holidays. I usually frost them and make smiley faces."

> ¾ **cup butter, at room temperature**
> ¾ **cup shortening, at room temperature**
> 2 **cups sugar**
> 4 **eggs**
> 1 **teaspoon almond extract**
> 5 **cups flour**
> 2 **teaspoons baking powder**
> 2 **teaspoons salt**
> **additional sugar for sprinkling on cookies**

Beat butter, shortening, and sugar in a large bowl until fluffy and well blended. Beat in eggs and almond extract. Whisk flour, baking powder, and salt together in another bowl. Stir flour mixture into first mixture until smooth. Chill dough 1 hour.

To bake cookies, heat oven to 375 degrees. Lightly grease baking sheets or line them with parchment paper. Scoop dough, 2–3 ounces per scoop, onto baking sheets, leaving 2 to 3 inches between scoops. Flatten the cookies and sprinkle with sugar. Bake 11–13 minutes. They should remain pale in color. Place the sheets on cake racks and let cookies cool until they firm up somewhat, then transfer them to the racks to cool completely. Repeat this process until all the dough is used up. Makes 34–36 large cookies or 20–22 humongous ones.

## THE BAKER'S FRIEND: PARCHMENT PAPER

Parchment paper is white or tan-colored, oven-proof, disposable paper that is sold by the roll in most kitchen supply stores. Once a baker tries it, there's no going back, for it eliminates the need to grease baking pans or sheets, and cookies will slip right off it. No sticking, no cleanup, and you can use the same sheet for multiple pans of cookies.
—T. A.

# *Triple Fudge Brownies*

## KATE'S CAFE, GLENWOOD CITY
### *Kate Platson-Phalin*

Kate's tried-and-true brownie recipe comes from *The Family Home Cookbook,* the first she ever bought. "I was stationed with my husband in Fort Bliss, Texas. It was just before he went to Vietnam, and I bought this from a door-to-door salesman. . . . I still have it, a little the worse for wear."

At Kate's Cafe, these brownies are in great demand by themselves and also as the base for Fudge Brownie Delight. "Pile vanilla ice cream, chocolate sauce, and whipped cream, a cherry—I use a bit of everything!—on top of a brownie," instructs Kate. "It's a beautiful thing when it's all done.

"I also bake them in a half sheet pan to make ice cream sandwiches. I cut the brownies with a two-inch round cookie cutter. Or I let the leftover brownie bits dry a little and put them on top of peanut butter pie. You've got to find another use for everything."

The frosting is similar to a ganache because it goes on warm and remains shiny even after it cools. "It gives a nice, deep layer of fudge on top of the brownie. It sets up fairly good in about 10–15 minutes. If a little of the fudge drips on the side of the brownie, people like that." If you're short on time, dust the brownies with powdered sugar. At Christmas, Kate makes them with special powdered sugar designs.

*Brownies*
- 2 **cups sugar, divided**
- 8 **tablespoons cocoa powder (Kate uses Hershey's)**
- 1½ **cups flour**
- 1 **teaspoon salt**
- 4 **eggs, lightly beaten**
- 1 **cup oil**
- ¼ **cup water**
- 2 **teaspoons vanilla extract**
- ½ **cup chocolate chips or shavings from your favorite chocolate candy bar (Snickers, Milky Way, etc.)**

Heat oven to 350 degrees. Grease and flour the bottom and sides of a 9-by-13-inch baking pan. Sprinkle it with a little of the sugar; this will give the bottom of the brownies a little texture. Place remaining sugar, cocoa powder, flour, salt, eggs, oil, water, and vanilla in a large mixing bowl. Stir until just combined. Stir in chocolate chips or candy bar shavings. Scrape batter into pan with a rubber spatula.

Bake 25 minutes. Remove from oven right away! Sides should have pulled away from pan slightly. Cool and frost. Makes 24—36 one-inch-high brownies.

*Quick Chocolate Fudge Frosting*
¾ **cup sugar**
6 **tablespoons butter**
6 **tablespoons heavy cream**
1 **cup milk chocolate chips or cut-up chocolate bar**
1 **teaspoon vanilla extract**

Place sugar, butter, and heavy cream in small (8-inch) sauté pan. Place over medium-low flame and slowly bring to boil. Remove from heat and stir in chocolate chips and vanilla. Let frosting cool somewhat before spreading over brownies.

# Chocolate Chip Cookies

## KATE'S CAFE, GLENWOOD CITY
### *Kate Platson-Phalin*

Kate's chocolate chip cookies are the big, beautiful, soft-textured kind that stay chewy even after they've been stored for three or four days. "If they last that long!" Kate laughs. Her customers "eat them so fast, I'm not sure if they even taste them." The recipe came from an old cookbook of her mother's.

Kate cautions home cooks not to overbake them. Pull them out of the oven when they're lightly colored. If they get a little dark, don't despair. "One lady who used to work for me likes them burnt," she says. To each her own.

If you like a lot of chocolate, use the larger amount of chips. Kate prefers milk chocolate chips from the Ghirardelli company. "A lot of other chips are waxy and they don't melt well into the batter."

> ½ **cup butter, at room temperature**
> ½ **cup shortening (Kate uses plain Crisco), at room temperature**
> 1 **cup brown sugar**
> ⅔ **cup white sugar**
> 2 **eggs**
> 1 **teaspoon vanilla extract**
> 1 **teaspoon salt**
> 1 **teaspoon baking soda**
> 2½ **cups flour**
> 6–8 **ounces (1–1½ cups) chocolate chips**

Heat oven to 350 degrees. Beat butter and shortening in a large bowl until well combined. Beat in brown sugar and white sugar thoroughly. Beat in eggs, vanilla, and salt. Heat 2 tablespoons of water in a small bowl or pan; stir in baking soda. Stir water/soda mixture into batter. (From Kate: "The soda is double acting and when you add it to the water, it takes some of the action out. The cookies get high and stay high. They stay chewy and don't fall flat.") Stir in flour and chocolate chips until just combined.

Use a scoop or large rounded spoon to scoop cookies into 2- or 3-ounce mounds onto ungreased baking sheets, leaving 3 inches between each mound. Bake in batches until light golden brown, 10–12 minutes. Cool the cookies for a few minutes on the sheets, then transfer them with a metal spatula to racks. Cool to room temperature. Makes about 3 dozen large or 2 dozen gigantic cookies.

# THREE

~ ~ ~

# Soups

## ALL ABOUT ROUX

Roux (pronounced *roo*) is a cooked mixture of flour and fat used to thicken liquids, be they soups, sauces, or stews. Liquids thickened with roux are relatively stable and won't thin out as they cook, making roux popular with restaurant cooks who need to keep a dish hot in a steam table throughout a meal period. Roux is a dependable, trustworthy thickening agent for home cooks, too.

To prepare a roux, first melt butter, oil, or some other type of fat, then stir or whisk in flour until the mixture is well combined. To remove the raw flour flavor, heat the roux slowly for several minutes over a medium-low flame, stirring frequently to prevent scorching. For white or light-colored sauces and soups, take care not to let the roux color. For some dishes, such as brown sauce, cook the roux until it begins to color a little and takes on a lightly nutty flavor. A Cajun-style roux is cooked until it is dark brown and takes on a

*(continued on facing page)*

# Corn Sausage Soup

## AMHERST CAFE, AMHERST
### *Diane Stroik*

On the origins of this recipe, Diane relates, "In September of 1983 one of my waitresses and I went to a food equipment show in New Orleans. While we were there, we tried this soup at a little restaurant. It originally had shrimp in it, but that's too costly for us little guys, and I think the sausage gives it a wonderful flavor."

Diane always "warns" her customers that this soup is spicy, with its kick of cayenne. "The girls seem to handle spicy better than the boys," she notes. "Except for Butch from the bank. He adds Tabasco to it." This soup seems to bring out the humor in folks along with the sweat. Diane's brother-in-law claims there's no need to heat it up because it's hot enough already, and another customer calls her to make it when he has to go to the dentist. "He says it numbs his mouth!"

This is one of those concoctions that gets even better by the second or third day, so don't be afraid to double the recipe. If tomatoes are in season, substitute 2 cups chopped vine-ripened tomatoes for the canned. Use fresh corn instead of canned or frozen, too.

> ⅓ cup vegetable oil
> 3 tablespoons flour
> 1½–2 cups chopped onion
> 1 large green bell pepper, chopped
> ½ pound smoked kielbasa or Polish sausage, sliced
> 2 tablespoons chopped fresh parsley
> salt, pepper, and cayenne pepper to taste
> 1 can (14–16 ounces) chopped tomatoes, undrained
> 1 can (15 ounces) corn, undrained, or 2 cups frozen corn
> 1–3 cups water or chicken stock, divided

Make a roux by heating oil in a soup pot over medium flame. Gradually whisk in flour and cook, stirring often, until roux turns golden brown, 3–5 minutes. Stir in onions and continue to cook, stirring often, until onions are tender, about 10 minutes. Stir in green pepper, sausage, parsley, salt, pepper, and cayenne. (Be careful with the cayenne!) Add undrained tomatoes, corn with half the liquid from the can (discard the rest of the liquid), and 1 cup of the water or stock. Bring to simmer, reduce heat, and let simmer very slowly. Add more water or stock as it cooks to reach desired consistency. The soup will be done in as little as 15 minutes, but develops more flavor if you simmer it for an hour or longer. Makes 6–8 servings.

# Chicken Dumpling Soup

## WOLF RIVER DINER, FREMONT

*Bob and Nance Klapper, owners, June Klapper Otto, manager*

This recipe originated with Bob's mother, Jean Klapper. "Throughout the generations we've tried to 'improve' Grandma's recipe, but our guests always ask for the original," Bob and Nance's daughter June says. "Chicken dumpling soup is always on our menu, winter or summer, and it goes fast no matter what the season. In fact, our guests buy it by the quart and gallon! We're happy to share it. It's a cozy, feel-good food."

If you're tempted to add a teaspoon or two of parsley, sage, rosemary, or other dried herbs to this soup, that's perfectly okay. You might want to use homemade chicken stock instead of the water and chicken base. You might even play with the amount of dumplings. That's the beauty of soup: it invites you to be yourself.

### Soup
- 1 **small chicken (about 3 pounds), halved or quartered**
- 1–1½ **cups chopped onion**
- 2 **cups chopped carrots**
- 1–2 **cups chopped celery**
- 3 **tablespoons chicken base or 3–4 chicken bouillon cubes**
- **salt and pepper**

### Dumplings
- 3 **eggs**
- ¾ **cup milk**
- 2–3 **cups flour**
- 1 **teaspoon salt**

Place chicken in a very large soup pot. Add enough stock or water to cover the meat, 5–6 quarts. Bring to slow simmer and cook 45–60 minutes, skimming surface occasionally to remove foam as it forms. Remove chicken from liquid—which has now become a lightly flavored broth—and let it cool. Cut up the meat, discarding skin and bones. (Alternatively, you can let the chicken cool in the broth before removing the meat. This will strengthen the flavor of the broth.) Set chopped chicken aside. Add onions, carrots, and celery to broth; simmer 10 minutes. Stir in chicken base until dissolved. Stir in reserved chicken. Bring soup back to a simmer and season with salt and pepper to taste.

(continued from facing page)

deep, almost smoky flavor—the perfect accent to spicy soups like gumbo. Keep in mind that the more you cook a roux, the less thickening power it will have because heat breaks down the starch in flour.

However dark or light you make it, cooked roux is whisked into a simmering liquid—or vice versa—until the liquid is smooth. Then the mixture is simmered to rid it of any remaining starchy flavor and to thicken it to the desired consistency.
—T. A.

At this point you can make the dumplings and serve the soup, but it will develop more flavor if you let it stand off the heat for an hour or two, or cool it down and then chill it overnight. Bring soup back to a simmer before making the dumpling dough.

To make dumplings, beat eggs, milk, flour, and salt with electric beaters, adding flour until dough pulls away from the sides of the bowl. Drop spoonfuls—each roughly a rounded teaspoon or level tablespoon—of the dough into the soup; simmer until dumplings are done, about 10 minutes. The dumplings will absorb broth, so the soup will thicken considerably as it cooks more or cools down. Add more water, chicken base, and seasonings as desired. Makes about one gallon.

### Chicken Soup for the Diner Soul

If there's anything more relished in diners than chicken soup, I don't know what it is. Indeed, a steaming cup of dumpling-crammed chicken soup can stir the soul, as is illustrated in this heartwarming, true story told by June Klapper Otto. It is posted on the cash register at the Wolf River Diner for all to marvel at.

Several years ago, I was approached by a man sitting on Table Seven at the diner. He greeted me soberly and thanked me wholeheartedly for our wonderful homemade chicken dumpling soup. I said, "Gee, you're welcome!" and proceeded to join him in a cup of coffee. I noticed two bowls of chicken dumpling soup with crackers crumbled in each, along with two glasses of soda. I was a little perplexed because the table was set for two, yet only the man sat across from me. He gently put a hand-knit bag on the table and announced to me that his wife's ashes were in this bag.

He continued to explain that he and his wife had shared eleven years of good times here at the diner over a cup of chicken dumpling soup. He said, as we wept, that he wanted to enjoy one more cup with his wife before he scattered her ashes over the Wolf River on the Fourth of July.

It was impressed on me that day that we are not just a place serving food. We create memories and preserve traditions—memories like a man and wife enjoying comfort food together, or an ice cream cone before the Webfooters Show or after a Little League game.

I am so proud of every staff member here. My life has been enriched by getting to know all of your spectacular personalities and unique strengths. Enjoy yourself with our fine guests! Share memories and pour a cup of happiness to all you serve.

—T. A.

# Turkey Corn Chowder

## MAIN STREET CAFE, SIREN
*Conny Roy*

Good recipes come from many sources, including food product companies. "This recipe came from a Farmers Brothers soup base many moons ago, and it's still very popular," Conny tells us. It's a favorite of the fish salesman who marks his next visit on the cafe's calendar to indicate when it should next be on the daily specials board. "He always takes a bucket of it home," she laughs.

Since home cooks don't have access to the same commercial products that cafe owners rely on, Conny's original recipe has been adapted for the home kitchen using a soup base made from scratch. For more on soup bases, see page 84.

*Soup Base*
- 3 **cups milk**
- 3 **cups chicken or turkey stock**
- 6 **tablespoons butter**
- 6 **tablespoons flour**

*Other Ingredients*
- 1 **tablespoon butter or bacon fat**
- ¾ **cup chopped celery**
- ½ **cup chopped onion**
- ¼–½ **cup crumbled, cooked bacon bits**
- 1½–2 **cups diced cooked turkey**
- 1½ **cups diced cooked potatoes**
- 1½–2 **cups frozen corn kernels, thawed**
- 1½ **teaspoons dried parsley flakes**
- **salt and white pepper**

To make the soup base, combine milk and chicken stock in saucepan; heat gently and keep warm. Meanwhile, melt butter in another saucepan over medium flame. Gradually stir in the flour; cook, stirring often, 3–4 minutes. Whisk in the hot milk-stock mixture and cook several minutes, stirring occasionally as it thickens.

While thickened liquid is cooking, prepare other ingredients. Melt 1 tablespoon butter or bacon fat in soup pot over medium flame. Add celery and onions; cook, stirring often, until tender. Stir in the soup base plus bacon bits, turkey, potatoes, corn, and dried parsley. Bring to simmer, reduce heat to low, and cook, stirring often, to blend the flavors for a few minutes. Season to taste with salt and pepper. Makes about 2 quarts.

## Making Chicken Stock

One day years ago, while working in a restaurant, I had just boned several chickens and was covering the scraps with water in a pot when a fellow employee, looking slightly appalled, asked what I was doing. "Making stock," I told him, explaining how the heating liquid would draw flavor from the bones to create a rich broth. "That's crazy," scoffed the novice cook. "You can't make something out of nothing."

Like a magic potion distilled from bat wings and snakebark sticks, the miracle of chicken stock is a little hard to believe. But the real enchantment, when stock is used in place of water, is its power to transform soups, sauces, stews, gravies, grain dishes, and numerous other preparations from good dishes into great ones.

Tasty, low in fat, and economical, chicken stock is also easy to make. If you can't boil water, all the better, for the secret to a clear, deep-flavored broth is gentle simmering. Don't believe that only restaurant cooks and homebodies have the time for it. Stock making is perfectly suited to today's multitasking schedules. Simply combine the ingredients, set the flame low, and let the stock bubble lazily for several hours while you go about your other business.

There are refinements, of course, and many tips for making great stock. If possible, start with naturally raised chicken from local sources. (You can also make poultry stock from other kinds of fowl, of course.) You'll get a decent batch of stock from mere bones (necks and backs add gelatinous body) and water (for better extraction start with cold), but the flavor is enhanced with meat, aromatic vegetables, and seasonings. Since these ingredients release their essence more quickly than bones, add them later in the cooking process.

Some additional tips: Don't add salt until the stock is done and ready for tasting (as a presalted liquid concentrates so does its saltiness). Don't use vegetables that smell skunky when overcooked, like broccoli and cabbage. Sautéing or roasting the ingredients until browned before simmering will improve flavor and color. Onion skins will also add color.

Skimming a stock removes coagulated proteins that collect, although the worst that can happen if you're not careful with this step is some cloudiness. Do you need to clarify stock (an elaborate process involving egg whites and parsley stems)? Not unless you have a compulsive behavior disorder or are making consommé.

Simmering broth will warm and perfume your kitchen. Collect bones and vegetables in your freezer until you have enough to make a big batch. Ladle your finished stock into plastic tubs or muffin tins for freezing, and lay in a supply of flavor that will improve your cooking for weeks to come.

A recipe isn't necessary to make a good stock, but here's a rough guide:

# Chicken Stock

2–3  quarts raw or leftover cooked chicken bones
  1  cup onion chunks
  1  cup carrot pieces
  1  cup other vegetables (celery, mushrooms, potato, etc.)
    several parsley sprigs
2–3  teaspoons dried herbs (rosemary, thyme, oregano, etc.)
    or 1–2 tablespoons fresh sprigs
12–15  peppercorns

Place bones in large, deep pot; cover with cold water. Bring to gentle simmer, skimming off scum. After about 2 hours of very slow simmering, add remaining ingredients. Continue simmering about 2 hours longer. Strain through double thickness of cheesecloth or coffee filters into bowl. Chill thoroughly, preferably overnight. Spoon off fat, or leave some for extra flavor, if desired. Stock can be stored in refrigerator 3–5 days or in freezer several months.—T. A.

# Clam Chowder

## BRICK HOUSE CAFE, BARRONETT
### *John and Dana Glaubitz*

John browses all kinds of cookbooks, including Betty Crocker and church publications, when he is itching to expand his selection of daily specials. But when it's something "more professional" he is hungry for, he turns to *Professional Cooking* by Wayne Gisslen, the culinary school bible, from which this recipe is adapted. John uses smoky Wisconsin bacon instead of the salt pork called for in the original, and he has created several spin-offs, too, like potato chowder, corn chowder, and country vegetable chowder.

| | |
|---|---|
| 4 | cans (each 6½ ounces) minced clams |
| 1 | bottle (8 ounces) clam juice |
| ½ | pound bacon, diced |
| 1 | cup finely diced onion |
| 6 | tablespoons flour |
| 3½–4 | cups peeled, diced red or white potatoes |
| 2 | cups milk |
| ½ | cup half-and-half |
| | salt and white pepper |

Drain juice from canned minced clams into a sauce pan; there should be about 1½ cups juice. Add bottled clam juice plus ½ cup water. Place over low flame to heat.

Meanwhile, place diced bacon and onions in large skillet over medium flame. Heat, stirring often, until bacon and onions are cooked, taking care not to let them brown too much. Reduce heat to low and gradually stir in the flour to make a roux. Cook the roux 3–4 minutes, stirring often and without letting it brown. Whisk in the hot clam juice-water mixture and raise the heat to medium. Bring to a simmer while whisking to remove lumps.

Stir in potatoes, cover, and let simmer, stirring often, until potatoes are tender, 10–15 minutes. Meanwhile, heat milk and half-and-half together until hot but not boiling. When potatoes are done, stir in the hot milk mixture. Reduce heat to low. Stir in the clams and heat through, but do not let it boil or it will curdle. Season with salt and white pepper to taste. Makes 8–10 servings.

# Ham and Corn Chowder

## COUNTRY CAFE, BLACK RIVER FALLS
### *Mark and Laura Chrest*

"Cream soups sell better than clear soups," says Mark. It is the Dairy State, after all, and his customers prefer thick, creamy, and chunky all happening in one soup. A chef from Boston taught Mark how to make this chowder. "But I kind of moved it around," he says. "I thought the Boston version would be too salty and garlicky for the Midwest."

- 3 tablespoons vegetable oil
- 1 cup diced onion
- 1 cup diced carrots
- ¾–1 cup diced celery
- 2–3 cups peeled, diced russet potatoes
- 3 bay leaves
- 2 cloves garlic, minced
- ½–1 teaspoon dried thyme leaves
- 1–1½ cups corn kernels
- 1–2 cups (about ½ pound) diced ham
- 2 cups heavy cream
- 4–6 cups 2% milk, divided
- 1 tablespoon chicken base
- 8 tablespoons (1 stick) butter
- ½ cup flour
- 3–6 dashes bottled hot pepper sauce (like Tabasco)
- salt and white pepper

Heat oil in a large soup pot over medium flame. Add onions, carrots, celery, potatoes, bay leaves, garlic, and thyme. Cook, stirring often, until onions are golden and nearly tender. Add corn, ham, heavy cream, 4 cups of the milk, and chicken base. Bring to simmer.

Meanwhile, make a roux by melting the butter in a small skillet over medium-low flame. Gradually stir in the flour and let it cook, stirring occasionally, for several minutes. Whisk the roux into the simmering soup until soup thickens. The soup will be pretty thick; thin it as desired with additional milk. Stir in hot pepper sauce and season with salt and pepper to taste. Makes about 2 quarts.

## ALWAYS SOUP, SOUP ALL WAYS

As I traveled around Wisconsin in search of notable cafes, I frequently met people who expressed envy for my occupation. Adjectives like *fun* and *interesting* peppered their enthusiasm. While it's true my journey was a great adventure, there were many days it felt like anything but. Marching into one cafe after another as both a stranger and a lone woman never ceased to be difficult, regardless of how many hundred times I had already done it. It was difficult to summon up charm when I missed my husband and son, my stomach hurt from chronic overeating, and the geezers around the coffee table turned and stared whenever I walked through a cafe door.

Not being a coffee drinker only compounded the awkwardness. I couldn't perch at the counter and hover over a bottomless cup while taking the measure of a place, as many of the folks I met out on the road admitted to doing. I ate a lot of pie before I realized a cup of soup would be a great substitute for a cup of coffee. Terese believes "the entire picture of a cafe comes from its soup, mashed potatoes and gravy, and pie." She's right. Find slow-brewed soup, peeled and mashed real spuds, and homemade pie, and you've found a cafe worth framing in a story.

And so I spooned soup. All kinds of soup. Chicken and noodle, vegetable beef, split pea, cream of potato, clam chowder. You name it, I ate it. Whenever I encountered something unusual on the daily menu board, I opted for that. Echoing repeatedly in my mind was the sage advice of an older woman I'd met over a bowl of Czechoslovakian chicken dumpling soup known as *shuleke* at the Country Style Cookin' Restaurant in Hillsboro: "Anything not customary is bound to be good." I'll always remember the shuleke, as well as the stuffed green pepper soup at Shelly's Northside Cafe in Baldwin. (When I requested the recipe, Shelly confessed it was frozen. I never would have guessed.) At the Four Seasons Cafe and Deli in Eagle River, I enjoyed Elly Mocello's Irish vegetable soup made with crumbs of corned beef, chopped cabbage, diced potatoes, carrots, and rutabagas. Other pleasant soup memories include the vegetable beef at Greenwood's Cafe in Reedsburg, Ham and Corn Chowder at the Country Cafe in Black River Falls (see recipe on page 51), and, at Kristine's Restaurant in Three Lakes, soup wizard Jeff Frye's Bavarian-style ham and dumpling.

Like teachers who remember only the exceptional students and the incorrigible ones, I have bad soup memories to go along with the good. There was a bowl of hamburger soup with elbow macaroni that had absorbed every last drop of broth so that they looked like pale, fleshy worms. It appeared only slightly worse than it tasted. In another cafe, I ordered the daily vegetable soup and watched as the owner dumped a can of Campbell's into a saucepan. There are few secrets in a cafe where the cook works in full view of the customers. I also remember a cup of chili that was so overpowered with chili powder that I fell into a paroxysm of sneezing so long lasting that the cafe owner refused my payment for the bill.

Unlike Hoosiers, who all but banish soup from cafe menus between April and October, Wisconsinites relish soup year-round. Cafe owners tell me that the hotter the weather, the better soup sells. My Chippewa Falls–born husband, Mark, offers a credible explanation. He often craves soup on even the hottest summer days, especially when he is worn out from paddling his canoe or pedaling his bike. He'll slide into a cafe booth, pick up the menu, flutter through its pages, and announce, "I feel like a soup." Never, "I'm hungry for soup" or "I'd like soup" or "I feel like soup," but always "I feel like *a* soup." Huh? What's *a* soup?

"I like *a* soup because it's a light meal that's also filling," Mark explains. "After I exercise I'm hungry but not yet ready to eat a large meal. Also, I like the way *a* hot soup runs down my throat and warms my belly. It just feels good and relaxes me. It's real comfort food."—J. S.

# Mushroom Barley Soup

## OAK STREET CAFE, JUNEAU
*Diane Moulai and Santo Pulvino*

Sadly, the Oak Street Cafe closed its doors in April 2005. During its four-year run, Diane and Santo insisted on only home cooking because, Diane said, "customers can't be bought." They could be sold on original soups like this one, however.

2 tablespoons vegetable oil
1 medium onion, chopped
1 stalk celery, chopped
½ pound fresh mushrooms, sliced
1 large clove garlic, minced
½ cup medium pearled barley
6 cups water
¼ cup soy sauce
1 teaspoon dried dill or 1–2 tablespoons
    chopped fresh dill
1–2 carrots, peeled and diced
1–2 tablespoons chopped fresh parsley
    salt and pepper

Heat oil in a soup pot over medium flame. Add onion, celery, mushrooms, and garlic. Cook, stirring often, 5–10 minutes. Add barley, water, and soy sauce. If you're using dried dill, add that now, too. Stir well, bring to simmer, reduce heat to low, cover, and cook slowly about 1 hour.

Stir in carrots and parsley. If you're using fresh dill, stir it in, too. Add more water, if desired, and continue to simmer slowly another 30–60 minutes. Add salt and pepper to taste. Makes 6 servings.

# Janette's Chicken Enchilada Soup

## DADDY MAXWELL'S ARCTIC CIRCLE DINER, WILLIAMS BAY

*Marshall and Janette Maxwell*

Food has power, sometimes healing power, as in the case of this rousing, south of the border–inspired soup from contributor Janette Maxwell. When she learned that a clerk at the shop near her cafe was feeling down, she took a bowl over to him. "He perked right up," she says. "So it's true, food really helps."

> 2   small (each 3 pounds) whole chickens, or 1 large (6-pound) whole chicken
> 6   quarts cold water or combination poultry stock and water
> ½   cup (1 stick) butter
> ¾   cup unbleached flour
> 8   ounces (about 2 cups) shredded or thinly sliced American cheese
> 8   ounces (about 2 cups) shredded cheddar cheese
> 2   cans (each 10 ounces) mild red enchilada sauce
> 2   cans (each 19 ounces) mild green enchilada sauce
> 1   tablespoon Cholula brand bottled hot sauce
> 1–3 teaspoons chicken base (optional)
>     salt to taste
>     garnishes: sour cream and tortilla chips (see below)

Place chickens in a very large soup pot; cover with water (or water-stock combination) and bring to simmer, skimming surface as needed. Simmer chicken 45 minutes, then turn off heat and let it cool in the liquid. When chicken is cool enough to handle, transfer it to a cutting board. Remove all skin and bones. Shred the chicken into strips by scraping the tines of a fork against the flesh. Set aside.

Strain chicken broth through cheesecloth or fine mesh strainer into a second pot. Clean and dry the original pot and return it to the stovetop. Add butter and melt it over medium-low flame. Whisk in flour and cook this roux, stirring often, several minutes. Meanwhile, bring broth to a simmer. Gradually whisk hot broth into roux. Let simmer several minutes, then reduce heat to lowest point and add cheeses a handful at a time, stirring constantly. When soup is smooth, stir in both kinds of enchilada sauce and the hot pepper sauce. If desired, add chicken base to taste. Add salt to taste. Stir in the shredded chicken and heat through. Garnish each bowl with sour cream and some tortilla chips. Makes about 6 quarts soup.

# Make-Your-Own Tortilla Chips

**shortening or oil for frying (Janette uses shortening)**
**corn tortillas**
**table salt or popcorn salt**

Add shortening or oil to a large, heavy pot or pan, to reach a depth of 2 inches. Heat over medium-high flame to 350 degrees. Cut tortillas into strips. Fat is hot enough for frying when one of the tortilla pieces begins to bubble immediately when you immerse its edge into the oil. Fry the pieces a few at a time, without crowding the pot. Turn them as they cook to lightly brown both sides; this should take just a couple of moments per side. Drain each batch on paper towels and salt them lightly while they are still warm. Cool completely and store in an airtight container.—T. A.

# Stuffed Green Pepper Soup

## OLD STORE CAFE AND DELI, DALE

*Deb and Bob Chonos*

Although it changed hands in 2004, we continue to remember the Old Store Cafe and Deli for Bob's multitiered and wacky namesake burger featured on page 124. And while Deb used her imagination with soups, she typically kept the ingredients straightforward and the seasonings simple, knowing that's what her regular customers preferred. "We served stuffed green pepper soup at least once a week because people asked for it," Deb says. "My husband, Bob, hates stuffed green peppers, but even he loves this soup."

1   pound ground beef, browned and crumbled
1   green pepper, finely chopped
1   can (15 ounces) tomato sauce
3   cans (each 11½ ounces) or about
        4 cups tomato juice
2   cups cooked rice

Combine first four ingredients. Simmer ½ to 1 hour. Add rice; simmer 10 minutes or longer. Makes 6 servings

### SOUPING IT UP

In small town cafes, owners and cooks don't mess with what works. On the other hand, when it comes to soup, messing around is almost inevitable. Creative cooks just can't resist adding a handful of this or a splash of that, adjusting the soup's ingredients to use up leftovers or changing them to please their own "customers." It could be that's where the phrase "souped up" comes from. We offer this souped-up version of Stuffed Green Pepper Soup.

1   pound ground beef
¾   cup finely chopped onion
2   teaspoons minced garlic
1   large sweet red pepper, finely chopped
1   teaspoon dried oregano

1 can (15 ounces) tomato sauce
3 cans (each 11½ ounces) or about 4 cups
 spicy V-8 juice
2 cups cooked rice
 salt and pepper to taste
 salad croutons

Brown ground beef with onion and garlic over medium-high flame. Combine with sweet red pepper, oregano, tomato sauce, and tomato juice in soup pot. Simmer, stirring often, ½ hour or longer. Stir in rice; continue simmering about 10 minutes. Season to taste with salt and pepper. Serve each bowl topped with croutons. Makes 6 servings. —T. A.

# Homemade Beef Broth

## WENDY'S PLACE, MINONG
*Wendy and Terry Holman*

Classic cafe food is plain but never tasteless. Wendy says she uses few spices but flavors her gravies and soups with homemade beef broth, made from roasts prepared for daily specials. Her Philly Cheese Steak Sandwich (page 127) and Hamburger Vegetable Soup (page 60) are perfect examples of how real broth pumps up the flavor in recipes.

 **4-pound eye-of-round beef roast**
3 tablespoons packaged beef stew seasoning (Wendy uses
 Schilling brand)
1 medium onion, sliced
 salt and pepper

Heat oven to 325 degrees. Place roast in pan with fitted cover. Add 6–8 cups water, or enough to cover at least three-quarters of the roast. Stir in beef stew seasoning, onion, and salt and pepper to taste. Cover, place in oven, and cook until meat is fork-tender, 2½–3 hours. Remove roast to a plate; strain broth, and, if desired, skim off fat. (It's easiest to remove after broth has been chilled.) Refrigerate meat overnight and use for Philly Cheese Steak Sandwiches or other dishes. Makes 6–8 cups.

# Pinto Bean and Ham Soup

## LOG CABIN CAFE, CRANDON
### Susan and Larry Palubicki

Like the Biscuits and Gravy featured on page 17, this rib-sticking satisfier was brought to northern Wisconsin by Kentucky migrants more than a century ago. It is prepared by cook Tammy Wiegand from this family recipe used for many years by both her grandma and her husband's grandma. The cafe's generous ten-ounce bowl is served with saltine crackers and a deep-fried bread stick, and occasionally corn bread, the traditional Appalachian side dish.

"The longer this cooks, the thicker it gets," says cafe owner Susan Palubicki. "If it lasts until the second day, it will get as thick as porridge. That's when my son likes it best."

- 1 cup diced onion
- 1 cup diced celery
- 1 cup diced carrots
- 2½ cups diced ham
- 1 pound pinto beans, rinsed twice
- 2 teaspoons chicken base or 2 chicken bouillon cubes
- 1 teaspoon minced garlic
- ½ teaspoon crumbled sage leaves
- ¼ teaspoon white pepper
- ¼ teaspoon baking soda (optional)
- salt and pepper to taste

Combine onions, celery, carrots, ham, and 12 cups water in large soup pot. Bring mixture to a simmer, skimming surface often to remove the froth. Stir in beans, chicken base, garlic, sage, and white pepper. Bring to simmer again, skimming surface as needed. Partially cover the pot and simmer the soup slowly until beans are tender and mixture begins to thicken, about 2 hours. About a half-hour before the soup is done, you can stir in the baking soda to help the beans soften. If you need to add more water as it cooks, add boiling water so that the soup will continue simmering without interruption. Season to taste with salt and pepper. Makes 8–12 servings.

## BEAN SOUP SCIENCE

There's no denying the pleasure of bean soup, especially during an unrelenting winter in Wisconsin. A big, bubbling pot of split pea or pinto bean with ham lends comfort just when we need it most. But eating bean soup is only part of the pleasure. Heating your favorite cast-iron kettle, slicing celery, watching pebblelike legumes transform slowly into liquid nurture—in short, cooking bean soup is enjoyable, too.

The late great food writer Laurie Colwin called it thrilling, in fact. She was referring, in *More Home Cooking,* to how easy it is to throw together a batch of lentil soup. "There is almost nothing to do," Colwin gushed, but I don't think she was talking just about saving time. Making bean soup is a little like playing God: take a rib here, wave a hand there, and behold! you've created a bowl of nourishment. A whole much greater than the sum of its very simple parts.

Supernatural power aside, however, it is science that explains how tough little starch granules homogenize into creaminess with the addition of water and slow, steady heat. If it's the science behind making bean soup that gives you a kick, then check out Russ Parsons's *How to Read a French Fry: And Other Stories of Intriguing Kitchen Science*—and be prepared to have many myths debunked.

Salting the water before cooking? No problem, Parsons says; it adds flavor and has no effect on cooking time. Adding tomatoes and other acidic ingredients? Only very large amounts will actually toughen beans. Baking soda? Sure, it softens beans faster; but take care, it can also turn them into mush.

What about presoaking beans to speed up cooking? Well, that depends. Cooking time is more affected by a bean's age—the older it is, the longer it takes—and type. Lentils, for example, require no soaking while presoaked garbanzo beans can take hours before they get tender. Even the mineral content of your water can affect cooking time. In a nutshell, presoaking does shorten cooking time, but only by a little. "On the other hand," Parsons reminds us, "soaking also removes a marginal amount of nutrients and . . . a noticeable amount of flavor."—T. A.

# Hamburger Vegetable Soup

## WENDY'S PLACE, MINONG
### Wendy and Terry Holman

Measurements are not something Wendy Holman worries about when she makes this soup, but she does pause before adding the rutabaga. "There's one lady who hates 'baggies, but she loves the soup, and she always asks me if there's 'baggies in it." Wendy tells how the customer once, by mistake, ate a bowl that contained rutabaga and wouldn't believe Wendy when she learned the truth. "It was good!" said the woman. "It couldn't have had rutabaga. I wouldn't have eaten it."

Use Wendy's recipe for beef broth on page 57 in preparing this soup.

    1  pound ground beef
    1  cup chopped onion
  ½  cup chopped celery
    4  cups homemade beef broth
    1  cup chopped carrots
    1  cup chopped potatoes
    1  cup chopped rutabaga
2–3  cups tomato juice
    1  can (10¾ ounces) tomato soup
1–2  cups cooked elbow macaroni
      salt and pepper

Adjust the amounts and types of ingredients in this soup as desired. Brown hamburger in skillet over medium-high heat. Drain off excess fat, add onion and celery, and cook a few minutes, stirring often. Combine with beef broth, carrots, potatoes, rutabaga, tomato juice, and tomato soup in pot. Simmer until vegetables are tender. Add macaroni and salt and pepper to taste. Makes 8 servings.

# Beer Cheese Soup

## MAIN DISH FAMILY RESTAURANT, LUCK
*Jenell and Ralph Britton*

Travelers to the town of Luck have been known to call ahead to request this simple concoction based on commercial canned soup, with a twist or two. Jenell serves it every other week year-round at the Main Dish, with a handful of popcorn on top and, of course, crackers on the side.

      2  **cans (each 10¾ ounces) Campbell's condensed
          cheese soup**
 1½–2  **cups milk**
      ½  **cup beer**
          **pepper to taste**
   4–6  **tablespoons finely chopped raw or cooked onion
          (optional)**
   4–6  **tablespoons finely chopped ham or cooked
          bacon bits (optional)**
          **popped popcorn**

Combine soup, milk, beer, pepper, and optional additions in soup pot. Bring to simmer, stirring often. Simmer over low heat 10–15 minutes to meld the flavors. Serve each bowl sprinkled with popcorn. Makes 4 servings.

# Wilson's Chili

## WILSON CAFE, POUND
*Larry and Sherrie Wilson*

In Wisconsin cafes, chili is almost as popular in the broiling heat of July as it is on subzero January days. It's often served as a daily soup special with a grilled cheese sandwich. Sherrie says this chili "tastes great with cheddar cheese."

 2 **pounds hamburger**
1–2 **tablespoons vegetable oil**
 1 **cup chopped onion**
1½ **cups chopped green peppers**
 2 **cups ketchup**
 1 **can (14–16 ounces) diced tomatoes, with juice**
 1 **can (28 ounces) crushed tomatoes or**
   **tomato sauce**
 2 **cans (each 15 ounces) dark red kidney beans,**
   **with liquid**
 2 **tablespoons chili powder**
 1 **tablespoon paprika**
2–3 **teaspoons cayenne**
 ¼ **pound spaghetti, broken into thirds**
  **salt and pepper**
  **grated cheddar cheese**

Heat large skillet over medium-high flame. Add ground beef and brown it, stirring to crumble the meat as it browns. Drain off fat. Meanwhile, heat vegetable oil in soup pot over medium flame. Add onions and green peppers; cook, stirring often, until they begin to get tender, about 10 minutes. Stir in ketchup, diced tomatoes, crushed tomatoes or tomato sauce, kidney beans, chili powder, paprika, and cayenne. Bring to simmer, stirring often. Reduce heat to low, partially cover the pot, and simmer slowly 1–2 hours.

 Cook spaghetti in lots of boiling, salted water. Add to chili. Serve chili with cheddar cheese. Makes about 3 quarts.

## CHILI WITH OR WITHOUT

On a Sunday afternoon in mid-October, in weather cold and rainy, five of us pedaled our way back to Eau Claire after tenting on the Mississippi River bank near Stockholm. The hills were steep and the relentless drizzle drew shards of rock and glass to the surface of the pavement, puncturing our tires one after another. It might not have been good weather for a bicycle trip, but it was perfect weather for chili.

We filed into the Durand Cafe, shaking water from our rain gear before peeling it off and plopping down on the counter stools. In minutes, steaming bowls of chili and triangles of grilled cheese sandwiches were brought out, and we lingered over them, delaying for as long as we could the moment we would have to head back out into the rain and get back on our bikes.

It was my very first experience with Wisconsin's small town cafes, and the first time I had eaten chili with noodles.

I grew up in a chili-without-noodles family, where elbow macaroni was reserved for macaroni salad and my mom's tomato and hamburger goulash (her contribution to every potluck we ever attended), and spaghetti noodles never made an appearance outside of spaghetti itself. My husband, on the other hand, grew up among chili-with-noodles folk who "stretched the pot" by adding elbow macaroni that swelled to soft, curly tubes. Needless to say, my husband, Mark, and I had serious ideological and experiential differences facing us when we married: would ours be a chili-with or a chili-without union? Since I do all of the cooking, Mark has graciously ceded to the without side of the coin, and our son, Peter, of course, has followed suit.

In *Chili Nation*, Jane and Michael Stern claim a Tex-Mex heritage for chili, placing its birthplace in and around San Antonio. With its ground beef, kidney beans, and tomato sauce—not to mention its noodles—midwestern chili is as far from the sirloin and pepper-packed Texas red as one can get. If chili is, as the Sterns believe, "this country's one truly shared national food," then the kettle in which it's cooked is the nation's true melting pot. As unlikely as it seems, we midwesterners may well have Greek, Macedonian, and other European immigrants in Cincinnati, Chicago, even Green Bay to thank for our favorite "chili mac."

In Cincinnati, Greek and Macedonian immigrants combined barbecue sauce with traditional spices like cardamom, coriander, cinnamon, cloves, and cumin, then stirred in ground beef and kidney beans to make a distinctly regional chili served over spaghetti noodles and topped with shredded cheese. In Green Bay in 1913, Lithuanian immigrant John Isaac produced a variation on the theme by drizzling his chili with spicy oil. In business ever since, Chili John's has become a Wisconsin institution. Oh, by the way, the next time you crush soda crackers to a pulp and stir them into your chili—

## TOPPING CHILI, CHILI TOPPING

Nothing tops chili. Nothing, that is, except any of the following: sour cream, chili powder, hot pepper sauce, corn chips, finely chopped raw onions, green onions, salsa, crumbled corn bread, tortilla chips, or crackers. But chili makes a great topping itself, too. Try leftovers on baked potatoes, omelets, hot dogs, burgers, hash browns, rice, noodles, and more.—T. A.

another midwestern chili tradition—think of John. It's said that he's responsible for persuading cracker manufactures to make the spoon-size oyster cracker. Aren't they a whole lot better than mush?

While Green Bay–style chili may be Wisconsin's unique contribution to our Chili Nation, plain old Wisconsin chili mac is far more likely to be the chili in every Packer backer's pot. We make it by simmering browned ground beef and kidney beans in a tomatoey liquid—ketchup, tomato sauce, tomato juice, or even condensed tomato soup—spiced with chili powder and maybe a little cumin, and "stretched" with broken spaghetti or elbow macaroni. Let's face it. Wisconsin-style chili isn't likely to rattle any culinary cages. As common in home kitchens as it is in school cafeterias, it's just plain fare for just plain folks. Topped with shredded cheddar cheese and sour cream, it's Dairyland's version of good old Texas red.—J. S.

# FOUR

~ ~ ~

# Salads

# Coleslaw

## VILLAGE KITCHEN, CASCO
*Chris and Gary Jacobs*

Every self-respecting Main Street cafe has a signature coleslaw that accompanies the end-of-the-workweek fish fry. In many kitchens, it also appears as a side dish throughout the week. But on Friday coleslaw is king. At the Village Kitchen, it is made in sixty-pound batches that disappear as quickly as Door County tourists after Labor Day.

When Chris makes this at home, she'll zip it up by adding diced onion, green pepper, or celery seed. The one thing that is not negotiable is the Miracle Whip. "Definitely not mayonnaise," she stresses. "Miracle Whip and Lawry's are the 'secret ingredients.'"

>    1 1/2  **cups Miracle Whip dressing**
>    3  **tablespoons sugar**
>       **salt and pepper**
>       **Lawry's Seasoned Salt**
>    6–8  **cups finely shredded or chopped cabbage**
> 1/4–1/2  **cup shredded carrots**

Mix Miracle Whip and sugar with salt, pepper, and Lawry's Seasoned Salt to taste. Toss with cabbage and carrots. Use this the same day you make it, as it will develop a strong taste after the first day. Makes 6–8 servings.

### DUEL OF THE DRESSINGS

I'd love to see a study that compares bottled mayonnaise users to those who prefer commercial salad dressing. Would it reveal any basic differences in people, I wonder?

Both are thick, creamy cold sauces or dressings that mimic the real thing: homemade mayonnaise. Both have richness and neutral flavor that blend well with a wide variety of foodstuffs, and they make a base for sauces that incorporate bolder flavors, like tartar sauce and blue cheese dressing.

Commercial mayonnaise, by federal law, must contain at least 65 percent vegetable oil. It must also contain pasteurized eggs or yolks that emulsify or thicken the sauce and an acidic component like vinegar to flavor it. Typically sugar, salt, pepper, and preservatives are added. Creamy salad dressing, on the other hand, contains a starch-based ingredient instead of the egg and is generally much sweeter than mayonnaise.

Most cafe owners and cooks who contributed salad recipes have a strong preference for one over the other. Moreover, loyalty to a particular brand can be fierce. For many mayonnaise lovers, Hellman's is best. For some aficionados of salad dressing, it's Miracle Whip or nothing.

The fresh, clean flavor of real mayonnaise will wake up your salads, yet few people make their own. But it's really quite simple. With a blender or food processor, it takes moments to make. Where the store-bought brands have a list of ingredients a paragraph long, from-scratch mayonnaise has only three: oil, egg, and lemon juice (plus a pinch of salt and pepper). For great flavor—but with affordability in mind—use a combination of olive oil and vegetable oil. The egg must be fresh and pure and the lemon juice straight from the fruit.—T.A.

# *Homemade Mayonnaise*

1 tablespoon fresh lemon juice
1 egg
1¼ cups oil (use a combination of olive oil
and vegetable oil)
salt and pepper to taste

Place lemon juice and egg in food processor or blender; blend 1 minute. With machine running, add olive oil in a *very* thin stream. After about half of the oil has been added, the mayonnaise will begin to thicken (you'll be able to hear it slap against the sides of the work bowl). Now you can add the oil a little faster. When all the oil is incorporated, season to taste with salt and pepper and blend again briefly. Keep refrigerated. It will last 1–2 weeks. Makes about 1½ cups.—T. A.

**ONE FROM
THE ROAD**

On a Friday night in
Wonewoc, I hap-
pened to drop in
at the Country Gals Cafe.
Determined not to make a
glutton of myself on the
offerings, I admonished my
waitress to bring only the
half portion of cod, which
came with my choice of
potatoes and the salad
bar. A little salad of iceberg lettuce, a tomato or
two, and perhaps some
shredded cheese sounded
just fine as an appetizer.
I picked up my plate and
headed into the adjoining
dining room where the
salad bar stretched out
along the side wall like
JV players on a bench.

My waitress did not
sufficiently prepare me
for the glory I saw there!
She didn't tell me that
owners Diane Hess and
her daughter Nicole Jack-
son spend most of Thurs-
day and Friday afternoons
preparing salads for not
only the Friday night fish
*(continued on facing page)*

# Pea and Bacon Salad

## COUNTRY GALS CAFE, WONEWOC
*Diane Hess and Nicole Jackson*

A winning salad from the Country Gals Cafe, which closed in 2005.

5–6  **slices bacon, fried until a little crispy, drained on paper
towels, and broken into small pieces**
1  **bag (16 ounces) frozen green peas**
1  **small white or yellow onion, cut in half and sliced very
thinly**
½–1  **cup Miracle Whip dressing
sugar to taste**

Combine bacon pieces, peas, and onions in a bowl. Mix Miracle
Whip and sugar—just enough to make it sweet but not too sweet—
in a small bowl. Stir dressing into salad, and let it sit an hour or longer
in the refrigerator to develop some flavor. Makes 6–8 servings.

# Piggly Wiggly Salad

## UNIQUE CAFE, BOSCOBEL
*Doyle and Nancy Lewis*

Fix this popular, old-timey salad for a potluck sometime. There's
bound to be folks in the group who recognize it from the deli case at
Piggly Wiggly grocery stores. You can serve it right after it's made,
but if you let it sit a while, the flavors will blend nicely. It will stay
fresh in the refrigerator a couple of days.

*Salad*
1  **head cauliflower, chopped into bite-size pieces
chopped florets from 1 bunch broccoli (reserve stems
for another use)**
1  **small red onion, finely diced**
1  **pound bacon, fried crispy, drained on paper towels,
and crumbled into bits**

*(continued from facing page)*

*Dressing*
1½–2 **cups mayonnaise (not salad dressing)**
⅓–½ **cup sugar**
3–4 **tablespoons white vinegar**
**salt and pepper**

Place salad ingredients in a large bowl. Whisk dressing ingredients in a smaller bowl until well combined. Mix dressing with salad mixture. Makes about 12 servings.

# Broccoli Raisin Salad

## COUNTRY GALS CAFE, WONEWOC
*Diane Hess and Nicole Jackson*

This was always on the salad bar at the Country Gals Cafe because customers protested when it was not. "Sometimes we'd get in ruts or slumps and then go and find a new recipe in a magazine," admits Diane. "But we came right back to where we started from because people complained that this or that was missing."

Diane's sister-in-law, Elaine Hepp, brought this recipe to the cafe after tasting it at a family gathering. It's important to make the dressing ahead of time so that the sugar dissolves and the flavors blend.

*Dressing*
1 **cup Miracle Whip dressing**
½ **cup sugar**
2 **tablespoons white vinegar**

*Salad*
**small florets broken or cut from 1 head broccoli**
½ **cup raisins**
½ **cup chopped walnuts**
¾ **pound bacon, fried crisp and crumbled**

Combine dressing ingredients; stir well. Chill the dressing as few as 2 hours or as many as 24 before combining it with the salad ingredients. If time permits, chill the salad another 2 hours or more before serving. Makes 8 or more servings.

fry but also the entire weekend. With gleeful abandon, I plunged in, building myself a lettuce salad topped not only with tomatoes, but also sliced cucumber, green pepper, mushrooms, hardboiled egg bits, and cottage cheese. I took this plate to my table and then headed back for more: potato salad, coleslaw, pasta salad, pea salad, broccoli salad with raisins and bacon, taco salad, Waldorf salad, Jell-O, and fruit salad.

Did I say it was all homemade? There are no jars opened and dumped into this salad bar, which I hereby anoint the Wisconsin queen.

—from *Cafe Wisconsin*

*(continued on facing page)*

## Salad Suspicion

How wonderful it is to stumble upon real homemade potato salad like Chris Jacobs makes (from Mom's recipe at that), not the kind that gets trucked to a cafe from a food service company. Like the legendary Christmas fruitcake that gets passed from one fruitcake-hater to the next, ready-stock potato salad scooped from white plastic tubs is something you just can't seem to get free of.

I love a good potato salad and have devised ways to determine whether what's on the menu was made by quick hands in the back kitchen or at a factory several states away. First, I look for the tell-all tub. Many times they are kept in the refrigerator case in a cafe's dining area, so no serious sleuthing is required to learn the truth. Or I might spy them in the kitchen—on a shelf, table, or near the kitchen pass-through window (which always leads me to wonder just how long they've been sitting at room temperature). If these cursory searches turn up nothing,

# *Potato Salad*

## VILLAGE KITCHEN, CASCO
*Chris and Gary Jacobs*

"My mom always made this when we were little," says Chris, who has become the one her family turns to whenever they want potato salad for a gathering. She makes it so often, in fact, she no longer uses measurements. "It gets kind of boring because I make it so much!" Mix the salad up a day ahead of time because the longer it sits, the better it gets, advises Chris. Your next picnic, like the Village Kitchen's top-notch Friday fish fry, would be naked without it.

$2\frac{1}{2}$ **pounds red potatoes (unpeeled)**
  1 **small white onion, diced**
  2 **stalks celery, halved lengthwise and chopped**
  3 **hard-cooked eggs, chopped**
  1 **cup Miracle Whip dressing**
  2 **tablespoons sugar**
  2 **tablespoons milk**
  2 **teaspoons prepared yellow mustard**
  1 **teaspoon white vinegar**
  $\frac{1}{2}$ **teaspoon salt, or more to taste**
  $\frac{1}{8}$ **teaspoon pepper, or more to taste**

Boil potatoes in lots of salted water until tender. Drain off the hot water, then immerse the potatoes in cold water to cool. Peel the potatoes and cut them into chunks. Place in large bowl with onion, celery, and hard-cooked eggs. Combine remaining ingredients in a smaller bowl, stir well, and pour over potatoes. Toss gently. Chill until serving time. Makes 10–12 servings.

# Macaroni Salad

## HAYSEED CAFE, WAUZEKA
*Corky Mead and Beth Groom*

*(continued from facing page)*

I ask the waitress if the potato salad has celery, radishes, or green onions. I like a little crunch and color to my salad. Or I ask if the potatoes are russets or red, peeled or skin-on. If she can't answer, I'm reasonably sure the potato salad is not one that will thrill me. You can't hide the makings of the real thing.—J. S.

On a summer day a few years ago, neighbors Corky and Beth decided to combine their two yard sales into one. Corky made macaroni salad for lunch. "It was the best macaroni salad I ever had," remembers Beth. "I said, 'It's so good, you should sell it.' And she said, 'I always wanted to run a restaurant.'" As it turned out, they shared a dream. The Hayseed Cafe is the result.

There's no set amount for the ingredients in this salad, Corky says. Although we've given measurements, you should use "just as much as you like." Corky sometimes adds 2–3 cups diced ham, tuna, or imitation crab. She doesn't give specifics about the peas, but we like them fresh or frozen (and thawed) and raw or very lightly cooked.

*Dressing*
- ¼ cup salad dressing ("Not mayonnaise," says Corky)
- 1 pint sour cream
- ½ cup sugar
- ½ cup white vinegar
- 2 tablespoons prepared mustard
- 1 teaspoon celery seed
- ½ teaspoon each salt and pepper

*Salad*
- 1 pound elbow macaroni, cooked, drained, rinsed, and cooled
- 2 or more cups shredded cheddar cheese
- ½ cup finely chopped onion
- 12–16 ounces peas
- salt and pepper to taste

Mix dressing ingredients in a large bowl. Add salad ingredients. Mix well. Chill until serving time. Makes 12–16 servings.

### SNICKERING AT SALAD

During our annual cross-country skiing trip, I entertained my family with stories about collecting recipes for the *Cafe Wisconsin Cookbook.* Among the quirkiest contributions was Diane Hess's Snickers Salad, a favorite at the Country Gals Cafe. I laughed at my family members' surprise when I told them the salad's unlikely ingredients—and received a surprise of my own when I spied my sister, Cathy, nod knowingly at her Mondovi-raised husband, Mike Weiss.

"What do you know about Snickers Salad?" I demanded.

Plenty, it turns out. Snickers Salad has been a mainstay at Weiss family gatherings for years. They'd been positively smitten ever since it first turned up at parish potlucks at Mondovi's Sacred Heart Catholic Church, where the recipe is in such demand that it's included in the *Centennial Cookbook.* A funeral dinner just isn't considered complete without a bowl of Snickers Salad on the table. And every May, when the Cemetery Committee enlists family and friends to clean up the cemetery prior to Memorial Day, it takes its place on the long tables set up end to end, filled with covered dishes brought to feed the workers.

"I was introduced to the salad when I became part of the Weiss family," Cathy explains. "I thought it was good, and I tried to figure out what was in it. I thought, 'Is it a salad or a dessert?' I always see it with the other salads at the cemetery potluck, so I figured that's what it must be.

"Once, I was at a yard sale that had a lot of kitchen utensils and cookbooks, and I started talking to the women running the sale. We wound up talking about favorite church recipes, and, of course, Snickers Salad came up. I asked, 'Is it a salad or dessert?' They laughed and said, 'It depends on which end of the table it's on!'"

Although Cathy has since encountered different variations of the salad at other potlucks, she reports that the defining ingredient—Snickers bars—is never discarded in favor of something else. This made me wonder just how many spins a funky little salad like this one could have. An Internet recipe search turned up a dazzling array of add-ins, including sliced bananas, grapes, and crushed pineapple.

The addition of more fruit seemed normal enough, but things quickly got out of hand. One recipe called for buttermilk, another for a large quantity of lemon juice. Others instructed me to add sour cream, cream cheese, marshmallow cream, or mayonnaise. These must be salad interpretations because the more dessertlike variations added toppings of chocolate chips, candy sprinkles, a drizzle of chocolate and/or caramel ice cream toppings, chopped peanuts, and crushed pretzels.

Comments from recipe contributors also reflected the "is it a salad or

dessert" quandary. My favorites include: "A great way to use up leftover Halloween candy." "A sneaky way to get the kids to eat some fruit." "If Snickers and salad are in the title, I just assumed it can't be bad, can it?"

Salad or dessert? You decide.—J. S.

# Snickers Salad

## COUNTRY GALS CAFE, WONEWOC
### *Diane Hess and Nicole Jackson*

"This was pretty popular around here," says Diane Hess of the former Country Gals Cafe. "We had it for quite a while. My sister-in-law found the recipe and then we tried it at the cafe. We had it every weekend on the salad bar, and if we didn't, we'd hear about it. You could substitute it as a light dessert. The Granny Smith apples are tart, and the other ingredients sweeten them up."

    5  **frozen Snickers bars (each 2.07 ounces)**
6–8  **Granny Smith apples (unpeeled)**
    1  **container (16 ounces) nondairy whipped topping, or more as needed**
    1  **box (3½ ounces) instant vanilla pudding mix**

Chop or pound the Snickers bar with a hammer into small pieces. Dice the unpeeled apples. Combine all the ingredients and stir well. (Do not prepare the pudding; just add the mix directly to the salad.) Refrigerate at least two hours or overnight. Add more whipped topping if necessary to thin the mixture a little. The apples will soften the mixture the longer it refrigerates. Makes 10 or more servings.

# Apple Salad

## UNIQUE CAFE, BOSCOBEL
*Doyle and Nancy Lewis*

Cherry juice gives this apple-packed Waldorf spin-off a "unique" look. Kids will especially love its pale pink color, as well as the addition of mini marshmallows. Salad creator Annette Wagner, who has worked at the Unique Cafe for twenty years, "give or take," is specific about the dressing. It must contain real mayonnaise, "not Miracle Whip."

"I made up this recipe a long time ago," says Annette. "I like to experiment."

*Salad*
- 2 **cups red grapes, cut in half**
- ½ **cup diced celery**
- ½ **cup chopped walnuts or pecans**
- 1 **jar (8 ounces) maraschino cherries, drained (reserve the liquid)**
- 2 **cups miniature marshmallows**
- 8 **medium McIntosh apples**

*Dressing*
- 2 **cups mayonnaise**
- 1 **cup whipped cream or whipped topping**
- ¼–½ **cup maraschino cherry juice**

Combine grapes, celery, nuts, cherries, and marshmallows in large bowl. Dice the unpeeled apples and add them to the mix. Combine dressing ingredients in another bowl; toss with salad. Chill at least 1 hour. Makes 12 or more servings.

# Jell-O Salad

## UNIQUE CAFE, BOSCOBEL
*Doyle and Nancy Lewis*

The salad bar at the Unique Cafe is just not complete without Jell-O. "It's a real comfort food," explains Nancy, who likes to "throw everything in it to give it some substance." If a few days go by without it, customers request its return to the lineup.

1 **small box (3 ounces) orange or lemon-flavored
    Jell-O gelatin**
1 **large box (6 ounces) instant vanilla pudding**
1 **cup hot water**
1 **can (15 ounces) mandarin oranges, drained
    (reserve the liquid)**
1 **cup nondairy whipped topping or real
    whipped cream**
   **miniature marshmallows (optional)**

Place Jell-O and vanilla pudding mixes in bowl. Stir in the hot water until mixes dissolve. Let it cool and thicken in the refrigerator 10–15 minutes. Stir in the mandarin oranges. Fold in the nondairy whipped topping or real whipped cream and, if desired, some mini marshmallows. You can thin the salad with a little of the reserved orange liquid, if desired. Makes 8 or more servings.

# Creamy Cukes

## CURVE INN CAFE, REDGRANITE
*Pam and Byrdie Chamberlin*

Fresh garden cucumbers make this simple salad shine. "Our best dishes are all made from family recipes—a little of this, a little of that," says Pam. "I do most of my cooking all by taste. The rest comes natural."

2 **tablespoons salt**
4 **medium cucumbers, peeled and sliced**
1 **medium or 2 small onions, finely diced**
  **Miracle Whip dressing**
  **sugar**
  **salt and pepper**

Combine 5–6 cups water with 2 tablespoons salt and stir to dissolve. Add the cucumbers and onions; toss gently but well, and chill 8 or more hours. Drain cucumbers well. Stir in Miracle Whip, sugar, salt, and pepper to taste. Makes 6–8 servings.

# A Beautiful Salad

## VILLAGE HAUS, FALL CREEK
*Sheri and Jim Coldwell*

With contrasting shapes, textures, and colors, this truly is a beautiful salad. Sheri grows many of the vegetables in her own garden or receives them as donations from her customers. When she runs short, she places a sign near the road asking for garden overflow.

Spring mix, also called mesclun, is a blend of young leaves and shoots such as arugula, endive, frisee, radicchio, and other varieties of flavorful salad greens.

> **hand-torn iceberg lettuce**
> **spring mix salad greens**
>
> *Toppings for Each Salad*
> 2 **slices of a scored cucumber**
> 3 **carrot slices (cut carrot into 3-inch pieces, then slice pieces lengthwise)**
> 3 **slices celery (cut celery into 3-inch pieces, then slice pieces lengthwise)**
> 3 **matchstick-cut rutabaga (cut rutabaga into planks, then cut planks into thin strips)**
>   **a few thin onion slices**
> 3 **tomato wedges, cherry tomatoes, or grape tomatoes**
> 1 **round slice of green pepper**
> 3 **fresh white mushrooms, sliced**
>   **a few broccoli florets**
>   **a few fresh or thawed peas**
>   **small handful of grated cheddar cheese**
>   **a few sunflower seeds**
>   **dressing of your choice**

Mix three parts iceberg lettuce with one part spring mix. Divide into individual salad bowls. Mound each salad with toppings. Toss with Thousand Island Dressing (page 82), Blue Cheese Dressing (82), or your own favorite dressing. Makes any number of servings.

## GIVE ME BEAUTIFUL OR GIVE ME NOTHING

Just two weeks into my second grand food foray through Wisconsin cafes, I began to crave green salads, crunchy raw vegetables, and ruby tomatoes that didn't taste, as Garrison Keillor once quipped, as though they'd been strip-mined in Texas. Sadly, a satisfying salad in a small town cafe is practically an anomaly. I was served a bowl of rusty iceberg lettuce with a mound of grated cheese so often that I nearly swore off salads altogether. After the day's eating was over—and most days that was by three o'clock—I often found myself in the grocery store buying a bag of spring mix and a tomato to go with the bottle of vinaigrette I kept in my cooler.

The salads that Sheri Coldwell assembles at the Village Haus in Fall Creek are masterful. She supplements hand-torn head lettuce with fresh greens, which in summer are picked from her own one-acre garden. Don't expect any less in winter. She mixes iceberg lettuce with pretty, tasty leaves in a deep glass bowl and tops them with an artistic assortment of julienned, sliced, and diced vegetables.

One Friday night in March, a group of old friends and I gathered around Sheri's largest table for pan-fried walleye. We were overjoyed with the Beautiful Salad and debated about the identity of the sweet cream-colored matchsticks. Was it jicama? Turnip? Parsnip? Since most of us were familiar only with stewed and mashed rutabaga (which we almost universally disliked), in its raw state it was not easily recognizable. The inventive addition thrilled us and, for Emily at least, inspired a multiweek frenzy of experimenting with rutabaga in a variety of dishes.—J. S.

# *Pico de Gallo (Mexican Salad)*

## GREENWOOD FAMILY RESTAURANT, GREENWOOD

*Ernesto and Linda Rodriguez*

Pronounced *PEE-koh day GUY-oh* ("rooster beak" in Spanish), this chopped salad is served as a side dish to rice, beans, and all kinds of Mexican main courses. It tastes best the second day, or after at least a few hours in the refrigerator, but you can serve it right away, too.

When Ernesto gave a cooking demonstration to the high school home economics class, he went through this recipe step by step. The students then followed his lead and made their own. The teacher loved it—the lesson *and* the salad.

Sadly, the Greenwood Family Restaurant closed its doors in 2005. Ernesto's seasoned hand in the kitchen continues to be missed.

3  **large tomatoes, coarsely chopped**
1  **large onion, finely chopped**
1  **ripe avocado, chopped**
½  **bunch cilantro, stems removed and discarded, leaves coarsely chopped**
2  **jalapeños, stemmed (but not seeded), finely chopped**
3  **teaspoons olive oil**
**juice of 1 lime, or more to taste**
**salt**

Toss tomatoes, onions, avocado, cilantro, jalapeños, and olive oil in bowl. Stir in lime juice and salt to taste. Chill before serving. This will keep 2–3 days in the refrigerator. Makes 3–4 cups.

# Mandarin Chicken Salad

LINDA'S WILMOT CAFE, WILMOT
*Linda Orvis*

Here's a crunchy fresh salad that's bright tasting and bright looking—
and good for you, besides. Linda presents it with Rye-Krisp crackers
and a cup of soup. If you have some leftover chicken from last night's
outdoor barbecue, go ahead and substitute it for the indoor "griddled"
chicken.

*Salad mix*
**torn iceberg lettuce**
**romaine lettuce**
**red leaf lettuce**
**green leaf lettuce**
**other lettuce or salad greens**
**shredded carrots**

*For Each Salad*
2 **sliced radishes**
4 **quartered slices of cucumber**
½ **tomato, cut into 4 wedges**
   **a few thin-sliced red onion rings**
   **one ring each of sliced red, green, and yellow sweet**
      **pepper**
½ **cup canned mandarin oranges, drained**
¼ **cup whole roasted, salted cashews**
   **6-ounce chicken breast, marinated in olive oil and**
      **lemon pepper overnight**
   **bottled raspberry vinaigrette dressing**

Combine lettuces, greens, and shredded carrots to make a salad mix.
Place at least two cups of salad mix in a large, individual serving bowl.
Scatter the vegetables, oranges, and cashews over the greens.

   Meanwhile, grill the chicken breast on a hot, oiled indoor griddle
(use the side that has raised grids, if you have one like that) or an outdoor grill. When it's done, cut it into strips and arrange them on
the salad. Serve with raspberry vinaigrette. Makes any number of
servings.

# Garden Pasta Salad

## COUNTRY GALS CAFE, WONEWOC
### *Diane Hess and Nicole Jackson*

"We didn't make anything that's hard to make," says Diane, who closed her cafe in 2005. "If it takes hours and hours, we were not going to make it." This colorful cold pasta salad comes together easily and is best during the summer when fresh produce is abundant. Then, advises Diane, "you could add any garden vegetables." Try substituting fresh Wisconsin parmesan for the Kraft and homemade dressing (next page) for the bottled.

> 3 cups (8-ounce box) multicolored rotini pasta
> 2 cups small broccoli florets (uncooked)
> ½ cup Kraft parmesan cheese
> ½ cup diced red bell pepper
> ½ cup diced green bell pepper
> ½ cup diced red onion
> ¼ cup each sliced green and black olives
> 1 cup bottled Italian or Caesar-style Italian dressing
> salt and pepper to taste

Bring a pot of salted water to boil. Add the pasta, stir, and boil until pasta is tender. Drain, rinse lightly with cool water, and drain well. When pasta is dry, toss it with the remaining ingredients. Chill. Makes 4–8 servings.

# Italian Dressing

Cafe cooks find a multitude of uses for an oil-and-vinegar dressing, especially one that's seasoned with garlic and herbs. It can be tossed with pasta, vegetables, or greens for a quick salad; used as a marinade for Italian-style baked chicken; drizzled over the inside of a sub sandwich; and much more. Here is a basic recipe to get you started. By all means experiment with a variety of vinegars and adjust the ratio of vinegar to oil to taste.

> **minced garlic to taste**
> 1 **part wine vinegar**
> **dried or fresh herbs to taste (basil, oregano, parsley,**
> **marjoram, etc.)**
> 3 **parts olive oil**
> **salt and pepper to taste**

Press the minced garlic and a little salt with a fork or the flat of a knife until it forms a paste. Combine with vinegar and herbs. Gradually whisk in olive oil. Season with salt and pepper.—T. A.

# Blue Cheese Dressing

## MAIN DISH FAMILY RESTAURANT, LUCK
*Jenell and Ralph Britton*

If you choose to make this with mayonnaise instead of salad dressing, you may need to add a couple of tablespoons of milk to thin it out a bit. Or, for more piquancy, substitute rice wine vinegar for the milk.

>   1   **cup bottled salad dressing**
>   ½   **cup sour cream**
> ½–1   **teaspoon horseradish sauce**
> ½–⅔  **cup (about 4 ounces) crumbled blue cheese**

Mix ingredients well. Makes about 1¾ cups.

# Thousand Island Dressing

## BONNIE'S DINER, PHILLIPS
*Shelley Moon*

Crispy, juicy, sturdy iceberg lettuce is the perfect foil for this thick and creamy Thousand Island dressing. Toss it with chopped leaves or blanket a whole wedge, then add any extras you like, salad bar–style, for a create-your-own first course. Shelley's chili sauce of choice is Heinz.

>   1   **cup mayonnaise**
>   1   **hard-cooked egg, pressed through a sieve**
>   ¼   **cup sweet pickle relish**
>   ⅓   **cup bottled chili sauce**
>   1   **tablespoon minced onion**
>   ¼   **teaspoon paprika**

Mix all ingredients. That's it! Makes about 2 cups.

# FIVE

~ ~ ~

# Daily Specials

## STOCK, BROTH, OR BASE?

It's your call. There's no doubt that a long-sim-mered homemade meat stock gives the best flavor and body to soups and sauces. There's also nothing like the feeling of satisfaction that comes from extracting deep-seated flavor from chicken or beef bones and vege-table scraps. Still, conven-ience is a powerful influ-ence in most kitchens today, whether home-based or professional. There's nothing evil about taking a shortcut, espe-cially since good-quality canned stocks and bases have come on the market in recent years. Do what the best cafe cooks do: If you use a canned or processed product, look for one with the least amount of additives and the greatest amount of "real food" ingredients. Then, taste before you add additional salt to the dish. There may already be more than enough from the product you've chosen.

Recipes for homemade beef and chicken broth are on pages 57 and 49.

—T. A.

# Don's Outpost Stroganoff

## OUTPOST CAFE, PRESQUE ISLE
*Terry and Kim Tassi*

Head cook Don Psenicka added some savory extras to a basic stroganoff recipe to come up with this incredible variation on the beef-with-noodles theme. His customers can't wait until it shows up on the daily specials board, which is once or twice a month at the Outpost. Don serves it over homemade egg noodles (see our recipe on page 146), with a grilled buttermilk biscuit on the side.

     4  tablespoons butter, divided
     2  pounds top round steak, cut into small cubes
 1½  cups diced onions
     1  tablespoon minced garlic
 2½  cups beef stock, or 2½ cups water and
             2–3 teaspoons beef base
  ½  cup dry red wine
     2  tablespoons Worcestershire sauce
  ¼  teaspoon each garlic salt, onion salt, and
             lemon pepper
  ½  pound fresh mushrooms, sliced
     3  tablespoons flour
     1  cup sour cream
         egg noodles
         chopped fresh parsley
         buttermilk biscuits (optional)

Heat a large skillet over medium-high flame for several minutes. Add 2 tablespoons of the butter and swirl pan to coat the bottom. Add beef and onions, raise heat to high, and brown the mixture for a few min-utes, tossing occasionally. Stir in garlic and cook for 1 minute, stirring once or twice. Stir in stock, wine, Worcestershire, garlic salt, onion salt, and lemon pepper. If the pan is full, transfer the mixture to a pot at this point, since you'll need room for additional ingredients later. Bring mixture to simmer, reduce heat to very low, cover, and cook until meat is tender, 45–60 minutes.

When meat is tender, stir in the mushrooms and simmer 15 min-utes. Meanwhile, make a roux. Heat remaining 2 tablespoons of but-ter in a small skillet over medium-low flame. Gradually stir in the flour and cook, stirring often, 3–4 minutes. Set aside. When mush-rooms are done and meat is very tender, drain liquid from meat mixture into a saucepan. Bring liquid to a simmer and whisk in the roux to thicken the sauce. Simmer, stirring often, 5–10 minutes. Now recombine the meat and sauce and stir in the sour cream. Add salt and pepper to taste. Gently heat through over low flame, stirring occasionally. Serve over homemade egg noodles with chopped fresh parsley sprinkled on top. Add a grilled buttermilk biscuit on the side, if desired. Makes 6–8 servings.

# Beef over Noodles

## Ideal Cafe, Iron River

*Mary and James "Mac" McBrair*

Mary likes to make this flavorful lunch special because "it mixes quickly and you can put it in the oven and forget about it." She occasionally doubles the sauce ingredients to make more gravy for the noodles. She uses real cream sherry—not cooking sherry—but dry sherry is also delicious. For a dish that's extra special, spoon the beef mixture over the homemade noodles on page 146.

- 2 cans (each 10¾ ounces) condensed cream of mushroom soup
- 1 cup cream sherry or dry sherry
- 1 envelope (1 ounce) onion soup mix
- 2 pounds cubed beef chuck roast or beef stew meat
- 8 ounces fresh mushrooms, sliced or quartered
  salt and pepper to taste
  cooked egg noodles

Heat oven to 325 degrees. Mix soup, sherry, and onion soup mix in an ovenproof pot or deep baking dish. Stir in uncooked beef and mushrooms; there's no need to brown the beef first. Cover tightly and bake until beef is very tender, 2½ to 3 hours. Season to taste with salt and pepper. Serve over hot noodles. Makes 7–8 servings.

# Rouladen-Style Beef Tips

## BONNIE'S DINER, PHILLIPS
### *Shelley Moon*

Shelley loves pickles, so she adds extra to this German-influenced dish developed by her father and stepmother. It always goes over well in the restaurant. When they started serving it, says Shelley, "customers were telling other customers, 'You have to order this,' and they would tell us, 'You have to have it more often.'" She says, "Many people have never heard of rouladen before, so we are teaching them something new."

The sauce is smoky-good from the bacon and lightly piquant from the pickles and mustard. Long simmering gives it a velvety texture plus deep flavor that is wonderful over hot egg noodles. Try the homemade noodles on page 146.

      4–5  slices bacon
      ½   cup flour mixed with 1 teaspoon salt and ½ teaspoon
             pepper
       2   pounds boneless beef round, cut into 1-inch cubes
       1   tablespoon butter
       1   cup chopped onions
       1   tablespoon minced fresh garlic or 1–2 teaspoons dried
             garlic powder
       3   cups homemade meatless spaghetti sauce (or one
             26-ounce jar bottled sauce)
       2   cans (each 14½ ounces) diced tomatoes, undrained
      ½   teaspoon black pepper
      ½   teaspoon dried basil
       1   tablespoon yellow or Dijon mustard
   ½–⅔  cup sliced dill pickles

Cook bacon in a large skillet over medium heat until brown and crispy. Remove bacon to drain on paper towels; cool, chop, and reserve. Transfer most of the bacon fat from the pan to a small bowl. Place seasoned flour in a paper bag, add the beef, and shake the bag to coat all the pieces. Raise heat under skillet to high. Shake off excess flour from beef. Brown the beef, using a little bacon fat for each batch, without crowding the pan. Transfer beef to a bowl as each batch is done. When all the beef is browned, deglaze the skillet with ½ cup water or juice from canned tomatoes, stirring well to release all the bits from bottom of pan. Add to beef and set aside.

Heat butter in a dutch oven or large, heavy pot. Add onions and fresh garlic; cook, stirring occasionally, until onions are tender. (If you're using garlic powder, add it when the onions are done.) Add reserved bacon bits and beef. Stir in spaghetti sauce, diced tomatoes, pepper, basil, mustard, and pickles. Bring to simmer, cover, and cook over low flame, stirring occasionally, until beef is very tender, 2–2½ hours. Serve over hot egg noodles. Makes 8 servings.

# Ham Balls and Noodles

## M & M Cafe, Monticello
### *Mike and Mary Davis*

"This was an attempt to make the daily specials more varied," says Mary. "It was pretty foreign to our guests at first, but they are willing to try anything and voted to keep them on the menu. We even had one company in New Glarus that wanted a 'ham ball alert' called in to their office when we served them. When we did that, four or five eaters would come running!"

If you like a little variation yourself, increase the amount of onion and horseradish in this recipe, or reduce the amount of sugar in the sauce, to suit your own taste. Sprinkle chopped fresh parsley over the dish for an attractive color contrast to the meatballs and noodles. For a homemade noodles recipe, see page 146.

1½ pounds ground ham
1½ pounds lean ground pork
  3 eggs, lightly beaten
 ½ cup milk
  2 tablespoons finely minced onion
  1 teaspoon horseradish
  1 teaspoon salt
 ¼ teaspoon pepper
  2 cups fresh or dried breadcrumbs
  2 cups brown sugar
  1 tablespoon mustard powder
 ½ cup cider vinegar
    hot, cooked wide noodles, tossed with butter

Heat oven to 350 degrees. Mix ham, pork, eggs, milk, onion, horseradish, salt, pepper, and breadcrumbs in a bowl. When it is well mixed, shape the mixture into meatballs that are slightly larger than a golf ball, or any size you prefer. Arrange meatballs in a single layer in a large baking pan or two smaller ones. Bake 30–40 minutes.

Meanwhile, mix brown sugar, mustard powder, vinegar, and ½ cup water in a saucepan. Bring to a boil over medium heat, stirring occasionally. When meatballs have baked for 30–40 minutes, pour hot sauce over them and continue baking 15 minutes longer. Serve immediately over hot buttered noodles or keep them warm in a crockpot or warm oven. Spoon some of the sauce over the meatballs and noodles when you serve them. Makes 8–10 servings.

# *Stuffed Meatballs*

## OLD STORE CAFE AND DELI, DALE
*Deb and Bob Chonos*

When she was still operating the Old Store Cafe and Deli—it changed hands in 2004—Deb's customers "asked for these all the time. The recipe happened by a fluke. Looking for something easy and different, we just messed around and came up with this. We always tried to stick with clever but easy things. We didn't do any putzy work because we were always really busy in the morning. We didn't cook ahead—we made everything fresh in the morning."

Deb used canned brown gravy for the sauce but says creamy mushroom soup would also be good. (It is. We tried it.) She served the meatballs with mashed potatoes or rice, but here's another idea: make extra stuffing, dot it with butter, and bake it while the meatballs are in the oven. Then serve the meatballs and sauce on top.

> 1–1⅓ **cups chicken broth or water**
> 2–3 **tablespoons butter**
> 4 **cups Brownberry Sage & Onion Stuffing**
> 2 **pounds ground beef**
> **about 4 cups brown gravy or 2 cans (each 18 ounces)**
> **creamy mushroom soup (*not* condensed)**
> **mashed potatoes or cooked rice**

Heat oven to 350 degrees. Heat chicken broth and butter to simmering. Place 4 cups dry cubed stuffing in a bowl. Gradually add the hot stock to the bread cubes and toss to make a moist stuffing. Let it cool while you divide the ground beef into 20 equal-size clumps. For each meatball, shape one portion of meat into a patty that's about 2 to 2½ inches in diameter. Place a tablespoon of the stuffing in center of patty and mold ground beef around it to completely enclose the stuffing. Brown the meatballs in a skillet or in a baking dish in the oven, about 20 minutes if you bake them. Pour gravy or mushroom soup over meatballs and bake uncovered for 25–30 minutes. Serve with mashed potatoes, rice, or additional stuffing. Makes 8 servings.

# Meatloaf

## TUCKER'S INN, LITTLE CHUTE
*Larry and Carol Van Lankvelt*

This classic comes from Little Chute, where the area's Dutch heritage shows up in last names like Larry and Carol's. There may not be anything particularly Dutch about meatloaf, but Larry notes that it's a favorite throughout the Fox Valley. "There are many recipes and most are very good. You can always find one to your own taste."

Until the Van Lankvelts sold Tucker's Inn in 2004, Larry kept this meatloaf on the daily menu and also ran it as a special every other week. "We had a few customers who made it a special point to be here for our meatloaf. One guy says he'd 'hit the mother lode' when we had it. My kids—age thirty-six and thirty-seven—won't eat any other kind."

That's how it is with meatloaf. It's a meal you treasure, and there's none as good as the kind you grew up on.

    2  cups dried bread cubes
    1  cup milk
  2½  pounds ground beef
    2  eggs
    3  tablespoons minced onion
    3  tablespoons minced celery
   ½  teaspoon Worcestershire sauce
   ½  teaspoon A1 Steak Sauce
   ½  teaspoon beef base
   ½  teaspoon garlic powder
       salt and pepper to taste

Heat oven to 350 degrees. Oil a large bread pan or baking dish. Mix bread cubes and milk in large bowl. Let stand 10 minutes, then squeeze the bread lightly and drain off the excess liquid. Add remaining ingredients and mix—hands work best here--until it is well combined and holds together. Press into bread pan or place in baking dish and shape it into a loaf. Bake about 1¼ hours. Let stand 5–10 minutes before serving. Makes 8 servings.

# Hot Beef

## MAIN STREET CAFE, SIREN
*Conny Roy*

Hot beef is the quintessential plate special in Wisconsin. The secret to its beefy toothsomeness and fall-apart tenderness is long, slow cooking. The longest, slowest method in the state just may be practiced by Mike Roy, Conny's father and former owner of the Main Street Cafe. He braises beef shoulder in a 200-degree oven overnight. "He puts it in about four or five in the afternoon and takes it out when he comes in at five in the morning," Conny says. Then he slices it and puts it on the steam table, ready to serve for lunch.

You can make a home version for dinner by starting the roast when you get up in the morning. Its Sunday-dinner aroma will greet you when you arrive home from work. Get a family member to peel and mash potatoes, and all you'll have to do is make the very simple gravy and slice the beef. Then layer it cafe-style on a blue plate and dig in while it's hot.

> **3- to 4-pound boneless shoulder blade roast**
> **or chuck roast**
> **salt and pepper**
> 1 **medium to large onion, thinly sliced**
> 3–4 **whole allspice**
> **homemade or canned beef broth, or combination of**
> **beef base and water**
> 2 **tablespoons cornstarch**
> 2 **tablespoons flour**
> 1/4 **cup potato water (the liquid used to boil potatoes)**
> **or plain water**
> **white bread**
> **hot mashed potatoes**

Heat oven to 200 degrees. Generously season the roast on both sides with salt and pepper. Place it in a roasting pan that's just a little bigger than the roast. Surround the meat with sliced onions. Add enough beef broth to come at least 1 inch up the sides of the roast (or about halfway up the roast). Cover tightly and place in oven. Cook until meat is very tender, about 10 hours. (If you're around, you can turn the roast over in the liquid about halfway through the cooking time.) You'll know it's done when a fork inserted into the flesh slips back out very easily.

When meat is done, transfer it to a platter, cover loosely with aluminum foil, and return it to the oven. (Alternatively, you can cook the beef one day and serve it the next. In fact, chilling the meat will make it slice more easily.)

To make the gravy, strain the liquid in the roasting pan into a saucepan. Bring liquid to a simmer. Mix cornstarch, flour, and ¼ cup water (use potato water for improved flavor) in a bowl or jar until smooth. Whisk some of this into the simmering liquid, adding more as needed to reach desired gravy consistency. Simmer gravy at least 10 minutes and season to taste with salt and pepper.

To make a cafe-style hot beef sandwich, slice roast across the grain with a sharp knife, as thick or thin as you like. Lay a slice of bread on the plate, top with beef and another slice of bread. Scoop mashed potatoes onto the sandwich or alongside of it, then ladle gravy over all. Serve immediately. Makes about 8 servings.

## BRING ON THE BEEF

What is the hands down, without-a-doubt, top choice main dish in Wisconsin cafes, more popular than burgers, soup and sandwiches, and daily specials?

Wisconsinites are head-over-heels crazy about hot beef—a humble pile of roast beef, mashed potatoes and gravy, and white bread. Hot beef is a regional quirk of appetite we share with our neighbors in the Upper Midwest and one that both amuses and bemuses outsiders. "We find it difficult to be charmed by plain roast beef," wrote Jane and Michael Stern in the first edition of *Roadfood* (1977), "but to Midwesterners it seems to be a never-ending source of eating pleasure."

I ate plenty of hot beef during my two eating adventures through Wisconsin, and I'll tell you, I encountered as much pain as pleasure. The worst hot beef imaginable was in a St. Croix River town where I was served chopped deli-style roast beef drowning in canned brown gravy, instant mashed potatoes, and four triangles of spongy white bread. The "beef" had the slightly pickled taste of brine beyond its prime. What are people thinking? Have they stopped thinking altogether? What's the point of running a restaurant if you're not actually going to cook?

As it happened, I'd been directed to this particular cafe by a representative of the local chamber of commerce. I often consult chambers for help in identifying a town's traditional cafes from other types of eateries, and I have a standard list of essential requirements that I recite, including a cafe's role as a community center, rather limited hours, and a menu of home-style food.

"Oh!" she exclaimed, indicating that she understood just what I was

looking for. "The kind of place where you can get hot beef any time of day!"

"Yes," I laughed. "That's it exactly!"

You can get hot beef any time of day at this particular cafe, it's true, but that doesn't means it's worth eating.

Thankfully, there are plenty of cafe owners like Conny Roy and her dad, Mike, at the Main Street Cafe in Siren who are as passionate about making great hot beef as Wisconsinites are about eating it. The best hot beef starts with a fresh beef roast, well seasoned and slow cooked in a hot oven under a watchful eye, one that leaks out plenty of rich broth for gravy. I like my beef rosy-hued and so tender it falls apart in shreds—I draw the line at crumbs— and I like it tucked between thick blankets of homemade white bread. If not that, then a quality bakery bread that won't turn to mush as it soaks up the gravy.

As charmed as Wisconsinites may be by "plain roast beef," the Sterns are equally charmed by our eating methods. In *Blue Plate Specials and Blue Ribbon Chefs* (2001) they write, "One weekday, at eleven in the morning [at the Downing Cafe in Downing, Wisconsin], we watched two hefty male table-mates in Oshkosh B'Gosh overalls tackle their beef platters using an identical utensil technique: fork grasped in a firm-fist right hand, the way you'd grip a motorcycle's handlebar, and a slab of soft white bread folded in the left hand. The fork is slid under a heap of beef sideways, like a shovel; the bread is used to push as much meat as possible into balance on the tines. About every three bites, the leading edge of the bread has become so soaked with gravy that the fork is used to sever the moistened part and add it to the next fork-load of beef."

We may not eat pretty in Wisconsin, but we sure do eat good.—J. S.

# *Roast Pork*

## CRYSTAL CAFE, PHILLIPS
*Mark and Becky Dittel*

Roast pork. Roast turkey. Roast beef. Three phrases that are magic on a cafe menu because everybody knows what they mean: good eating. Served over white bread with mashed potatoes and gravy, or as a full dinner with vegetables and a warm roll, this is both core and pinnacle of American farm-style cooking. We call it comfort food today, and it's relished as much for what it is—plain, plentiful, familiar—as for what it isn't—trendy, mass produced, overly health conscious.

> **3- to 4-pound boneless pork loin roast**
> **small amount oil**
> 2 **envelopes (each 1 ounce) onion soup mix**
> **flour**
> **salt and pepper**
> **mashed potatoes (see page 140)**

Heat oven to 275 degrees. Blot roast with paper towels to remove surface moisture. Heat a large pan over high flame several minutes. Add oil and swirl to coat bottom of pan. Brown the roast on all sides. (Alternatively, you may brown it under the broiler. If you do, Mark warns, "Be sure to remove the netting from the roast if it has one.") Meanwhile, combine dry onion soup mix with 6 cups water in a roasting pan. Add the browned roast, cover pan, and bake until meat is very tender, 3 or more hours. Remove meat to a platter. Strain the broth into a saucepan. Cool broth and meat, then cover them and refrigerate overnight.

To make gravy, bring broth to simmer. Make a slurry by combining 6 tablespoons flour with about ½ cup water in a jar. Cover with tight-fitting lid and shake until mixture is smooth. Whisk half of it into the simmering broth until thickened, then gradually add more slurry to reach desired thickness. Simmer the gravy, stirring occasionally, at least 10 minutes. Season with salt and pepper to taste.

To serve, cut the pork across the grain into thick slices. ("Cutting it across the grain is the key to the difference between tender and nontender pork," Mark explains.) Heat pork in the gravy, and serve it with mashed potatoes and more gravy. Makes 10–16 servings.

## SAUER POWER

There's no doubt about it. Wisconsinites have an affection for sauerkraut, the old-world brew of fermented cabbage that goes so perfectly with pork, sausage, and brats that one without the other is practically inconceivable. Growing up in Chippewa Falls during the 1950s and 1960s, my husband, Mark's, childhood straddled modern touchstones such as television and rock and roll with family farm traditions that included making kraut in an old Red Wing crock in the basement bathroom. He tells a boyhood story that I like to hear again and again (as our teenage son, Peter, sits by, shaking his head in utter disbelief) about how he'd gorge ecstatically on sauerkraut until he was nearly sick.

"I'd eat so much I had to lay on the couch afterwards because my belly was so full. It was also a good way of getting out of doing the dishes."

*(continued on facing page)*

# Pork Ribs and Sauerkraut

## KOFFEE KUP, STOUGHTON
*Kendall and Trish Gulseth*

Daily specials like this one are fast food that tastes slow. The slow part comes from being partially cooked the day before, refrigerated overnight to develop flavor, then further cooked in a steam table all morning. The fast part is that it's ready to be served, hot and full of soul, the moment you order it. But whatever you do, don't eat this fast. Kendall's ribs, served with real mashed potatoes and pork gravy, are worth lingering over every single bite.

Kendall adapts this recipe to make barbecued ribs by substituting barbecue sauce for the kraut. Use lots because once you've heated it with the ribs and beer, it makes a great gravy. Try the barbecue sauce recipe contributed by Helena Lawinger of the Red Rooster Cafe in Mineral Point on the previous page. And, for a primer on mashed potatoes, see page 140.

> **3** **pounds baby back rib racks**
> **5** **tablespoons flour**
> **salt and pepper**
> **2** **cans (each 14 ounces) sauerkraut, undrained**
> **½** **cup beer**
> **mashed potatoes**

Heat oven to 325 degrees. Place ribs in a roasting pan that has a cover to fit and is large enough to hold all the ribs in two layers. Add enough water to reach a depth of an inch or two, but do not submerge the ribs. Cover pan and bake until meat is very tender, 2–3 hours. (Kendall says, "If you can turn the bone in the meat, then it's done.") Cut the rib racks into smaller portions, then transfer them to a pan to cool off. Strain the cooking liquid, now a flavorful broth, through a fine-mesh strainer into a bowl and let cool. Cover meat and broth and refrigerate overnight.

The next day, skim the solidified lard from the top of the broth, reserving 3 tablespoons for the gravy. Save the rest for another use or discard it. To make gravy, heat 3 cups of the broth and keep it warm. Melt the lard in a saucepan over medium heat, stir in the flour, and cook, stirring often, 3–4 minutes. Whisk pork broth into flour mixture until thickened. Simmer, stirring occasionally, 10 minutes. Season with salt and pepper to taste. This gravy will be pale but delicious.

For the ribs, layer them with the sauerkraut in a dutch oven or baking dish in this order: one-third of the sauerkraut, half of the ribs, one-third sauerkraut, half of the ribs, one-third sauerkraut. Pour beer over ribs, cover dish, and heat over low flame or in oven until hot. Meanwhile, prepare mashed potatoes and reheat the gravy. Serve the ribs topped with sauerkraut and the potatoes with gravy. Makes 6 servings.

# Sausage, Potatoes, and Sauerkraut

## UNIQUE CAFE, BOSCOBEL
### *Doyle and Nancy Lewis*

Annette Wagner, right-hand woman in the Unique's kitchen, layers "rope-type" sausage like kielbasa with sauerkraut and parboiled potatoes in this slow-cooked dish that she first made for her family at home. It's easy to make and easy to vary. Annette adds onion chunks or diced, peeled Granny Smith apples, or even green peppers. We have tweaked ours by adding caraway and dark beer and by using bratwurst. Bring on the Packer game!

- 1 pound kielbasa, Polish, or other "rope-type" sausage, cut into 2-inch pieces
- 1 pound baby red potatoes, boiled until half done and cut into chunks
- 3–4 cups sauerkraut, undrained

The amounts are approximate, and if you don't own a crockpot, layer it in an oven-proof pot with a tight-fitting lid and bake it at 300 degrees.

*(continued from facing page)*

Like many cafe owners, Mark's mother, Eleanore, a child of the Depression, is a whiz at making something good out of little. It was seldom that the family could splurge on Polish sausage, so she'd purchase turkey legs and put them into her Eau Claire–made Presto pressure cooker along with sauerkraut, then boil up a side of potatoes. Though it was a simple meal, it was also a favorite.

If there was any money at all to be spent on sausage, it was spent in support of the church. In the Stanley-Thorp area, where Eleanore grew up as one of thirteen children of Polish immigrants, the family feasted at the annual parish supper at St. Mary Czestochowa in the crossroads village of Junction. "Those old Polish people knew how to make good sausage," Eleanore asserts. "My brother Tony kept track of how much he ate by counting the inches. It's been fifty years, and I've never had anything like it since."—J. S.

# *Cornish Pasty*

## RED ROOSTER CAFE, MINERAL POINT
*Helena Lawinger and Patti McKinley*

In April 2002, Helena's Cornish pasties were voted best in the state
by readers of *Wisconsin Trails* magazine. She offers them two ways:
as traditional, handheld individual turnovers, or layered pan-style like
a pasty casserole. Only cubed sirloin is used because, Helena says,
"the better the meat, the better the pasty."

*Crust*
4½  **cups flour**
1½  **teaspoons salt**
 ¾  **teaspoon baking powder**
1½  **cups lard, cut into pieces**
 ¾  **cup ice water**

*Filling*
2½  **pounds sirloin steak, cut into small cubes**
4½–5  **cups peeled, sliced potatoes**
 1  **small rutabaga, peeled, quartered and sliced**
1½  **cups chopped onion**
    **salt and pepper**
    **butter cut into small pieces**

To make crust, whisk flour, salt, and baking powder in bowl until well
combined. Use a pastry cutter or two knives to cut in the lard until
the mixture is crumbly. Stir in the ice water to form a dough. Cover
and chill dough until you're ready to assemble the pasties.

To make filling, combine steak, potatoes, rutabagas, and onions
in large bowl. Season generously with salt and pepper; toss well.

To form and bake pasties, preheat oven to 350 degrees. Transfer
dough to a floured work surface.

For the traditional, lead-miner's-style pasty, oil a large baking sheet
or line it with parchment paper. Divide dough into 8 equal portions.
Roll out each portion to the size of a dinner plate. Divide filling among
the dough rounds. Scatter butter pieces over filling. Using extra flour
if needed to prevent sticking, fold dough over filling. Press and crimp
to seal the edges all around. Place on baking pan; bake 1½–2 hours.
Serve hot. Makes 8 individual pasties.

For pan-style pasties, oil a 9-by-13-inch baking pan. Divide dough
in half. Roll out half the dough to fit the bottom of the pan. Transfer

to pan. Spread filling over dough. Scatter butter pieces over filling. Roll out other half of dough and place it on top of the filling, tucking the edges in. Bake 2–2½ hours. Makes 9 servings.

## PASTIES PAST AND PRESENT

Pasties were brought to southwestern Wisconsin in the 1820s and 1830s by immigrants from Cornwall who came to work the region's lead mines. These Cousin Jacks were the state's original badgers, men who dug tunnels into the earth to extract its valuable minerals. It took hearty fare to sustain them through exhausting hours in the dank, dark mines. Pasties filled the bill.

As the national dish of Cornwall, the pasty has a long and close association with miners. According to folklorists Yvonne and William Lockwood in "Pasties in Michigan's Upper Peninsula," tradition says women wrapped potatoes, meat, and onions in pastry as a substitute for the sandwich and carried them hot from the hearth to the mines. Standing at the mouth of the open shaft, they'd drop the pasties to the men waiting down below. The pasties must have been darned durable and the mine shaft not only vertical but incredibly straight to withstand the drop. More believable is the story that miners carried the pasties in pails or pockets and heated them up for dinner on a shovel held over a candle flame.

As with pie, it's the crust that either makes or breaks a pasty. It's impossible to have a good pasty with a lousy crust. No matter how tasty the contents, if the crust lacks flavor, is dry and crumbles, or is too tough to sink your teeth into, the pasty is a miserable failure. A successful crust must be both sturdy and flaky. Some pasty makers swear by shortening. Others wouldn't consider anything but lard or suet. Crust recipes can be so closely guarded that they become secret, passed down only to family members and among church-women.

Helen Lawinger, a devotee of lard, and her daughter Patti McKinley have been making pasties at the Red Rooster Cafe in downtown Mineral Point since 1972. As edible symbols of the town's Cornish heritage, pasties are old hat to the locals, who eat them at home but only rarely when they go out to eat. Tourists, on the other hand, often have to be told what pasties are. Patti reports that once they try them, they come back, sometimes filling empty coolers so they can enjoy pasties at home throughout the year.

Served the traditional way without condiments or the newfangled way with ketchup, chili sauce, or gravy (to purists, there's only the right way and the wrong way), pasties are found in the lead mining region of southwestern Wisconsin and also along the northern border with Michigan, where they filtered south out of the Cornish settlements in the lead and copper mining region of the Upper Peninsula. Along both the Michigan-Wisconsin border and in the UP, the pasty was picked up by later European immigrants, particularly the Finns, who adopted it with such gusto that it now sometimes is identified as Finnish in that region. And, as Northwoods and Great Lakes tourism developed into a major industry, the pasty developed into an important regional symbol. In 1938, in Hurley, Wisconsin, an Italian entrepreneur opened the first commercial pasty shop. You read right: an Italian American. From humble beginnings, the Cornish pasty has emerged from the pocket of the lead miner into an important and dynamic symbol of not only Cornish and Finnish ethnic tradition but also of regional culture.—J. S.

# *Midwest Style Barbecued Ribs*

## RED ROOSTER CAFE, MINERAL POINT
*Helena Lavinger and Patti McKinley*

The sauce in this recipe may also be used on barbecued chicken.

- ½ **cup brown sugar**
- ½ **cup red wine vinegar**
- ¼ **cup prepared mustard**
- 1 **cup ketchup**
- 3 **tablespoons Worcestershire sauce**
- 2 **tablespoons butter or vegetable oil**
- 3 **green onions, finely cut**
  **salt and pepper**
- 4 **pounds baby back ribs**

Make a barbecue sauce by combining brown sugar, red wine vinegar, mustard, ketchup, Worcestershire sauce, butter or oil, and green onions in sauce pan. Add a little salt and pepper. Bring to a low simmer and cook, stirring occasionally, 15 minutes. Heat oven to 325 degrees. Cut ribs into serving-size pieces and place them, meat side up, in a roasting pan. Season with salt and pepper. Bake 1½–2 hours; drain off accumulated fat. Brush sauce over ribs and bake or grill the ribs a few minutes longer. Makes 4–6 servings.

# OJ's Barbecued Chicken

## OJ's Midtown Restaurant, Gillett
### *Owen and Joan Farrell*

The addition of chili powder to roast pork, hot beef, and meatloaf has become Owen's trademark, ever since the day he accidentally knocked a can of the seasoning off a shelf and into a pan of gravy—and liked the results. We do, too! Owen leaves the chili powder out of this recipe for barbecued chicken, however, and instead makes it exactly the way his grandmother did. Served with mashed potatoes and plenty of extra sauce, it is a popular addition to Owen and Joan's catering menu.

- ½ cup sugar
- 4 tablespoons ketchup
- 4 tablespoons molasses
- 4 tablespoons soy sauce
- 1 tablespoon salt
- ½ teaspoon pepper
- 3 pounds chicken, cut up
- 1 tablespoon cornstarch mixed with
    - 2 tablespoons water

To make sauce, mix first six ingredients with ½ cup water. Place chicken pieces in large bowl. Add sauce and toss to coat all the pieces. Cover and let marinate in the refrigerator 8 or more hours. Heat oven to 250 degrees. Line one or two deep baking pans with aluminum foil. Arrange chicken pieces on pans; spread sauce over them. Bake until chicken is brown and tender, basting two or three times, 2 to 2½ hours. Remove chicken to a platter and keep it warm. Pour sauce from baking pan into saucepan. Add 1¼ cups water and bring to simmer. Whisk in the cornstarch mixture to thicken the sauce. Serve sauce with the chicken. Makes 4–6 servings.

# Southern Style Pan-Fried Chicken

## FAYE'S DINKY DINER, EAGLE RIVER
*Faye and Dale Hillner*

A native of Memphis, Faye brings the South to the Northwoods when she serves up this down-home, no-frills lunch special every Wednesday at the Dinky Diner. (With just twenty seats, it's Wisconsin's dinkiest.) "People come just for the chicken," she tells us. "Customers say it is the best around. As far as we know, no one else serves it."

So revered is Faye's pan-fried chicken in and around Eagle River that folks will drop in on Thursdays to see if there's any left. When there is some—which isn't often—she reheats it in the deep fryer and serves it in a basket with french fries.

> **chicken quarters**
> **cold water**
> **flour**
> **salt and pepper**
> **garlic powder**
> **Crisco**

Cover chicken with cold water and let it soak about 10 minutes. Meanwhile, make the breading in a deep bowl. Combine flour with plenty of salt and pepper plus garlic powder to suit your taste. In a large cast-iron skillet over medium flame, heat enough Crisco to generously cover the bottom of the pan. When shortening is hot enough to make a drop of water sizzle when it hits the fat, roll the chicken in the breading until well covered and place in the pan. Cook the chicken in batches, without crowding the pan, and turn it as needed until it's brown and crispy on all sides and done all the way through, about 20–30 minutes. Drain on paper towels and serve hot. Makes any number of servings.

## CHICKEN FAST AND SLOW

In *Fried Chicken,* food writer John T. Edge celebrates America's favorite Sunday dinner ("fried chicken and churchgoing are long intertwined") in all its surprising varieties, from slow-cooked, southern pan-fried chicken like that made by Faye Hillner at the Dinky Diner in Eagle River to the millions of bone-in and boneless pieces pulled out of fast-food pressure fryers coast to coast.

Pan-fried chicken once "evoked a rural idyll, a time and place where many cooks had the luxury, the inclination to devote hours on end to the preparation of Sunday supper," Edge writes. Fast-food chicken, on the other hand, requires little time and even less skill. Face it. The teenage boy behind the Kentucky Fried Chicken counter isn't there to fulfill your spiritual and physical needs. To him, fried chicken is all about making car payments.

It was KFC founder Colonel Harland Sanders who revolutionized fried chicken. In the late 1930s, Sanders took it out of the pan and put it into the pressure fryer so he could make more faster while retaining a pan-fried flavor. So tasty and popular was Sanders's pressure fried chicken that Duncan Hines featured his Corbin, Kentucky, restaurant in *Adventures in Good Eating* from the first edition in 1939 straight through until 1952, the last researched and written by Hines himself. The year 1952 was pivotal for both men, as well as the American public: Hines retired and sold out to big business, and Sanders traded in his sole enterprise for franchises. Going out for fried chicken would never be the same.

(The Colonel's original Corbin restaurant is now fully restored as the 1940s-themed Harland Sanders Cafe, a combination Kentucky Fried Chicken outlet and museum.)

Sanders's magical combination of pressure cooking with deep-fat frying is shared by Broasted chicken—both a cooking method and industry trademark. Established in 1954 and headquartered in Beloit, Wisconsin, since 1977, the Broaster Company boasts that its specially marinated and crispy-crunchy crusted chicken is more tender, juicy, and flavorful than chicken that is deep fried. I've eaten a lot of Broaster chicken in pursuit of why it's so darned popular and have concluded that, like the emperor and his new clothes, once the crust cracks away there's nothing much to brag about underneath.

Thanks largely to KFC and businesses like the Broaster Company, the mass production of fried chicken resulted in widespread availability and standardization of taste, so that pressure fried chicken is what most Americans have come to like. "We do chicken right," KFC trumpets, and we're lulled into believing that it's true.

Until, that is, we get a taste of the real stuff made by cooks like Faye Hillner in a sizzling cast-iron skillet. Every Wednesday, Faye dips into the traditions of

## A Little Chocolate with Cheese

**M**ole (pronounced *MOH-lay*) is the intriguingly spicy sauce that is traditional in the Mexican states of Puebla and Oaxaca. It comes in many flavor variations and colors but most typically is a smooth, dark, reddish-brown concoction made with chilies, garlic, onion, pumpkin or sesame seeds, and a small amount of chocolate. (Yes, chocolate, but not the sweetened kind.) Mole can be complicated to make, but, happily, delicious bottled versions are imported to the U.S. and can be found in Latino markets and on the ethnic food shelves of large grocery stores.

*Queso fresco* (pronounced *KAY-so FRAYS-ko*) is a fresh, mild-tasting Mexican cheese that crumbles easily but won't melt away into smoothness when it's heated. Rather than overburdening the enchiladas, it adds a nice salty, crumbly accent to Ernesto Rodriguez's winning specialty.—T. A.

her Tennessee childhood—but not too deep, because pan-fried chicken hovers at the surface of every southerner's life—and prepares fresh pan-fried chicken from the time she arrives in the early morning until the door closes at one o'clock. She typically fries enough chicken to fill forty orders, and in a diner with only twenty seats, that's a lot of chicken. Served with sides of real mashed potatoes, corn, and cornbread, Faye's lightly crusted fried chicken—the seasoned flour coating fuses with the skin and doesn't fall away from the meat—is the centerpiece of what Edge refers to as the "archetypal family meal" served southern style. Add a glass of sweetened iced tea and a wedge of sweet potato pie (you can make your own using the recipe on page 184), and honey, you'll think you've died and gone to heaven.—J. S.

# *Chicken Mole Enchiladas*

## Greenwood Family Restaurant, Greenwood
### *Ernesto and Linda Rodriguez*

If you think of gooey, cheese-burdened fast-food enchiladas as Mexican fare, you're in for an exciting surprise. Ernesto's enchiladas, ordered by adventure eaters at the Greenwood Family Restaurant until it was sold in 2005, are filled with fresh-cooked chicken, spiked with *mole,* and topped with authentic south-of-the-border garnishes like sliced radishes and *queso fresco.*

> 1 **chicken (3–4 pounds), cut into quarters**
> 1 **tablespoon vegetable oil**
> 2 **jars (each 8 ounces) mole sauce**
> 24 **corn tortillas**
> **sesame seeds**
> **about 2 cups crumbled queso fresco**
> **thinly sliced radishes**
> **thinly sliced onions, separated into rings**
> **small romaine lettuce leaves**

Place chicken in a large pot; cover with cold water. Bring to simmer, skimming surface as needed. Simmer chicken 40–50 minutes. Remove chicken from liquid and let it cool, reserving the liquid.

Heat oil in a large, deep skillet over medium flame. Add mole and 8 cups of the chicken liquid. Whisk until smooth. Reduce heat and simmer about 15 minutes, stirring often. The mixture should end up "not thick and not thin," says Ernesto. Meanwhile, remove bones and skin from chicken. Shred the meat by placing a piece of it on a cutting board and scraping it downward with a fork. Cover shredded meat and place it in a warm oven, or reheat it in a microwave when you're ready to serve the enchiladas.

To assemble and serve enchiladas, wrap the tortillas in aluminum foil and heat them in a warm oven. (Alternatively, you can heat them one at a time in a hot cast-iron skillet for a few seconds on each side.) For each serving, submerge a warm tortilla in the mole, then let the excess drip off. Transfer tortilla to serving plate, spread about 3 tablespoons shredded chicken in the middle, and drizzle with a little of the mole sauce. Roll it up. Repeat once or twice to make two or three enchiladas for a single serving. Drizzle a little more mole over enchiladas. Sprinkle with sesame seeds and scatter 2–3 tablespoons of queso fresco over the top. Top with a few radish slices and a few sliced onions, and place a leaf of romaine lettuce on the side for a garnish. Repeat as needed for more servings. Makes 8–12 servings.

## A Taste of Mexico

During the decade or so between the first and second editions of *Cafe Wisconsin,* Mexican restaurateurs in search of affordable restaurants moved out of large urban areas such as Chicago, Milwaukee, and Rockford, Illinois, into Wisconsin's smaller cities and towns. These restaurants, including many small town cafes, were perfectly suited to their family-operated way of doing business.

Among them were Ernesto and Linda Rodriguez, owners of the former Greenwood Family Restaurant in Greenwood. They were operating their own restaurant in neighboring Marshfield when a new bypass absorbed the building and lot. "We had to go out looking for another place," Linda remembers. "We looked all over. I hated this place when I first saw it because it was so small and cold. I couldn't see how it would do. But then I began to see what it could be, and we bought it. We closed down for five weeks, and my brother Kevin—he's a contractor—did all the remodeling. Everyone was waiting for us to reopen. Our first day was a Tuesday, and that Friday there was a line out onto the street. I was frantic. I was running around this place like a cat on a hot tin roof."

They soon found that the locals like to eat early and get home to do the evening farm chores. As the days settled into a predictable pattern, Linda's blood pressure evened out, and the grand-opening kinks disappeared. Their six-page menu mixed traditional Wisconsin food with Italian, Greek, and authentic Mexican specialties served every Saturday night. Entrees included enchiladas, burritos, and other familiar favorites accompanied with the traditional rice and beans, fresh salsa, and colorful pico de gallo. A traditional

Mexican dessert that quickly became a customer favorite was fried ice cream (see page 191).

Saturday Mexican specials were popular, especially with the area's Mexican migrants and senior citizens. Linda theorizes that the older people are the ones who are familiar with Mexican food because they have traveled in that country. Linda believes the younger generations are reluctant to try it because their idea of Mexican is Taco Bell and Taco John's. "I could tell when people walked in the door whether they were going to order Mexican," she says. "I wasn't offended when they didn't. Chances are they'd order broasted chicken or hot beef. Even though we had a hundred things on the menu, they'd always go for that."

For other authentic Mexican fare from Ernesto and Linda, see the recipes for Chicken Mole Enchiladas (page 102), Refried Beans (page 148), and Mexican Rice (page 148).—J.S.

# Marshall's Pork Chipotle Stew

## DADDY MAXWELL'S ARCTIC CIRCLE DINER, WILLIAMS BAY

*Marshall and Janette Maxwell*

"I love the flavor of chipotle peppers," says Marshall, who created this chunky, soul-satisfying stew served with warmed corn tortillas, rice, and a green salad. What he's not crazy about is carrots ("it's just a taste thing"). For some folks, carrots add welcome sweetness and color to the mix, but you can leave them out if you want. Marshall does.

Chipotles are smoked, dried jalapeño peppers available in small cans at Latino food markets or well-stocked grocery stores. They are rich, distinctive, and very spicy.

This recipe makes enough to feed a crowd but is easily halved. If your group likes it hot, make additional salsa to offer with the stew. Sour cream and chopped cilantro wouldn't hurt, either.

> *Salsa*
> 1  can (**28 ounces**) **whole peeled tomatoes (or substitute 2 pounds vine-ripened tomatoes, peeled, partially seeded, and coarsely chopped)**
> 1  **cup chopped onion**
> 1  **jalapeño, seeded**
> ¼  **cup chopped cilantro**

1   tablespoon garlic powder, granulated garlic, or
    fresh minced garlic
1   or more teaspoons chili powder
½   teaspoon salt
2   canned chipotle peppers

*Stew*

5   pounds fresh boneless pork butt or country-style
    rib meat
   salt and pepper
   vegetable oil
2   cups chopped onions
1   cup diced carrots (optional)
3   or more cloves garlic, minced
1½–2   pounds red or other waxy-type potatoes, peeled,
    if desired, and cut into 1-inch cubes
⅓   cup chopped cilantro
1   teaspoon salt

To make the salsa, blend the first seven ingredients in a food processor or blender on high speed until well combined. Add the chipotles and blend another 30 seconds.

To make the stew, trim fat and cut pork into large, 2-inch cubes, then pat dry with paper towels. Season the meat generously with salt and pepper. Heat a large, heavy (preferably cast-iron) pan over high flame several minutes. Add a teaspoon or two of oil and swirl pan to coat the bottom. Brown the meat in batches, a few minutes per side. Do not crowd the pan or the meat will steam instead of brown. Add a bit more oil between batches as needed. As each batch is finished, remove the meat to a large roasting pan with fitted lid. When all the meat is browned, reduce the flame to medium low, and add a bit more oil. Stir in the onions, carrots (if desired), and garlic. Cook, stirring often, until vegetables begin to soften a bit. Add the mixture to the roaster, scraping up any bits on the bottom of the pan. Add potatoes, cilantro, salt, and prepared salsa to the roaster. Stir to mix well. Bring to simmer (you may need to do this over two burners), stir well again, cover, and simmer until meat and vegetables are tender, 1½ or more hours. You can also cook the stew in the oven at 350 degrees or lower for 2 or more hours. It can be held at 200 degrees for several hours until ready to serve. Makes 16 or more servings.

# *Mexican Lasagne*

## M & M CAFE, MONTICELLO
*Mike and Mary Davis*

Mary thought this recipe shared by a friend "would entice our customers out of their meat-and-potatoes mode." It worked, and now it's featured at least once a month. A mild chunky-style salsa is used at the M & M Cafe, but if you want to turn up the heat, go ahead and use a spicier one. A handful of chopped cilantro leaves also adds a bit of kick. (Note: No-cook lasagne noodles are ones that do not require precooking before being used in a recipe.)

1½ **pounds ground beef, browned, drained, and lightly salted**
1 **can (15 ounces) refried beans**
2 **teaspoons dried oregano**
1 **teaspoon cumin**
¾ **teaspoon garlic powder**
12 **no-cook lasagne noodles**
2½ **cups bottled salsa**
2 **cups water**
1 **container (16 ounces) sour cream**
1 **bunch green onions, chopped**
1 **small can (3 ounces) sliced ripe olives**
2 **cups (about 8 ounces) shredded Monterey Jack or cheddar cheese**

Heat oven to 350 degrees. Oil a 9-by-13-inch baking pan. Combine cooked ground beef, refried beans, oregano, cumin, and garlic powder in a bowl. Place 4 of the no-cook lasagne noodles in the prepared pan. Spread half of the meat mixture over the noodles. Place 4 more noodles over the meat and top it with the remaining meat. Place final 4 noodles over this. Mix salsa and water in the same bowl you used for the meat. Pour it evenly over the lasagne. Cover tightly with aluminum foil and bake 1½ hours. Combine sour cream, green onions, and olives; spoon over the hot casserole. Spread cheese evenly over the top. Continue to bake until cheese melts, 5–10 minutes. Remove from oven and let stand 10–15 minutes before serving. Makes 10–12 servings.

# Stuffed Squash

## VILLAGE HAUS CAFE, FALL CREEK
*Sheri and Jim Coldwell*

Sheri is a great a gardener as well as a great cook. When her one-acre plot goes into harvest mode and her customers bring her armfuls of overrun, she finds creative ways to put everything to use in the cafe. This is one of the dishes she makes when the cornucopia empties on her doorstep. It is so popular, Sherri says, "I sometimes send out post-cards to people when I make it. If I didn't, I'd have a lot of people mad at me."

You can play with the type and amount of ingredients, and even use some frozen vegetables if you're short on fresh. This recipe makes a lot, but it is easily halved. Of course, if *your* garden is overflowing, consider doubling the recipe and inviting your neighbors over.

|   |   |
|---|---|
| 6 | acorn squash |
| 1½ | pounds bulk Italian sausage |
| 1 | cup finely chopped onion |
| ¾ | cup finely chopped celery |
| ½ | cup finely chopped red or green sweet pepper |
| ¾ | cup diced rutabaga |
| ½ | cup sliced carrot coins |
| ½ | cup chopped green beans |
| 1 | cup frozen peas |
| 1 | cup diced tomatoes |
| 3 | tablespoons garlic powder |
| 2 | cups freshly grated parmesan cheese |
| 2 | teaspoons dried sage |
|   | salt and pepper |
|   | breadcrumbs |
|   | butter, cut into small pieces |

Heat oven to 350 degrees. Cut squashes in half lengthwise and scrape out the seeds with a spoon. Place halves, skin side up, in one or two large baking pans. Pour a little water in the bottom of pan(s) and bake squash 45 minutes.

Meanwhile, heat a large, heavy skillet over medium-high flame. Add sausage and brown it, stirring often so it breaks up as it cooks. Drain off fat. Add onions, celery, and sweet pepper. Cook, stirring occasionally, 5–10 minutes. Add rutabaga, carrots, and beans. Cook, stirring often, about 10 minutes. Remove from heat. Stir in peas, tomatoes, garlic powder, parmesan, and sage. Add salt and pepper to taste. Mix well.

Stuff the partially baked squash halves with the stuffing, heaping up the stuffing on top. Place stuffed squash back into the pan(s). Sprinkle with breadcrumbs and dot with bits of butter. Bake another 45 minutes. Dig in! Makes 12 servings.

# Spaghetti and Meatballs

### KOFFEE KUP, STOUGHTON
*Kendall and Trish Gulseth*

Quality Black Angus ground beef is the only kind Kendall uses in his meatballs. He makes them big and beautiful, as large as a tennis ball. But if golf balls are more your size, that's fine, too.

*Sauce*
- 2–3 tablespoons olive or salad oil
- 1 cup finely chopped onions
- 3 cans (each 1 pound) diced tomatoes
- 2 cans (each 6 ounces) tomato paste
- 2 teaspoons dried, crushed oregano
- 1 teaspoon garlic powder
- 1 teaspoon sugar
- 1½ teaspoons salt
- ½ teaspoon pepper

*Meatballs*
- 2 pounds ground beef
- 3 eggs
- ½ cup finely diced onions
- ½ cup dried breadcrumbs
- ¼ cup oatmeal
- ½ cup parmesan cheese ("from the green can")
    or 1 cup freshly grated
- 1 tablespoon dried, crushed oregano
- 2 teaspoons dried thyme
- 2 teaspoons garlic powder
- 1 teaspoon onion salt

⅛ **teaspoon ground allspice**
2 **teaspoons salt**
1 **teaspoon pepper**
1–2 **tablespoons dried parsley (optional)**

*Also*
**cooked spaghetti**
**additional parmesan cheese**

To prepare sauce, heat oil in a large, heavy saucepan over medium flame. Add onions and cook, stirring often, until tender. Stir in remaining sauce ingredients, bring to simmer, lower heat, partially cover pan, and cook, stirring occasionally, 1 hour or longer.

To prepare meatballs, heat oven to 350 degrees. Wash your hands and use them to gently but thoroughly combine all the meatball ingredients in a large bowl. Form the mixture into "tennis balls" or "golf balls" and arrange them without touching on a baking sheet. Bake 35–45 minutes. Add meatballs to sauce. Keep on low heat, gently stirring once in a while, or cool it down and chill to reheat later or the next day.

Serve sauce and meatballs over spaghetti and pass the parmesan. Makes 8 or more servings.

# Pizza Stuffed Shells

## COUNTRY CAFE, BABCOCK
*Sherri Dessart*

Sherri added her own "inventions" to a recipe she found in a magazine to create this Italian-style dish served with garlic bread and a tossed salad at the Country Cafe. She admits that it's "putzy" to put together, but it's so good, we doubt you'll mind.

> 24 jumbo pasta shells
> 1 teaspoon olive oil
> 3 Italian sausages (about ¾ pound), casing removed
> 1 tablespoon minced garlic
> 10 ounces mushrooms, sliced
> 1 jar (15½ ounces) pizza sauce
> 1 can (14½ ounces) chopped tomatoes
> 1 each small red, yellow, and green sweet pepper, finely diced
> 1 medium onion, finely diced
> 1 container (15 ounces) ricotta cheese
> 6–8 ounces thin-sliced pepperoni, finely diced
> ½ cup freshly grated parmesan cheese, divided
> 1 large egg, beaten
> 4 ounces shredded mozzarella

Boil pasta in large amount of salted water until barely tender. Drain, rinse with cool water, and set aside. Heat large skillet over medium-high flame. Add olive oil and swirl to coat skillet bottom. Add sausage and brown it, chopping it with a spoon to break it up. Stir in garlic and mushrooms; cook, stirring often, until mushrooms are tender. Add pizza sauce and tomatoes (with the juices). Simmer 10 minutes. Meanwhile, combine sweet peppers, ricotta, pepperoni, half the parmesan, and the egg; stir to mix well.

Heat oven to 350 degrees. Layer half the tomato-sausage sauce in the bottom of a 9-by-13-inch or similarly sized baking dish. Stuff the shells with the sweet pepper–cheese mixture and arrange them over the sauce. Spread remaining sauce over stuffed shells. Bake 40 minutes. Sprinkle shredded mozzarella and remaining parmesan over top and continue to bake until cheese is melted, about 10 minutes. Makes 8 servings.

# Creamed Cod

## KOFFEE KUP, STOUGHTON
*Kendall and Trish Gulseth*

According to Kendall, Norwegian-style creamed Icelandic cod "is like a thick chowder." Just one of many "white foods" that characterize traditional Scandinavian cooking, it may look bland, but it's oh, so rich.

At the Koffee Kup, creamed cod is ladled over your choice of mashed potatoes, homemade biscuits, or toast. Kendall says most of his customers go for toast, but we say, why go for bread when you could have from-scratch mashed potatoes (page 140) or Kendall's own hot baking powder biscuits (page 23)? On the other hand, browned toast does add a little color to the dish.

Take care to cook the roux slowly over a low flame so that no browning of the flour occurs. See page 44 for more about roux.

- 3 **cups 2% milk, plus additional milk as desired**
- 6 **tablespoons butter**
- 6 **tablespoons flour**
- $\frac{1}{8}$ **teaspoon ground nutmeg**
- 2 **pounds frozen cod, thawed**
  **salt and white pepper to taste**
  **toasted white bread, homemade biscuits, or**
  **mashed potatoes**

Heat milk in microwave or on stovetop; keep it warm. Melt butter in a heavy saucepan over medium-low flame. Using a wooden spoon, gradually stir in the flour. Reduce heat to low and cook the roux, stirring often, 3–5 minutes. Use a wire whisk to gradually whisk in the warm milk. Raise heat to medium and bring the mixture to a simmer, stirring often. Whisk in nutmeg. Simmer until mixture thickens. Cut the cod into chunks and add it to the white sauce. Simmer slowly, stirring occasionally, 10–15 minutes. The cod will break up as it cooks. If mixture is too thick, add additional milk to reach desired consistency. Season to taste with salt and white pepper. Serve hot over toast, biscuits, or mashed potatoes. Makes 6–8 servings.

### Norwegian "White Food" Syndrome

With its heavily glaciated terrain dominated by a jagged, fjord-filled coastline on the west, rugged mountains broken by fertile valleys on the east, and small, scattered plains in between, Norway is a land of striking contrasts. As you might expect, traditional foods of Norwegian peasant origin vary by region, yet, surprisingly, there are enough commonalities that people from every district feel at home at the national dining table. This is due in large part to the importance of the sea, which proved to feed the Norwegian people far more reliably than the land.

Out of the sea came salmon *(Atlantisk laks)* and white fish such as haddock *(hyse)*, tusk *(brosme)*, and particularly cod *(torsk)*, which when dried sustained many a family through the sunless winters. Lutefisk is sun-dried cod reconstituted by soakings in water and potash lye, followed by several additional cycles of soaking and rinsing in clean water. Boiled and served with butter, the gelatinous lutefisk is considered a national badge of ethnic identity and bravado by some, a national disgrace by others.

Lutefisk is just one of several "white foods" that characterize traditional Norwegian cookery. It is familiarly paired with lefse, thin flat rounds like tortillas, of which there are many varieties in Norway today. In Wisconsin, it is frequently made from potatoes, as it is at Countryside Lefse of Blair, which supplies lefse to the Norske Nook in nearby Osseo. As versatile as the Mexican tortilla, lefse can be eaten with butter and sugar, wrapped around a filling in the style of a sandwich wrap, and used as a kind of edible utensil, used to scoop up, push, and pick up food from a plate.

Many people prepare and eat lefse throughout the year, but lutefisk is primarily relegated to fundraiser dinners sponsored by Lutheran churches and Sons of Norway lodges from mid-October to mid-November. It is also served twice in the late fall at the Norske Nook in Osseo, as well as at the Nook's Rice Lake and Hayward locations. If lutefisk is your thing—and believe me, it is not for everyone!—be sure to call ahead for the dates. Be prepared to defend your attraction to lutefisk against those who have come for the *kjøttkaeker,* or Norwegian meatballs. Lightly spiced with seasonings like ginger and nutmeg, they can be served in either brown gravy or a white, cream-type sauce. Other white or whitish foods commonly served with lutefisk are herring (pickled or in cream sauce, or both) and boiled or creamed cabbage.

Boiled dumplings known as *klubb* or *kumle*—made from shredded raw potatoes mixed with a little flour—are a traditional white food that appears to have been replaced in cafes by another popular white food: boiled or mashed potatoes. On the other hand, *blodklubb*, made with pork blood, is a significant part of Syttende Mai dinners sponsored by the Stoughton Sons of

Norway. In rural Argyle, the Yellowstone Lutheran Church substitutes "klub" in gravy for lutefisk at its annual family style Norwegian supper.

Potatoes were introduced to Norway in the middle of the nineteenth century and quickly became a favorite, finding their way into stews and clear broth and milk or cream-based *suppe*. *Fisksuppe*, or fish soup, is an old standby, as is *plukkfisk*, a dish made by combining fish, potatoes, onions, and seasonings with a cream sauce. The creamed cod made by Kendall Gulseth at the Koffee Kup in Stoughton is similar to *plukkfisk*.

As in Wisconsin, dairying has a long tradition in Norway, and milk, cream, butter, and cheese figure prominently into its food traditions. Served either hot or cold, *risengrøt* or *riskrem* is a cream-based pudding made with flour, *rommegrøt*, a sour or sweet cream pudding made with rice, and *flotgrøt*, a similar pudding made with fruit. All remain popular in many Wisconsin households of Norwegian heritage, especially at Christmastime.

Christmas is the time of year when Norwegian food traditions are dusted off and celebrated—particularly the preparation of special baked sweets rich with butter and cream. My own family is German, but we did not hesitate to adopt Norwegian cookies like *krumkake* (the making of which has been inherited by my brother, Tom), *Berlinerkranser*, and occasionally *sandbakkels*. You can find these holiday delights, and perhaps *fattigman, rosetter, kringler, julekake*, and others as well, at the Norske Nook and, until it closed in June 2006, they were available at Borgen's Norwegian Cafe and Bakery in Westby.—J. S.

# Friday Fish Fry

## VILLAGE KITCHEN, CASCO
*Chris and Gary Jacobs*

Like thousands of good cooks across the state, Chris serves up a weekly fish fry to diners who would hardly recognize a Friday without it. Chris offers a greater variety of deep-fried fillets than most cafes, including lake perch, pike, redfish, and "plain old cod," and two kinds of breading: a thin, "dry-style" coating and a thicker, "wet-style" beer batter. She knows most home cooks won't bother with a deep fat fryer, and notes either breading works if fish is pan fried in a small amount of oil. She gives her customers the same options.

Chris's mom is the fish batter queen at the Village Kitchen. She relies on McCormick brand Golden Dipt breading mix as the base for her beer batter but adds a commercial product not available in retail grocery stores. Her dry breading, however, is easily accomplished in family kitchens, and that's what we've relayed below.

> **vegetable or peanut oil**
> 1–2  **cups milk**
> 1  **egg**
> **salt and pepper to taste**
> **McCormick Golden Dipt All-Purpose Breading Mix**
> **fresh or thawed and drained fish fillets**
> **lemon wedges**
> **tartar sauce (see page 144)**

Heat oven to 200 degrees. Line a baking sheet or large ovenproof platter with a triple-thickness of paper towels. Pour enough oil into a large, heavy skillet to reach ¼-inch up the sides. Heat over medium-high flame until a tiny sprinkle of breading mix sizzles when it hits the hot oil, about 5 minutes. Meanwhile, beat milk, egg, salt, and pepper in large bowl. Place some of the breading mix in another bowl. When oil is hot enough, cook the fish in batches and without crowding the pan. Dip fillets first into milk mixture, then into breading mix. Coat them thoroughly, shaking off the excess, and add them to the hot oil. Cook until brown and crispy on underside, then turn fillets with a pair of tongs and cook on the other side. Adjust the heat as necessary; thin fillets will take just a couple of minutes per side; thicker ones a bit longer. Drain fish on paper towels and keep them warm in the oven while you fry the remaining batches. Serve hot with lemon wedges and tartar sauce. Makes any number of servings.

## Thank God It's Friday Fish Fry

Fridays have a smell in Wisconsin. It is the tradition-rich blend of hot oil and fish—Icelandic cod or native freshwater favorites—repeated ad infinitum from border to border, in taverns, church halls, VFW posts, small town cafes, and all variety of other places where people gather to celebrate the end of the workweek.

Although it has spread over the border into Minnesota and pops up here and there throughout the country, the Friday night fish fry is truly a Badger State phenomenon. Many folks attribute the ritual to the state's heavy Catholic population, which prior to the changes brought by Vatican II was forbidden to eat meat on Fridays. Another popular explanation credits tavern keepers who lured post-Prohibition customers back to the family-friendly neighborhood beer hall by offering free or cheap fried fish. For many, this was the only affordable opportunity to treat the family to a rare night out. Until advances in the commercial fishing and frozen food products industries made it possible to truck in ocean fish, Wisconsin's ample lakes provided fresh perch, walleye, Lake Superior whitefish, and other favorite freshwater fish to feed the hungry masses. In the spring, its Great Lakes streams provided millions of smelt, which have been so tremendously overfished that they're now pretty much relegated to a once-a-year splurge at the local Knights of Columbus hall.

The results of an online poll posted on the *Whad'Ya Know?* website, an offshoot of the popular call-in radio program of the same name hosted by Michael Feldman, Wisconsin's own wit of the airways, show that fish eaters are "almost dead-in-the-water even" regarding their favorite fish. Tops was walleye, followed by catfish, "good old cod," and, tied at 18 percent of the vote each, perch and whitefish.

I'm content with cod, most common at all-you-can-eat gut-busters, but I am always thrilled when I find out-of-the-ordinary choices like the beer-battered redfish (also known as ocean perch) at the Village Kitchen in Casco. I was directed to the Village Kitchen by a fellow adventure eater, who praised the fish fry as something not to be missed. Two nuns were sitting at the counter when I arrived, and it wasn't long before the parish priest walked in wearing his blacks, his clerical collar tucked into his shirt pocket. You know you've found the best fish fry in the area when the place is filled with Catholics!

A ritual with a long history imbued with tradition, Wisconsin's Friday night fish fry is perhaps above all an important social event, where individuals come together to renew and strengthen bonds of family, friendship, and community. "She enjoyed the Friday night fish fry at the Lox Club as so many friends would stop and say hello," reads a Kaukauna woman's obituary filled with the ephemeral everyday details that matter most in a well-lived life. ("She was known for her homemade bread, pies, and her ability as a seamstress to sew any dress pointed out to her in the catalogue," the reader learns.) I suspect the Friday night fish fry at the Lox Club may never be quite the same. —J. S.

# Three-Cheese Tuna Bake

## M & M Cafe, Monticello
### *Mike and Mary Davis*

This is not your ordinary, empty-the-larder tuna casserole. If you're Catholic, it may have you wishing for the return of meatless Fridays year-round. But to be honest, it's far too good for pious penitence. Substitute three or four cups of chopped, cooked chicken or ham for the tuna, and you'll be in a parallel Three-Cheese heaven.

Mary recommends the use of 4 percent cottage cheese, as "the low-fat stuff tends to be watery."

>     3 tablespoons butter
>     ½ cup chopped onion
>     ½ cup chopped green pepper
>     ½ teaspoon dried basil
>     1 can (10¾ ounces) cream of mushroom soup
>     1 can (4 ounces) mushroom pieces, undrained
>     ½ cup milk
>     12 ounces wide egg noodles
>  1½–2 cups small-curd cottage cheese
>     4 cans (each 6 ounces) tuna, drained
>     16 slices (each ⅔ ounce) processed American cheese
>     ½ cup grated parmesan cheese

Heat butter in skillet over medium flame. Add onion, green pepper, and basil. Cook, stirring often, until tender. Stir in soup, mushrooms (plus their liquid), and milk. Meanwhile, cook noodles in lots of boiling water. Drain.

Heat oven to 350 degrees. Butter a 9-by-13-inch or similarly sized baking dish. Place half the noodles in the dish. Dot with half the cottage cheese and half the tuna. Place half the cheese slices over tuna. Sprinkle with half the parmesan. Repeat layers. Spread soup-vegetable mixture over top. Bake 45–55 minutes. Makes 12 servings.

## Do I Have to Eat It?

Tuna casserole is a standard Friday offering during Lent at Wisconsin's cafes, a kind of low-budget break from the traditional fish fry well suited for obligatory remorse. It's easy to be sorrowful while counting your sins over a helping of flaked tuna, canned soup, and rice—topped, of course, with crushed potato chips.

When I was a kid, I did not look forward to Friday dinner in the weeks preceding Easter because I knew, more times than not, this would be what Mom had planned. Eventually, Kraft blue box mac and cheese was substituted for the rice—a dish that was frequently replicated on a Coleman stove during family camping trips. I came to think of tuna casserole as a kind of desperation food, or what you ate when everything else was restricted by either papal decree or the cooking environment.

Tuna casserole and macaroni and cheese all but disappeared from my kitchen and camping repertoire once I was married. This despite the fact that in Indiana, where I have lived since 1990, macaroni and cheese is Hoosier comfort food, as much a mainstay on the picnic table as a cherished staple at Thanksgiving, Christmas, and Easter dinners. I did not miss it, did not look back with nostalgic longing, did not fill my plate at all-you-can-eat food bars and Amish buffets.

And then Mary Davis shared her recipe for Three-Cheese Tuna Bake. On a Friday in Lent, I pulled the recipe from the file and layered egg noodles, cheese, and tuna into a cake pan.

"What's for supper?" my teenage son asked when he arrived home famished from track practice. "Tuna casserole," I answered.

"Oh, yuck! Do I have to eat it?"

He did. We did. We liked it so much that I made it again before Easter. In just two outings, it has become a family favorite. I'm thinking that mixed together in a saucepan instead of baked in the oven, it would be great on a camping trip.—J. S.

# SIX

~ ~ ~

# Sandwiches and Burgers

### TOGETHER AT LAST

Debating among the daily specials written on the board at the Stacker Cafe, I considered the oppressive July heat and opted for the soup and sandwich special. I have to sheepishly admit, though, that when "I first read the offerings and saw egg and ham salad sandwich, I was confused. I thought I had to choose between egg salad and ham salad, but Paula set me straight. It was an egg salad sandwich with bits of ham in it. So simple, so obvious, yet I had never before encountered it. What a great way to tweak an old standby. The Stacker Cafe deserves applause.—from *Cafe Wisconsin*

# Ham and Egg Salad Sandwich

## STACKER CAFE, CORNELL
### *Paula and Ed Jenneman*

With some recipes, measurements just get in the way. So it is with the Stacker Cafe's ham and egg salad, prepared fresh as a daily special by cook Phyllis Zakrzewski. When you make it, do what Phyllis does: use as much as you like of everything and just mix it all together.

**hard-cooked eggs**
**celery**
**onion**
**ham**
**mayonnaise**
**salt and pepper**

Peel and chop the eggs. Finely dice the celery, onion, and ham. Mix with mayonnaise and season with salt and pepper to taste. Makes any number of servings.

# Andyjacks Cherry Wraps

## PERRY'S CHERRY DINER, STURGEON BAY
*Perry Andropolis*

If you think dessert is the only way to enjoy Door County's most famous crop, you'd best try Perry's grilled chicken-cherry wraps, invented one night when he was a little bored, a little hungry, and a lot creative. Dip them in Marzetti's brand caramel apple dip, found in the produce section of the grocery store, for a surprising and unique accent. The wraps are named for Perry's dad, Andrew (nick-named Jack), who with his mother, Ann, operated Andropolis Restaurant for many years before Perry converted it into the 1950s-themed diner.

- 3 **ounces (about ½–⅔ cup) diced, cooked chicken breast**
- ½ **cup frozen sweetened tart cherries, thawed**
- ¼ **cup walnut pieces**
- 1 **twelve-inch herb-flavored sandwich wrap**
- 1 **ounce Marzetti's caramel apple dip**

Heat a large griddle or two cast-iron pans over medium flame. When hot, add chicken, cherries, and walnuts; toss and cook to heat through. Heat wrap on other end of griddle or in second skillet. Place chicken mixture in center of wrap, roll it up, cut it in half, and serve with caramel apple dip. Makes 1 serving.

# Barbecued Hamburgers

## OJ's Midtown Restaurant, Gillett
*Owen and Joan Farrell*

You're going to need extra napkins for this saucy, good-eating dish reminiscent of sloppy joes. The ground beef is seasoned like meatballs, formed into patties, baked in a rich, sweet homemade barbecue sauce, and tucked inside burger buns. Joan's mother created it years ago to use up the elk, venison, and other wild game that the men in the family brought back from a hunting trip out west. These days Joan uses ground chuck and cooks the burgers in big roasters to serve at graduations and weddings.

The recipe makes enough sauce for up to three pounds of meat. Joan specifies that she uses Open Pit barbecue sauce, but cooks who like a more piquant sauce may add 1 tablespoon each red wine vinegar and prepared mustard to the mix. For a smoky flavor, add a few drops of liquid smoke.

*Sauce*
- 4 cups ketchup (one 36-ounce bottle)
- ⅓–½ cup brown sugar
- 1 tablespoon Worcestershire sauce
- 1 tablespoon bottled barbecue sauce (such as Open Pit)
- 1 tablespoon beef base
- ¼ teaspoon each salt and pepper

*Burgers*
- 2 pounds ground chuck
- 2 eggs
- ½ cup finely diced onion
- ½ cup finely diced celery
- ½ cup crushed soda crackers
- ½ cup milk
- 1 teaspoon salt or more to taste
- ½ teaspoon pepper or more to taste

*Also*
- 1 large green pepper
- 1 medium onion
- 10 burger buns

Mix all sauce ingredients in a deep saucepan. Bring to low simmer, partially cover, and let simmer about 15 minutes, stirring occasionally.

Lightly but thoroughly mix all the burger ingredients in a large bowl. Form mixture into 10 patties. Heat a large frying pan over medium-high flame for a few minutes. Brown the burgers in batches on both sides, without crowding the pan. Take care to just brown them; don't cook them all the way through.

Heat oven to 325 degrees. Slice off the top of the green pepper, carefully remove the core and seeds, then slice the pepper into 10 rings. Slice the onion into 10 rings.

Oil a larger roaster or casserole dish. Spread a little of the barbecue sauce on the bottom. Place the hamburger patties over the sauce. Place a pepper ring and an onion ring on each patty. Spread the remaining sauce over the burgers. Bake until peppers and onions are soft and sauce is bubbly, 50–60 minutes. Serve burgers on buns with some of the sauce. Makes 10 servings.

## HOME OF THE HAMBURGER

On any given day, Wisconsin cafe owners are likely to serve as many burgers as daily specials, if not more. As sandwiches go, it's Dairyland's all-time favorite, especially topped with a melted slice of cheese. The next time you bite into a beef patty sandwiched between two halves of a white bun, thank Charlie Nagreen of Seymour, who is said to have invented the hamburger at the Outagamie County Fair in 1885. "Hamburger Charlie" flattened his meatballs and put them between two slices of bread so people could eat them while strolling through the exhibits. His salesman's pitch was a jaunty little ditty that went like this: "Hamburgers, hamburgers, hamburgers hot / Onions in the middle, pickle on top / Makes your lips go flippity flop. Come on in, try one order. Fried in butter, listen to it sputter." His ditty was surprisingly close to that used by Kewpee Hotel Hamburgs, a two-hundred-stand chain founded in the 1920s: "Hamburg / Pickle on top / Makes your ❤ go flippity flop."

Other communities across the USA lay claim to being the home of the hamburger, but the fine folks of Seymour remain firmly loyal to their local hero. Every August since 1989 they've played with their food by hosting the Seymour Burger Fest, a one-day party punctuated with a hamburger-eating contest, competitive cook-off, the world's largest hamburger parade, a giant ketchup slide, and other won't-believe-it-'til you-see-it events like the 1990 wedding between "Bunard" and "Patti" held on the grandstand. Attendants included Oscar Onion, Peter Pickle, Kenny Ketchup, Missy Mustard, Charlene Cheese, and Susie Sauerkraut.

At Burger Fest two years later, twins Barbie Q and Chuckie Weldon were born. The proud parents passed out ten thousand free baby burgers. Surely you weren't thinking cigars?

Burger Fest fun includes two world record hamburgers grilled in 1989 and 2001. Weighing in at 5,520 pounds, the first was surpassed ten years later by an even bigger burger made in Saco, Montana. Seymour regained the title in 2001 with an 8,266-pound behemoth burger that fed nearly thirteen thousand people. So far it has withstood any would-be aspirants to the title, but then that's a mighty big bun to fill.

Not a town to let fame lie fallow eleven months out of the year, Seymour celebrates its association with hamburger history with a special exhibit at the local museum. It replaces the Hamburger Hall of Fame that sadly closed its doors in 2004. Its Main Street site is still marked by the world record-setting grill topped with a giant fiberglass burger, a popular backdrop for fun family photos. Even better, pose the kids in front of the twelve-foot statue of Hamburger Charlie himself, dedicated at Burger Fest 2005. They sure grow 'em big in Seymour.—J. S.

## Bob Burger

Bob and Deb Chonos, owners of the former Old Store Cafe and Deli in the Outagamie County town of Dale, sometimes stood in the back kitchen rolling their eyes in amazement at the wacky requests their customers made. "We'd ask each other, 'How in the world did they come up with that?'" Bob tells me. He's really not one to laugh, however, seeing as how he is the inventor and namesake of the Bob Burger—without a doubt the quirkiest burger in Wisconsin. He has a sense of humor and knows how to laugh, which is important because I poked a lot of fun at his expense. But then I also ate a Bob Burger, so I'm allowed.

What is a Bob Burger, you ask? It is a monster of a burger and "a slippery little devil," according to Bob. It's hard to eat because it refuses to stay neatly stacked and ordered. I had to finish mine with a fork. Bob starts with a good-size burger and layers it from plate up in this order: bun bottom, peanut butter, sliced banana, hamburger patty, American cheese, bacon, fried egg, lettuce, tomato, mayonnaise—all crowned by the bun top. And he wonders about some of the things his customers concoct!

The Bob Burger is so weird, I just had to try it when I dropped in at the Old Store Cafe and Deli in 2002. Bob whipped it up in the kitchen and brought it out to me stacked a good five inches high on a white china plate. I had a hard time wrapping my hands around it, but I succeeded in gingerly taking a bite. The first one consisted of mostly bun bottom, peanut butter, and banana, since I approached it from an upward angle. With both Bob and Deb watching me closely, I reported, "Nothing strange here." I've always liked peanut butter and banana sandwiches. With the next bite, I got the full sensation . . . and it was amazingly good. A third bite and fourth convinced me that as strange as it seemed, Bob had a winner with the Bob Burger. The flavors of all the apparently incompatible ingredients blended into a pleasant surprise. I was savoring a Bob Burger, not tasting the individual items.

The obvious question is, just how on earth did the Bob Burger get invented? "I just built it up over the years," Bob says matter-of-factly (as if there could be any other way). "Years ago a friend introduced me to peanut butter and bacon. When I was in the Air Force, we had a sack burger, which was a burger with a fried egg. Then when I was in Spokane at an A & W, I just threw all of that out there, and they made it for me. When the girl brought it out, she just stood there watching. I said, 'What, I didn't pay you enough?' 'You paid me enough,' she said. "I just have to watch you eat it!'"

With Deb initially in charge of the menu and the kitchen, the Old Store Cafe and Deli didn't boast the Bob Burger. But one day, Bob made one up for himself and another guy saw it and said, "Make me one of those." Thus, the ball started rolling, picking up speed when a friend, a local radio broadcaster, encouraged everyone over the air to stop in for the "famous" Bob Burger. He said it as joke, but the Bob Burger soon became the talk of the town—and the talk in neighboring towns as well.

When the expansion of Highway 10 kept customers from reaching the Chonoses' door, forcing the Old Store Cafe and Deli to close in 2004, quite a few people expressed sorrow at the pending loss of the Bob Burger. "It was so odd, but it certainly made the rounds," Deb notes. If you're one of those who pine for Bob's gift to Wisconsin, take heart. You can now make your own at home. Think of Bob when you do.—from *Cafe Wisconsin*

## Burgers: Have Them Your Way

**D**iner burgers are at once ubiquitous and the embodiment of individuality. Many cafes celebrate their idiosyncratic spirit with specialty burgers created in-house by owners, employees, and customers. What kind of burger are you?

**Blue Burger**—third-pound beef patty, blue cheese, grilled onions, and mushrooms (Brick House Cafe, Barronett)

**Bonnie's Gourmet Burger**—quarter-pound beef patty with hickory-smoked bacon, American cheese, fried onion, lettuce, tomato, and mayo on a toasted bun (Bonnie's Diner, Phillips)

**Brick House Burger**—This is a double burger—a bacon burger plus a mushroom burger plus more. From bottom to top, it's layered this way: bun bottom, rings of sliced onion, third-pound beef patty, bacon, American cheese, third-pound beef patty, sautéed mushrooms, American cheese, lettuce, sliced tomato, bun top. Whew! (Brick House Cafe, Barronett)

**Country Burger**—third-pound beef patty, two slices of ham, and your choice of cheese (Brick House Cafe, Barronett)

**Pizza Burger**—third-pound beef patty, spaghetti sauce, white American cheese. While the burger is frying, use a handheld food chopper to "rough up" the surface so the spaghetti sauce will stick. (Brick House Cafe, Barronett)

**Reuben Burger**—beef patty, swiss cheese, corned beef, sauerkraut, and Thousand Island dressing (Faye's Dinky Diner, Eagle River)

**Eagle River Burger**—beef patty, bacon strips, swiss cheese, grilled onions, and mushrooms (Faye's Dinky Diner, Eagle River)

**Kitchen Burger**—beef patty, brat patty, American cheese, sliced raw onion, and anything else you want (Village Kitchen, Casco)

**Wittenburger**—beef patty, Wisconsin cheese, Nueske's famous sugar-cured, applewood-smoked, thick-cut bacon made just up the road (Gus and Ann's Restaurant, Wittenberg)

**Hanke's Wisconsin Patty Melt**—two quarter-pound beef patties overlapped and grilled side by side, topped with grilled onions and Wisconsin four-way cheese, served on grilled sourdough bread. Owner Diane Gray explains that "a slice of four-way cheese looks like a little window, with panes of cheddar, Colby, mozzarella, and Monterey Jack." The beef is ground fresh daily at Hanke's SuperValu, from which the sandwich gets its name. (Diane's [formerly Gus and Ann's] Restaurant, Wittenberg)

—T. A.

# Philly Cheese Steak Sandwich

### WENDY'S PLACE, MINONG
*Wendy and Terry Holman*

The meat lovers at Wendy's Place really go for this "exotic" import from the city of brotherly love. Wendy uses her own homemade beef and broth featured in the recipe on page 57.

- **2–3 tablespoons butter**
- **2 cups sliced onions**
- **2 cups sliced green peppers**
- **salt and pepper**
- **12–16 ounces roast beef, shaved or sliced as thinly as possible**
- **hot beef broth (optional)**
- **4 buttered steak buns, lightly toasted or grilled**
- **4 slices swiss cheese**

Heat 2 tablespoons butter in large skillet or on griddle over medium-high heat. Add onions and peppers; sauté until barely tender. Season with salt and pepper to taste. Heat sliced beef in same skillet with a little more butter, or dip them in hot broth. Divide beef among steak buns and top with cheese, then vegetables. Makes 4 servings.

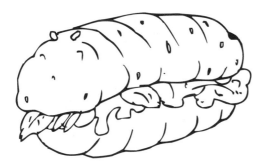

# Chicken Strip Sandwich

## WENDY'S PLACE, MINONG
*Wendy and Terry Holman*

This hearty grilled sandwich made with thick Texas Toast is a hit with the Minong lunch crowd. Wendy uses Hidden Valley Ranch Salad Dressing and Seasoning Mix, which she blends with rich buttermilk and real mayonnaise.

**grilled or deep-fried chicken strips**
**cooked bacon strips**
**butter**
**large, thick-sliced white bread**
**swiss cheese slices**
**ranch dressing**

Heat a griddle or cast-iron skillet over medium flame until hot. For each sandwich, grill 3–4 ounces chicken strips and 3–4 bacon strips on one end of the griddle. (Alternatively, you may deep-fry the chicken strips.) Meanwhile, butter two slices of bread on both sides. Grill one side of both slices on the other end of the griddle until golden brown. Flip the bread slices over and top one of them with two slices swiss cheese plus the cooked chicken and bacon. Place the other bread slice on top, with the undone side facing up. Grill on both sides until cheese is melted and toast is golden brown. Serve with ranch dressing. Makes any number of servings.

## BEER, BRATS, AND BEYOND

People don't just celebrate with beer in Wisconsin, they celebrate because of beer. Breweries, in fact, were common here even before the state became a state, thanks to early European immigrants. They quickly learned that the area's cold temperatures and clear waters were ideal for brewing up their favorite drink. And the rest, as they say, is history.

Today, while foamy brown ales, lagers, stouts, and pilsners are enjoyed nearly everywhere and at nearly any time in the state, quaffing isn't the only way we savor beer. Indeed, as any self-respecting brew lover will tell you, beer is food . . . so why not use it as an ingredient?

Cafe cooks do. Certain beer-spiked dishes, in fact, are familiar in many a diner. In the recipe on page 61, beer cuts the richness of cheese soup and gives it a pleasant tang. It adds moisture and flavor to the quick bread recipe on page 38. Beer makes fish fry and onion ring batters crispy, and enhances slow-simmered dishes like Kendall Gulseth's Pork Ribs and Sauerkraut (page 94).

One beer-soaked specialty known and beloved by all is grilled bratwurst. (Okay, maybe a few residents out there don't relish them, but if they know what's good for them, they won't admit it.) Indeed, if there was such a thing as a state aroma, surely Wisconsin's would be the smell of simmered-in-beer, charcoal-broiled brats. Tucked into a bun, topped with brown mustard and raw onions (and, if you like, sauerkraut), brats should be declared the official state sandwich.

The topic of brats-in-beer isn't without controversy, however. Some folks simmer their sausages in a beer-and-onion bath first, then grill them until the skin is deep brown and so brittle it bursts at the touch of a tooth. Others swear by the grill-first, simmer-later method, claiming the hot barbecued brats soak up more beer flavor that way. Either way, you also have to decide what kind of beer to use, how much water (if any) to add to it, and if you can get away with adding a nice big blob of butter to the mix. If you think such questions can be easily resolved, then tune in sometime while two brat cooks debate the merits of their opposing opinions. You'd think world peace was at stake.

Of course in Wisconsin, these are what we call good problems.

For more about cooking with beer, see page 38.—T. A.

# *Farmer Sandwich*

## LINDA'S WILMOT CAFE, WILMOT
*Linda Orvis*

This hearty sausage open-faced stack and the ham-and-asparagus melt on page 131 are proof positive that Linda Orvis has a way with sandwiches. She enjoyed this at a friend's house years ago and has been making it ever since.

Linda uses smoked sausage in the cafe but suggests substituting bratwurst, kielbasa, or Polish sausage for a varied taste.

> 1 **Granny Smith apple**
> 2 **slices whole wheat bread**
> **softened butter**
> 1–2 **teaspoons finely diced red onion**
> 1 **4-ounce fully cooked smoked sausage link**
> 3–4 **tomato slices**
> 2 **slices cheddar cheese**

Heat broiler, or heat oven or toaster oven to 400 degrees. Heat a large, flat griddle or large, cast-iron skillet over medium flame until hot. Peel the apple, core it with an apple corer or small, sharp knife, and cut it into rings.

Butter one side of each of the bread slices. Place the bread slices butter side down on one part of the grill and cook until toasted, on the bottom only. Meanwhile, place the sausage on another part of the griddle and cook it, turning occasionally, until heated through and lightly browned. Add the apple rings to the grill and heat them briefly, without letting them get soft or mushy. When the sausage is done, slice it diagonally into 6 pieces.

Next, layer the ingredients on a baking pan as follows: one slice of bread (grilled side up), apple rings, red onion, sausage pieces, tomato slices, and cheddar slices. Broil or bake sandwich until the cheese is melted. Cut the second slice of grilled bread into four triangles and serve them alongside the open-faced sandwich. Makes 1 serving.

# Asparagus Gratinee

## LINDA'S WILMOT CAFE, WILMOT
### *Linda Orvis*

Just as some musicians can hear a song and then play it, some cooks can see a dish and then prepare it. Linda was idly looking through food magazines on a rack near her grocery store checkout when she came upon this open-faced sandwich. She thought the picture looked good, so she recreated it at the cafe—without even reading the recipe.

Linda laughs about how she found it: "As if my two thousand cookbooks aren't enough, I have to look at magazines in the stores!" But she clearly has an instinct for what will go over at her restaurant, no matter where she finds her inspiration. One of the cafe regulars wrote an article in the local newspaper identifying her Asparagus Gratinee as one of his favorite menu items. He also praised Linda's Farmer Sandwich (previous page) and Mandarin Chicken Salad (page 79).

Linda uses frozen asparagus, but we opted for pencil-thin fresh spears. This simple but clever sandwich immediately became one of our favorite dishes, too.

> 2 **slices marbled rye bread**
> **softened butter**
> 5 **asparagus spears, frozen and thawed, or fresh**
> 3 **ounces sliced ham**
> 3 **slices swiss cheese**

Heat broiler, or heat oven or toaster oven to 400 degrees. Heat a large, flat griddle over two medium flames (or heat two cast-iron skillets) until hot. Butter one side of each of the bread slices. Place the bread slices butter side down on one part of the grill and cook until toasted on the bottom.

Meanwhile, add a little butter to another part of the grill and add the asparagus spears to the hot butter. Cook them, turning occasionally, until tender if they are fresh or until heated through if they are thawed. Heat the ham on the griddle, too, until lightly browned.

Next, layer the ingredients on a baking pan as follows: one slice of bread (grilled side up), ham, asparagus, and cheese. Broil or bake sandwich until the cheese is melted. Cut the second slice of grilled bread into four triangles and serve them alongside the open-faced sandwich. Makes 1 serving.

## RECIPE VS. RHYTHM

I nside the brain of every cafe cook is a big box of recipes. Sometimes they get written down and shared with kitchen staff or a lucky customer, but just as often the details of a dish's preparation are evident only to the person who makes it every day.

Competent cooks use all five senses to see, smell, taste, touch, and even hear when a roast is properly browned or a sauce has thickened enough. They also have another faculty, a kind of sixth sense or rhythm that develops deep within their bones after years of practice. These cooks understand that no measurements, no written-down recipe is enough. Indeed, it's only the beginning.

Recipes are maps. They can guide you to a successful dish, but they can't take you there. You have to travel there on your own, and each time you do, the journey will be a bit different for any number of reasons. This is particularly true about the recipes in this book because they come from casual, family-run kitchens whose cooks "go with the flow." That is, they use up yesterday's ham in the split pea soup, add beef base to a gravy to pump up its flavor, omit rutabaga from a pasty for a regular who doesn't like it. Anything from the weather to the variety of apple available this week at the grocery store can affect the finished dish.

Sometimes there are so many variables that there isn't a recipe at all. When we asked Elly Mocello of the Four Seasons Cafe and Deli in Eagle River for the recipe for her popular Berry Berry Pie, she replied, "Your request for our Berry Berry Pie cannot be forwarded. I use whatever berries I have on hand, and depending on them and [the amount of] juice, I add sugar and thicken and season it accordingly. So literally it is made from 'feel.'"—T. A.

# SEVEN

~ ~ ~

# Side Dishes and Extras

# Ol' Settler Bean Casserole

## RED ROOSTER CAFE, MINERAL POINT
*Helena Lawinger and Patti McKinley*

There's a lot of flexibility with this easy-to-prepare recipe for baked beans. If your family likes them meaty, go for the larger amounts of bacon and hamburger. Same thing for the brown sugar and green onions. You might even opt to include the bacon fat for a real pioneer flavor. It's all up to you.

1–2  pounds ground beef
¼–½  pound bacon
   2  cans (16 ounces) pork and beans
   2  cans (16 ounces) butter beans
   2  cans (16 ounces) kidney beans
   1  cup brown sugar
1–2  bunches green onions, chopped
2–3  teaspoons molasses

Brown the ground beef over high heat; breaking it up as it cooks. Fry the bacon, drain it on paper towels, and crumble it. Combine beef and bacon with remaining ingredients. Bake at 350 degrees for 45–60 minutes. Makes enough for a crowd.

## OPEN READING AT THE LITERARY CAFE

Do you have an appetite for reading? Allow us to recommend the daily special: two books that serve up tasty helpings of life in fictional Wisconsin towns where the local diner serves as an important social, political, and cultural center.

*Hope Was Here,* a Newbery Honor Book by Joan Bauer, is a story for young adult readers, but even grownups will find it worth their time. Abandoned by her mother as an infant, Hope moves from Brooklyn to Mulhoney, Wisconsin, with her Aunt Addie, an exceptional cook hired by G. T. Stoop, owner of the Welcome Stairways diner. With Addie in the kitchen whipping up soul-satisfying food the likes of brown sugar pecan pancakes, butterscotch pie, and Too-Good chili, G. T. campaigns to unseat Mulhoney's corrupt mayor. Using courage and humor, G. T. attempts to persuade residents that, despite his diagnosis of leukemia, he is a better choice. When the mayor ridicules him by pointing out that "town business is a little more complicated than flipping burgers on a grill," G. T. responds, "You learn courage and decision making quick when you've got two dozen burgers on the grill."

As she joins other high school students in campaigning for G. T., Hope discovers that good meatloaf and honorable politics have a lot in common. Both must be cultivated with concern and care and must not be abused. Addie counsels Braverman, the teenage grill cook, about the finer points of making meatloaf: "You don't shove it in a pan with tomato juice and oatmeal. You mold it with care. You mix it with onions and spices and Worcestershire sauce and form it into a free-standing loaf and never put it in a loaf pan. You slather it with barbecue sauce, which caramelizes over the loaf when it cooks."

"Politics," G. T. knows, "isn't about power, control, or manipulation. It's about serving up your very best."

In *Murder Over Easy,* Madison writer Marshall Cook fictionalizes the actual 1997 killing of a diner owner in Marshall, Wisconsin. His Nancy Drew is Monona Quinn, a former columnist for the *Chicago Tribune,* a new outsider in the small town of Mitchell, Wisconsin, and the editor of the *Mitchell Doings.* When Charlie Cornell, the owner of the village cafe, turns up dead, Monona believes someone has a taste for murder. But who would want to kill Charlie, an active community volunteer and friend to the friendless who "meant much more to Mitchell than good food and a gathering place"?

Charlie's cafe "had been as close to a social center as a little town like Mitchell had," the daily gathering spot for the Mitchell Caffeine Irregulars, the Communal Crossword Puzzle Club, and the "mid-morning round table, where Mitchell's movers and shakers downed endless cups of coffee, chewed over crops, prices, and local politics, and solved the world's problems." Charlie himself had a gift for people and a gift for cooking, his mother, Charlene, confides to Monona's husband, Doug. "Omelets were his specialty, of course, but he could cook anything. He made wonderful stirfries. Never used a recipe. He was like a fellow who plays the piano without needing any music. Little pinch of this, a shake of that. He just had the touch."

For everything but pie, that is. "Charlie said nobody made pies like his mama," Charlene coos. When Doug asks the secret to her success, she tells him what every successful pie maker already knows: "It's no secret. You use all fresh, and you don't beat up the crust. The less you handle it, the better. That and scoops of sugar and tubs of real butter."

There may be no mystery to making pie as good as dear old Mom's, but what about the mystery of Charlie Cornell? Place your order for *Murder Over Easy,* dig in, and find out.—J. S.

*(continued on facing page)*

## POTATO PANCAKES PLAIN AND FANCY

Pancakes aren't just for breakfast anymore—especially when they're potato pancakes. The Swiss call them *roesti,* the Eastern Europeans call them *latkes,* and the Irish call them boxty. Wisconsinites call them delicious. In the morning we like them with applesauce, syrup, jam, or fresh fruit and yogurt. Plain or zipped up with herbs and other add-ins, we like them with Friday fried fish, Sunday ham dinner, and as a meal all by themselves. We offer these suggestions for perking up potato pancakes:

- Add chopped fresh parsley, dill, rosemary, or tarragon
- Replace some of the potatoes with grated zucchini, carrots, or parsnips
- Add diced ham and grated cheese
- Throw in a handful of diced onion

# Potato Pancakes

## STACKER CAFE, CORNELL
*Paula and Ed Jenneman*

Though they're on the breakfast menu, people eat these with applesauce or syrup any time of the day at the Stacker Cafe, named for the world's only remaining pulpwood stacker—a cross between a derrick and a conveyor belt—found in Cornell's Mill Yard Park.

> 2 baking potatoes (each 6–8 ounces)
> 1 egg
> ¼ cup flour
> 6 tablespoons butter-flavored oil, divided
> salt and pepper
> applesauce

Peel potatoes. Grate them on the large holes of a handheld box grater into a bowl. Do not squeeze out the liquid. Stir in the egg, flour, and 4 tablespoons of the oil. Add salt and pepper to taste. Heat remaining oil in a large, heavy skillet or on a griddle. Divide batter into 3–4 pancakes and spoon them onto the griddle. Flatten them somewhat and cook until golden brown on both sides, about 4 minutes per side. Serve with applesauce. Makes 3–4 pancakes.

# Cheesy Hash Brown Bake

## OJ's Midtown Restaurant, Gillett
### *Owen and Joan Farrell*

You're bound to get raves about this buttery baked hash brown casserole from OJ's. It's so good it's bad, as they say. If you want to be a little less bad, substitute low-fat cream of chicken soup and low-fat sour cream, and use half the butter. Don't stint on the cheese though. For best flavor make it a nice sharp white or yellow cheddar.

Joan Farrell notes that the dish freezes well, so you can make it ahead and bake it as needed. "You can bake it frozen or thawed," she says.

> 2 **pounds frozen hash browns (use chunky or shredded ones)**
> 1 **can (10¾ ounces) Campbell's condensed cream of chicken soup**
> 1 **pint sour cream**
> 2 **cups shredded cheddar cheese**
> 1 **cup finely chopped raw onion**
> ½ **teaspoon salt**
> ½ **teaspoon pepper**
> 1 **cup (2 sticks) butter, melted (divided)**
> 2 **cups crushed cornflakes**

Heat oven to 350 degrees. Butter a 9-by-12-inch or similarly sized baking dish. Mix hash browns, cream of chicken soup, sour cream, cheddar cheese, onion, salt, pepper, and half the melted butter in a large bowl. Spread mixture into prepared pan. Combine remaining butter with crushed cornflakes; spread mixture over the hash browns. Bake until casserole bubbles around the edges, 45–50 minutes. Makes 12–16 servings.

*(continued from facing page)*

- Go Dutch—add grated apples and cinnamon and top with whipped cream
- Go Greek—add chopped fresh spinach and feta cheese
- Go southern—replace the potatoes with sweet potatoes and nutmeg, brown sugar, and pecans
- Go crazy—top with peanut butter and jelly —T. A.

*(continued on facing page)*

## HINTS FOR SUCCESS: POTATO POWER

What's the best spud to cook with? It depends what you're making. Elly Mocello swears by baby reds for her fried House Rox Potatoes, a signature side dish at the Four Seasons Cafe. Thin-skinned red potatoes and long, yellow fingerling potatoes (they're sometimes referred to as "waxy" potatoes) have a firm, hold-their-shape texture that also makes them ideal for salads and stews. For fluffy baked potatoes and really tender french fries, your best bet is the sturdy, starchy russet. Russets, or "bakers" as they are commonly called, are used in the Sand Creek Cafe's Classic Hash Browns (page 9) and the Stacker Cafe's Potato Pancakes (page 136). All-purpose white potatoes and the buttery-tasting yellow cultivars such as Yukon Golds and German Butterballs can be mashed, baked, boiled, or roasted.

# Potatoes Au Gratin

## VILLAGE HAUS, FALL CREEK
*Sheri and Jim Coldwell*

Gratinéed potatoes are the fancy-pants way to prepare spuds in a down-home cafe. Sheri contributed a deluxe dinner-crowd version that calls for twenty-five jumbo baking potatoes and is cooked in a full-size commercial baking pan. We've cut back the recipe to family size.

To thicken and flavor the sauce, Sheri uses a powdered "peppered white gravy mix . . . the kind you use for biscuits and gravy, or chicken fried steak." You'll also find it called country gravy mix.

One Thanksgiving, Sheri substituted brussels sprouts for the potatoes and created an instant favorite. Her instructions are below.

> 3 large (each 10–12 ounces) baking potatoes
> 1 small onion
> 5 tablespoons butter, cut into pieces
> 1 package (about 2.64 ounces) country gravy mix
> ¼ pound sliced American or other cheese
>   milk

Heat oven to 350 degrees. Butter a 9-by-3-inch baking dish or one that's large enough to hold all the ingredients (or spray it with non-stick coating). Peel and slice the potatoes. Rinse them well and drain thoroughly. Thinly slice the onion. Spread a third of the potatoes in the pan. Scatter half the onions over potatoes. Dot surface with about 2 tablespoons of the butter pieces. Sprinkle half the gravy mix evenly over all. Top with half the cheese slices. Repeat these layers. Make a final layer with the last third of the potatoes and the last tablespoon of butter. Pour milk over potatoes, using enough to come about halfway up the sides of the pan. (Do not cover the potatoes with milk.) Cover dish tightly with aluminum foil or lid. Bake 50–60 minutes. Remove cover and stir potatoes well. Continue baking, uncovered, until potatoes are tender and casserole is thickened and golden brown on top, 45–60 more minutes. Let stand 5–10 minutes before serving. Makes 6 servings.

For Brussels Sprouts Au Gratin Sheri instructs: "Follow the process for potatoes au gratin, but first blanch the cleaned brussels sprouts before beginning the layering process. I don't put the onions in this recipe, although when I uncover it, I put Durkee fried onions on top and bake it until the onions are crisp. Yum yum."

# House Rox Potatoes

## Four Seasons Cafe and Deli, Eagle River
### *Elly and Jerry Mocello*

What's in a name? Both flavor and function in the case of these rocking potatoes. Elly, who got this recipe from a restaurateur in Colorado, says, "Because the potatoes are cut into cubes, they resemble rocks; thus, the name." The flat sides of the pieces help them brown in the pan; thus, the flavor. Elly adds, "Cast iron works best for browning the potatoes, and then the seasoning becomes enhanced, too." The red potato jackets speckled with the spice mix and fresh green parsley make an attractive presentation.

*Rox Seasoning*
- ¼ **cup black pepper (medium grind—not fine, not coarse)**
- 4 **teaspoons garlic salt**
- 1 **scant teaspoon garlic powder**
- ½ **teaspoon Lawry's Seasoned Salt**

*Potatoes*
**small red potatoes**
**olive or vegetable oil**
**butter**
**chopped fresh parsley**

Combine seasoning ingredients in a container with a shaker top. Cook potatoes in boiling water until tender. Drain and cool them. Chill until ready to use. To finish the cooking, cut up the potatoes into a chunky dice. Heat a griddle or cast-iron pan over medium flame. Add some oil and butter—enough to coat the bottom of the pan. Add the potatoes and let them cook on the first side until nicely browned, then sprinkle with Rox seasoning to taste. Toss and cook until browned all over, adding more seasoning as desired. Just before the potatoes are done, toss in some fresh parsley. Makes any number of servings.

*(continued from facing page)*

Never store potatoes in the refrigerator. Their starches can turn to sugar that will give an off-flavor. Instead, keep them in a basket or paper bag in a dark, cool, well-ventilated cupboard. Do not store potatoes and onions together. Onions emit gas that quickens the decay of potatoes.—T. A.

# *Mashed Potatoes*

You'll get the fluffiest mashed potatoes from large brown baking potatoes, but Yukon Golds and other all-purpose yellow-skinned varieties have a buttery flavor that makes them a viable alternative.

The best tool for mashing light, lump-free potatoes is an old-fashioned potato ricer, because it's virtually impossible to overwork the spuds with one of these. The worst tool to use is a food processor, which will whirr your potatoes into glue in a nanosecond. In-between choices include a handheld potato masher and electric beaters, but take care not to overdo it. A sturdy fork will yield what's known as smashed potatoes—just the thing for those who love the lumps.

> 2 **pounds potatoes**
> 4–6 **tablespoons milk, half-and-half, or buttermilk**
> 2–3 **tablespoons butter**
> **salt and pepper**

Peel potatoes and cut them into even-sized chunks. Place potatoes in pot, cover generously with water, and add a tablespoon of salt. Bring to boil and cook until a fork inserted into a chunk slips out easily, 10–15 minutes. Meanwhile, heat milk and butter together. Keep the mixture warm. When potatoes are done, drain off all the water and place the pot over a low flame. Shake the pot for a moment or two to dry the potatoes off completely. Quickly pass potatoes through a potato ricer into a bowl or mash them with a potato masher or electric beaters until no lumps remain. Fold in hot milk mixture and salt and pepper to taste. Serve immediately. Makes 6 servings.—T. A.

## MASHED POTATO MATTERS

Mashed potatoes is one of my favorite test foods for judging the quality of a cafe. Owners who are taking the extra time to peel, chop, boil, and mash potatoes are are just my kind of cooks. I cheer the philosophy of Joan Nehls of Joan's Country Cookin' in Hustisford who says, "I feel I might as well use my time while I'm here."

Are the mashed potatoes real? I must have asked this question hundreds of times, and I've heard nearly as many answers. Since instant potato buds and flakes are made from real potatoes, I'm often assured that the mashed potatoes served at a cafe are indeed "real." When they're brought to my table mounded in a perfectly shaped globe, sides as smooth as a scoop of vanilla ice cream, I know I've been misled. Real mashed potatoes have lumps that preclude a slick appearance. Another fairly reliable indication of real is bits of peels or skins that add texture and color. Joan Nehls began adding them to the real mashed potatoes she prepares every day when her food salesman pushed packaged potato skins. "I said, 'Potato skins? Why would I want to buy them?' 'To put in your mashed potatoes,' he said. And I thought, heck, I've got potato skins—I've been throwing them away—and so I put them in."

The addition of bits of peels is just one of many tricks used by some cafe owners to "doctor" instant, canned, even frozen mashed potatoes into tasting more like the real thing. Other camouflaging tactics include the addition of butter, milk, cream, sour cream and/or broth, and salt and pepper and other seasonings. Owners rationalize the deception by telling me it is not cost effective to pay employees to labor over russets and reds, that real mashed potatoes don't keep well on steam tables, that leftovers can't be reused, and that doctored fake mashed potatoes actually taste better than real. I stubbornly remain a hard sell. No matter how much they're fussed over, fake mashed potatoes always taste like Pringles to me. Real mashed potatoes have a musky, earthy flavor that simply can't be duplicated.

On the other hand, I acknowledge that there are some people who actually prefer instant. A cafe owner in Nappanee, Indiana, in the heart of Amish country, prepares only real mashed potatoes in her restaurant because that's what the tourists expect, yet her own boys grew up on instant at home. They refuse to eat the potatoes at the cafe because of their lumps. When Mom mashes real potatoes for family dinners at Thanks-giving and Christmas, she appeases her now grown sons by making them a pot of instant.

One benefit to instant potato buds and flakes is their interminable shelf life. But there's nothing more versatile than spuds delivered by the produce truck. Real potatoes can be baked and twice baked, cut raw for homemade french fries and potato chips, boiled and diced for American fries and potato salad, shredded for hash browns and potato pancakes, mashed and served with gravy (a side dish written cryptically on menu boards as MPG), shaped into dumplings or pierogi, or folded into batters for doughnuts and even chocolate cake. For this reason, many cafe owners find real potatoes far more economical than instant products that must generally be ordered in quantities too large to store in undersized kitchens.

Not the least of real mashed potatoes' many charms is its strong associations with home and family. "It's real comfort food," says Terese. "I just love mashed potatoes and gravy. Who doesn't? A regular lunch for me in a cafe is a bowl of soup and an order of mashed potatoes and gravy. Once I ordered mashed potatoes and gravy and a malt, and my friend laughed, 'What kind of a meal is that?' To me, a bowl of soup, mashed potatoes and gravy, and a piece of pie provide the entire picture of a cafe. You know if it's good on just these three things."—J. S.

# German Potato Salad

## Village Kitchen, Casco
*Chris and Gary Jacobs*

German potato salad is less a salad than a warm, sweet-sour side dish. At some cafes it's offered as a potato choice with Friday fish fries and other hearty daily specials. At the Village Kitchen it's served occasionally as a side dish with Belgian *trippe,* a pork-and-cabbage sausage that is a legacy of the Belgian immigrants who settled in the area in the mid-1800s. Chris says it's always the same people who order trippe, but "we're getting the younger generation, too. They say, 'Oh, my grandma used to make this!'"

|  |  |
|---|---|
| 1½–2 | pounds red potatoes |
| 4–5 | slices bacon, cut with scissors into small pieces |
| 1 | scant cup diced onion |
| ¼ | cup white vinegar |
| 3 | tablespoons sugar |
| 1 | teaspoon salt |
| ⅛ | teaspoon pepper |
| 2 | tablespoons cornstarch |

Boil unpeeled potatoes in water until tender. Drain and let cool a few minutes, then dice the potatoes, place in a bowl, cover, and keep warm. Meanwhile, fry bacon pieces in hot pan until crispy. Remove bacon with a slotted spoon to drain on paper towels. To make dressing, add onion to the fat in the pan and cook over medium flame, stirring occasionally, until tender. Sir in vinegar and 2 tablespoons water. Stir in sugar, salt, and pepper. Heat until dressing boils. Mix cornstarch with ⅔ cup water and add to dressing, stirring until it thickens. Add additional water to reach desired consistency. Pour dressing over potatoes and toss gently. Makes 6 or more servings.

## LOCAL FLAVOR, LOCAL SUPPORT

You know trippe when you smell it. A fairly pale, soft-textured sausage with delicate skin, trippe packs a distinctively odorous punch because of its high cabbage content. Relatively unknown outside the lower Door County and Green Bay area, this Belgian-influenced specialty is beloved by descendents of Walloon Belgians who settled here. As one myself, I grew up eating trippe and can certify that it smells gassy but tastes great.

A real taste of local flavor that has escaped the fate of so many other regional specialties, trippe, with eggs, can be ordered for breakfast every other Thursday morning at the Village Kitchen in Casco. It occasionally gets daily special status at lunch and dinner time, too. For all her trippe needs, owner Chris Jacobs turns to Marchant's SuperValu in nearby Brussels. Specializing in fresh dressed meats and specialty sausages including trippe, Belgian pie, headcheese, and sulze, Marchant's bears the slogan "spreading a little heritage."

When cafe owners offer local specialties on their menus, they help preserve and celebrate unique food traditions that might otherwise wither in today's fast-food culture. They also play a role in an economic network of support that helps preserve local businesses and farms.

At Joan's Country Cookin' in tiny Hustisford, for example, owner Joan Nehls always uses real whipping cream from Radloff Cheese Factory, a neighbor in town. "They send us lots of business, so we help out each other," she says. Up in Babcock, in the heart of Wisconsin's cranberry country, Sherri Dessart of the Country Cafe heartily agrees. Sherri buys fresh cranberries directly from a local grower, bakes them into pies, breads, and muffins, and sells them by the pound during the harvest months of October and November. She also supports local farmers during the growing season by buying fresh produce from farmers' markets in Wisconsin Rapids and Marshfield.

In Wittenberg, Diane Gray, owner of Diane's (formerly Gus and Ann's) Restaurant, uses only Nueske's sugar-cured, applewood-smoked bacon. Made just up the road for over seventy years, Nueske's famous bacon has been featured in *Cuisine* and *Saveur* magazines and in the *Chicago Tribune* and *New York Times*. In addition, weekend breakfasts at Diane's just aren't complete without Nueske's smoked sausage links and smoked pork chops.

Another one-of-a-kind Wisconsin specialty food is the lefse—soft Norwegian flatbread made from potatoes—made by Countryside Lefse of Blair, suppliers to the Norske Nook in Osseo. In business since 1965, Countryside Lefse rebounded after a fire destroyed its downtown building in 2003. It remains one of the few companies in the nation making lefse from real potatoes, not instant, and rolling it by hand.

Specialty bread of another kind is produced for the Amherst Cafe in Amherst. When Pauc's corner bakery closed some years ago, leaving owner Diane Stroik without the sunflower bread that had become synonymous with her cafe, she took Pauc's recipe to Amherst Family Foods and convinced its bakery to make it for her. Diane also buys all of her meats, sausage, and thick-sliced bacon from Waller's Meat Locker in nearby Nelsonville. "I like to spread the revenue around to local business," Diane explains. "After all, we're all in this together."—T. A.

# Herbed Green Beans

## IDEAL CAFE, IRON RIVER
*Mary and James "Mac" McBrair*

"I like to try new ways to dress up vegetables," Mary tells us. But when she finds a good thing, she likes to stick with it. She's used this recipe for thirty years. "I occasionally use it as part of my lunch specials. People like the change from plain vegetables. Some of my customers have nicknamed it 'Herb's Beans.'"

  1  **package (16 ounces) frozen green beans or 1¼ pounds fresh green beans, trimmed and cut into pieces**
  2  **tablespoons butter**
 ½  **teaspoon dried savory**
 ¼  **teaspoon dried oregano**
 ¼  **teaspoon dried basil**
 ¼  **teaspoon garlic salt**

Cook beans in boiling, salted water until nearly tender, 3–7 minutes; drain well. Melt butter in large skillet. Add herbs and garlic salt; cook, stirring once or twice, a few minutes. Stir in drained beans. Cook, stirring once or twice, until beans are tender, 2–3 minutes or longer. Makes 4 servings.

# Tartar Sauce

## OJ's MIDTOWN RESTAURANT, GILLETT
*Owen and Joan Farrell*

Creamy, sweet, and pickly, tartar sauce is a must-have with fish sandwiches and Friday night fish fry.

  2  **cups Miracle Whip dressing**
 ¼  **cup sweet pickle relish**
  2  **tablespoons ReaLemon lemon juice**

Mix ingredients. Makes 2¼ cups.

# Corn Fritters

## CLINTON KITCHEN RESTAURANT, CLINTON
*Connie and Jim Farrell*

"This is one of my grandmother's favorite recipes and a true favorite among young and old customers," says Connie. She serves these old-fashioned corn fritters with baked ham and maple syrup. (Leftovers are great for breakfast.) The fritters lend themselves to a south-of-the-border theme when you add dollops of salsa and sour cream.

>       **oil for deep-frying**
> 2⅓   **cups flour**
> 1½   **tablespoons baking powder**
> 1     **teaspoon salt**
> 2     **eggs**
> 3     **cups milk**
> 3     **cups fresh corn kernels (if using frozen, thaw and drain well)**
>       **maple syrup**

Pour oil into deep-fat fryer or heavy pot to a depth of 2 or more inches. Heat over medium high flame while you prepare the batter. Whisk flour, baking powder, and salt in a large bowl until well combined. Beat eggs in a separate bowl; mix in milk. Make a well in the flour, pour in the milk-egg mixture, and, using a large rubber spatula, gently fold the two mixtures together. Fold in corn. Test the oil. It's ready when a tiny amount of batter dropped into it sizzles upon contact. Drop the batter from a large spoon into the oil. Take care not to crowd the pan. Fry the fritters in batches, flipping them a few times, until puffed, rounded, and golden brown, about 3–4 minute per batch. Drain on paper towels and serve warm with maple syrup.

# Homemade Egg Noodles

Savory homemade egg noodles are going the way of real mashed potatoes. But if fewer cooks are taking the time to make them, they are all that more welcome when a cafe chef or home cook serves the real thing. Use these in soups and casseroles, or as the base for the noodle dishes in chapter 5.

You can mix the dough by hand using a pastry cutter to cut the butter into the flour, but if you have a food processor, the speed and ease of this recipe will have you wondering if you should ever buy packaged dried noodles again. As for rolling out the dough, it's easy and fun.

1½  cups flour
1½  tablespoons frozen or very cold butter, cut into tiny
       pieces
 ¼  teaspoon salt
  2  large egg yolks
  2  large eggs
     additional flour for rolling out dough

To make the dough, place flour, butter, and salt in food processor. Pulse the mixture 4 or 5 times. Add the egg yolks and eggs and pulse again just until the dough forms a ball around the blade of the food processor. Take care not to overmix the dough.

To roll out the dough, flour a work surface and rolling pin. Divide the dough into 3 portions. Roll out each portion into a rectangle about 10-by-13-inches in size (it shouldn't be paper-thin), using additional flour as needed to prevent the dough from sticking to the work surface. Let the rectangles dry on a rack for 15–20 minutes.

To cook the noodles, bring a large pot of salted water to boil. When the noodle "sheets" have dried out as directed, dust the excess flour off their surfaces. Roll each one up from the long end and slice the rolls crosswise, making noodles as wide or narrow as desired. Gently toss the cut noodles with your fingers to open the spirals. Cook them in the boiling water until barely tender, about 2–3 minutes. Drain well. Makes 1 pound, or about 4–6 servings.—T. A.

# Croutons

## UNIQUE CAFE, BOSCOBEL
*Doyle and Nancy Lewis*

Any kind of bread can be used to make these croutons. "We use white and wheat bread. Sometimes we use the ends of bread loaves that wouldn't get used," explains longtime cook Annette Wagner. They're savory and crisp, but not hard like store-bought croutons, and perfect for salads, soups, and snacking. "Everybody likes them," Annette promises.

> 3 tablespoons butter
> 1½ tablespoons salad oil
> 1 teaspoon garlic powder
> ½ teaspoon each dried basil, thyme, and parsley
> 3–4 slices bread, cut into cubes and dried out for a
>     few hours or longer

Heat oven to 350 degrees. Melt butter with oil, garlic powder, and herbs. Toss with bread cubes. Spread out on a pan and bake until golden brown, about 10 minutes. Makes 1½–2 cups croutons.

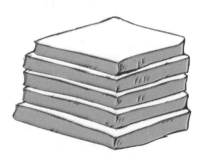

# Refried Beans

### GREENWOOD FAMILY RESTAURANT, GREENWOOD
*Ernesto and Linda Rodriguez*

These refried beans are the perfect side dish for the Mexican specials that were prepared at the Greenwood Family Restaurant, sold by the Rodriguezes in 2005. They wouldn't have been out of place with some of their American, Greek, or Italian dishes, either.

> **pinto or black beans**
> **olive oil**
> **finely chopped onion**
> **finely chopped jalapeño**
> **salt and pepper**

Soak beans overnight in cold water. In the morning, cook them according to package directions until soft. Heat some oil in a fry pan, add onions and jalapeños—as much of each as you want—and sauté them until tender. Start adding scoops of cooked, drained beans to the pan. Use a potato masher to mash the beans, watching carefully as they fry so they don't scorch. Season with salt and pepper to taste. Makes any number of servings.

# Mexican Rice

### GREENWOOD FAMILY RESTAURANT, GREENWOOD
*Ernesto and Linda Rodriguez*

Do not be tempted to take a peek while this rice is cooking. It will be done when the liquid is absorbed and each grain is "split open." It should be dry, not saucy. As an alternative to the stove top, Linda often cooked this traditional Mexican dish in a 375-degree oven for 20 minutes.

> 1 **tablespoon olive oil**
> ¾ **cup finely chopped onion**
> 2 **cups long grain white rice**
> 2½ **cups chicken broth**
> 1–1½ **cups tomato sauce**
> ½ **cup finely diced carrots**
> 1 **serrano chile, seeded and minced**
> 1 **teaspoon salt**

Heat olive oil in saucepan over medium flame. Add onion and cook, stirring occasionally, until lightly colored. Stir in rice and cook, stirring often, until rice is golden with some browning in spots, 5–10 minutes. Stir in remaining ingredients, bring to simmer, cover, reduce heat to lowest flame, and cook about 20 minutes. Turn off heat and let stand 5–10 minutes. Makes 8 servings.

# Salsa

## GREENWOOD FAMILY RESTAURANT, GREENWOOD
*Ernesto and Linda Rodriguez*

Make this as hot or as mild as you like. The ratio Ernesto prefers when he's making it for himself is two jalapeños for every tomato! Linda advises that leaving in the chili's membrane and seeds will increase the fire.

- 6–8 **tomatoes**
- 3 **jalapeños, or more to taste**
- 2 **teaspoons minced garlic**
- 2 **teaspoons salt**
  **chopped fresh cilantro to taste (optional)**
  **finely chopped onion to taste (optional)**

Heat oven broiler. Place tomatoes and jalapeños on a pan under the hot broiler. Roast them, turning often, to blacken them all over. Let cool a bit then pull off the skins. Place in a blender or food processor with garlic and salt, including the seeds from the peppers. Blend until smooth; this is not a chunky salsa. Add optional chopped cilantro and onion, if desired. Makes about 2 cups.

# Refrigerator Pickles

## UNIQUE CAFE, BOSCOBEL
*Doyle and Nancy Lewis*

When the Unique's regulars bring in mounds of surplus cucumbers to share, these sweet refrigerator pickles are the result. "These go on the salad bar," says cook Annette Wagner. "We use both the small pickling cucumbers and the regular ones. The store-bought ones don't keep too well."

Although these could hardly be easier to make, Annette does specify that canning salt should be used. Regular table salt typically has anticaking additives that don't dissolve as easily as canning salt and can cloud the brine. If you like your pickles tangy, use less sugar. Kept cold, the pickles will keep up to a year. "But of course they don't last that long!"

- **7 cups sliced, unpeeled cucumbers**
- **1 cup thinly sliced onion rings**
- **2 tablespoons canning salt**
- **2 cups sugar**
- **1 cup white vinegar**
- **½ teaspoon celery seed**

Mix cucumbers, onion rings, and canning salt well. Let stand two hours. Drain well. Divide into 2 or 3 pint glass jars, if desired. (Avoid containers that are metal, as they can react with vinegar.) Meanwhile, combine sugar, white vinegar, and celery seed in saucepan. Bring to a boil. Remove from heat and let cool. Pour this over the pickles. Refrigerate the pickles. Makes 2–3 pints.

# EIGHT

~ ~ ~

# Pies and Other Desserts

# Amish Cream Pie

## M & M Cafe, Monticello
### *Mike and Mary Davis*

"M & M" stands for Mike and Mary, but we think it also means "mmm-m-m." This unusual baked cream pie is the most-requested pie at the cafe. Mary says, "I no more than make the Amish cream pie and it's gone." Some of her regulars eat a piece every day. It's so popular, in fact, that customers have been known to call ahead and reserve a piece.

Mary adapted the recipe from one she clipped out of the *Wisconsin State Journal* and a similar version she found in *Cooking from Quilt Country* by Marcia Adams. Sugar cream pies like this are legendary in Adams's home state of Indiana, where old-time Hoosiers refer to it as a "desperation" pie because it can be made when the larder's pretty near empty.

For an even richer pie, substitute half-and-half for the milk. To reduce the amount of fat, evaporated skim milk can replace some of the half-and-half.

> ¾ **cup sugar**
> ¼ **cup cornstarch**
> ½ **teaspoon salt**
> 2 **cups half-and-half**
> ½ **cup milk (or substitute more half-and-half)**
> 8 **tablespoons (½ cup) butter, cut into chunks and softened**
> ¼ **cup packed brown sugar**
> 1 **teaspoon vanilla extract**
> **9-inch baked pie crust**

Heat oven to 325 degrees. To make the pie filling, place sugar, cornstarch, and salt in a medium saucepan and whisk until well combined. Gradually stir in half-and-half and milk until mixture is smooth. Heat over moderate flame, stirring constantly, until mixture is thickened. Remove from heat and whisk in butter, brown sugar, and vanilla until well blended. Pour filling into baked pie shell; sprinkle with cinnamon. (Mary says prebaking the crust was part of the original recipe and suspects it's necessary for a crisp crust.) Bake until edges are bubbly, 20–30 minutes. Cool completely and chill, if desired. Makes 8 servings.

# Unique Cream Pie

### UNIQUE CAFE, BOSCOBEL
*Doyle and Nancy Lewis*

Bananas and coconut make beautiful pie together. When Nancy combined the two to create this beauty, Doyle wanted to give it a different kind of name. It's been the Unique Cream Pie ever since. Nancy tries all kinds of flavor combinations in her cream pies— pineapple and banana, peaches and vanilla, spiced apples and vanilla, to name a few. While the variations are popular, she acknowledges that "the just plain banana cream pie seems to fly out of the cafe."

- 2 **cups whole milk**
- 1 **package (5–6 ounces) instant vanilla pudding**
- 2–3 **cups sweetened real whipped cream or nondairy whipped topping, divided**
- ½ **cup shredded coconut (sweetened or unsweetened)**
- 2 **large bananas**
- 1–2 **tablespoons lemon juice**
- 1 **9- or 10-inch deep-dish pie shell, baked**
- 3–4 **tablespoons shredded coconut, lightly toasted**

Pour milk into a bowl, add pudding mix, and whisk by hand or beat with electric beaters until thick, about 5 minutes. Gently fold about 1 cup (more or less to your liking) of the whipped cream into the thickened pudding. Gently fold in ½ cup shredded coconut. Slice the bananas, toss them with the lemon juice, and spread most of the bananas into the bottom of the pie shell. Spoon the pudding–coconut mixture over the bananas. Spread the remaining whipped cream over the pudding. Decorate with the remaining bananas and the toasted coconut. Refrigerate until set, 1 or more hours. Makes 8 servings.

## AND THE WINNER IS . . . WHIPPED CREAM

Whipped cream versus nondairy whipped topping? There's no contest. Offered a choice, even folks who grew up on the sweet, convenient tubs of frozen topping will go for a dreamy mound of genuine whipped heavy cream. Yes, it's more work. Yes, it's less stable. But oh yes, it's so-o authentically delicious.

For many cooks a container of thawed nondairy whipped topping is a welcome necessity. Whipped cream from aerosol cans is another choice when you're in a pinch. Additives and preservatives notwithstanding, convenience is important, especially to busy cafe cooks. But when flavor and purity score higher than your schedule, here's the way to go:

Choose heavy cream over whipping cream, if it's available; heavy cream has a higher fat content that helps guarantee a fluffier and more stable whipped product. But avoid ultra-pasteurized heavy cream. It's heated to an extra-high temperature in order to give it a longer shelf life, and once it's whipped it deflates much faster than pasteurized cream. The higher heat treatment also causes a loss of flavor and nutrients.

Use only glass, stainless steel, or copper bowls. Avoid plastic, which doesn't chill well, and aluminum, which can react with the cream. Chill the bowl and beaters in the refrigerator or freezer. The colder the equipment, the colder the cream, and the colder the cream, the easier it will whip. Use medium speed and beat the cream steadily, moving the beaters around and up and down to incorporate as much air as possible. Tip the bowl occasionally, too, to get to the cream on the bottom.

For maximum volume, add sugar and any flavorings after the cream has thickened somewhat. For every cup of cream, add 1–2 tablespoons of sugar or 2–3 tablespoons of powdered sugar. A tablespoon or less of maple syrup or honey are also great choices. Keep liquid additions like extracts and liqueurs to a minimum as they'll dilute the cream.

Stop beating as soon as the mixture is thickened and the cream can stand up in a mound when you lift a beater out. Overwhipping will make the whipped cream less stable, or worse, turn it into butter. Store any leftover whipped cream in a tightly covered glass jar.—T. A.

## Cool Whip . . . The Consumer's Champion

Like Terese, I too love real whipped cream, but I must admit to using Cool Whip for at least 90 percent of my whipped topping needs. And I do mean Cool Whip, not the store brands. I'm a stickler for the real fake thing.

While Terese and I aren't exactly in opposite corners of the ring, we thought we'd let whipped cream and Cool Whip (eponymously speaking) battle for superiority on their own. So, in the far corner: real dairy whipped cream. In this corner: hydrogenated coconut and/or palm oil and high fructose corn syrup.

A mainstay in grocery store freezer cases and in many home refrigerators, Cool Whip was invented in 1966 by Bill Mitchell, a General Foods chemist. Within three months of its debut in the Kraft lineup, sales of Cool Whip summited the whipped topping chart. American housewives loved its time-saving convenience, lower price, good taste, fewer calories, longer shelf life, and the fact that it was more stable in recipes than the real thing. And if all this wasn't enough, there was an added bonus: all those reusable plastic tubs were perfect for storing kitchen leftovers and household trinkets.

With countless recipes developed in Kraft test kitchens and made available in cookbooks and magazine ads, Cool Whip revolutionized desserts and salads. First came simple Jell-O and Pudding in a Cloud, followed quickly by molded Jell-O salads; layered tortes, parfaits, and trifles; ice cream and Cool N' Easy "cheater" pies; baked cookies made with cake mix and Cool Whip; and chicken and Waldorf salads using Cool Whip for half the mayonnaise. The introduction in 1975 of Jell-O brand pistachio pudding coincided nicely with the Nixon administration's political gaffe, resulting in Watergate Cake with Cool Whip–laced Cover-Up Icing and the related Watergate Salad. Another iconic cake, the Cool Whip Flag Cake topped with blueberries and strawberries, arrived on the scene slightly later.

Writing in the *Atlantic Monthly* following Bill Mitchell's death in July 2004, Mark Steyn notes the interdependency of the products in the Kraft repertoire that "live happily within a self-contained universe." Make a Cool Whip dessert or salad from a Kraft recipe and you'll inevitably find yourself needing another Kraft product. "It's like modular furniture," writes Steyn. "Sometimes you put Cool Whip in the Jell-O, sometimes you put Jell-O in the Cool Whip. But it's an all-or-nothing-world. It would be unsettling and intrusive to replace the Cool Whip with Martha [Stewart's] recipe for *crème anglaise*."

Can't imagine middle class, Yankee Doodle Cool Whip taking the place of royal English custard? How about standing in for Wisconsin's dairy best real whipped cream? For some folks, like Terese (and me 10 percent of the time), there's no contest. For many others, Cool Whip is the *crème de le crème,* the no-work, no-worry topping for pies and the never-fail fold-in for everything from Snickers Salad to chocolate peanut butter pie. According to Kraft, six tubs of Cool Whip are purchased every second in America. During the weeks between Thanksgiving and Christmas, enough Cool Whip is purchased to top 2.4 billion slices of pumpkin pie. Although the dairy industry isn't keeping tabs, it appears that the folks buying and whipping real cream are a jab away from a knockout.

Here's another interesting set of facts: Since 1996, the entire production of Cool Whip has been centralized in a single Kraft plant in Avon, New York. Prior to that time and beginning in 1966, half the Cool Whip in the United States was made at a Birdseye plant in Waseca, Minnesota. This may explain why more Cool Whip is sold in Minneapolis than any other city in the country. Number four on the list is Syracuse, New York, located just seventy miles from Avon.—J. S.

# Chocolate Peanut Butter Pie

## BONNIE'S DINER, PHILLIPS
### *Shelley Moon*

Super-rich and creamy, this pie is for kids of any age—and so popular at Bonnie's Diner that it's nearly always on the daily specials board. If you choose to use real whipped cream in this recipe, you'll need 2 to 2½ cups heavy cream to yield a total of 4 to 5 cups whipped for the top two layers. See pages 153 and 154 for instructions, and whip the cream while the chocolate layer is cooling.

*Chocolate Layer*
⅔ **cup sugar**
¼ **cup cornstarch**
3 **tablespoons cocoa powder**
   **pinch of salt**
3 **egg yolks**
2⅔ **cups milk**
1 **tablespoon butter or margarine**
1 **teaspoon vanilla extract**
   **9- to 10-inch baked pie crust**

*Peanut Butter Layer*
½ **cup peanut butter**
½ **cup powdered sugar**
2 **cups nondairy whipped topping, thawed, or 2 cups whipped cream**

*Whipped Cream Layer*
2–3 **cups nondairy whipped topping, thawed, or 2–3 cups whipped cream**
   **small amount solid chocolate (baking chocolate or candy bar)**

To make chocolate layer, combine sugar, cornstarch, cocoa powder, salt, egg yolks, and milk in saucepan. Stir the mixture over medium flame until it thickens and bubbles. This will take about 6–8 minutes. Stir it often while it's beginning to cook, then stir constantly as it warms up and gets close to bubbling. But don't let it boil longer than a minute or so. (Alternatively, you may combine the ingredients in a microwave-proof bowl and heat it 3 times for 3 minutes each time, stirring after every 3 minutes.) Stir in butter and vanilla. Spread filling in prepared pie crust. Cool completely before adding other layers.

To finish the pie, beat peanut butter and powdered sugar together. Fold in 2 cups of nondairy whipped topping or whipped cream. Spread over cooled chocolate layer. Spread remaining 2–3 cups nondairy whipped topping or whipped cream over this and grate some chocolate over the top. Chill before serving. Makes 8 servings.

## CREAM PIE WOES

More than ten years ago I received a cookbook as a gift for joining a local woman's club. As close friendships developed with several of the elderly members, I was often treated to gifts of pie. Loraine's thick, rich butterscotch pie topped with golden meringue was easily my favorite, as it was with her children and grandchildren, who always demanded it for Christmas dinner. I tried several times to make the pie from the recipe in the book, religiously following Loraine's simple instructions. While the cooked filling was still hot, I poured it into a baked pie shell and covered it with meringue. But each time I cut the pie into slices, the filling fell away like the ocean at low tide. I had made pie, but what I got was butterscotch soup.

As rich and heavy as fudge, the chocolate cream pie at a local cafe made me determined to try my hand at cream pie once again. Loraine gave me her no-fail recipe, and I confidently measured the ingredients into my saucepan. Once again, I got soup.

Doomed to repeat my failures, I put cream pie out of my repertoire. I couldn't make it at home, so I enjoyed it on the road. I ate them all: banana, coconut, butterscotch, pineapple, chocolate, peanut butter. It was the chocolate peanut butter pie at Bonnie's Diner that put me back in the kitchen.

On my hands and knees, I pulled the double boiler off the bottom shelf of the cupboard. It had been dormant for so long it was covered with dust. I washed it, set it on the stove, and filled it with carefully measured ingredients. This time, I thought, I will make a great pie. I'd loved the pie at Bonnie's, so I knew the recipe had to work. My peanut butter–loving husband would be so happy to top off dinner with pie. I followed the instructions and then set the filling on the back patio to cool in the winter chill. My neighbor's cat, Emma, who much prefers us, normally resides there but was sleeping under our bed upstairs. I learned to check on her whereabouts the day I retrieved a lemon pie from nature's refrigerator and discovered Emma up to her whiskers in meringue.

An hour later, I retrieved the pot. There would be no pie tonight. My filling was a flop. "It's not even thick enough for pudding," Mark lamented as he spooned it out of the bowl. No pie. No pudding. This time I had made chocolate peanut butter soup.

The abandoned baked pie shell sat on the stovetop for more than a week before I decided to use it to make butterscotch pie. I used Connie Farrell's recipe from the Clinton Cafe—and got butterscotch soup. Darned tasty but I couldn't cut a slice.

Why am I a failure at fillings? Terese has solutions to my pie-making woes below.—J. S.

## CREAM PIE ANSWERS

You know what they say: "If I had a dime for every time someone asked me . . ." The culinary question that might have made my fortune is the one Joanne asks above about cream pie fillings.

If you've ever hovered over a simmering mixture of egg yolks, sugar, cornstarch or flour, and milk, waiting patiently for it to thicken to glossy perfection, only to watch it thin out later on, take heart. You're definitely not the only one to experience this disheartening problem, as Joanne's story indicates.

I'm no scientist, but I've learned that both undercooking and overcooking can be the cause of cream filling failures. The authors of the 1997 edition of *Joy of Cooking* note that if the mixture doesn't simmer for at least thirty seconds, amylase, an enzyme present in egg yolks, "will react with the starch, thinning out and discoloring the filling within twenty-four hours." This explains why most recipes direct you to let the filling simmer for a minute or so before turning off the heat.

But nine times out of ten, a cook's tendency is to overcook rather than undercook a mixture. In this case, the culprit is too much heat, which breaks down the cornstarch in the filling. This is why you shouldn't allow a cream pie filling to bubble on past that first minute.

Vigorous beating after the starch bonds have formed and thickened the filling can also cause the bonds to disintegrate and turn your filling into soup. So no excessive beating, please. But note: while the filling is heating up, gentle, near-constant stirring is necessary in order to prevent scorching.

One more thing: according to *Joy of Cooking,* a cream pie "filling is also likely to thin out if allowed to cool before being poured into the crust." Pour the hot filling directly into the prebaked and cooled crust. Contrary to popular belief, it will not cause a crust to go soggy.

If you want to avoid the guesswork of timing and stirring, use the microwave instead of the stovetop. This is what both Shelley Moon of Bonnie's Diner in Phillips and Joan Farrell of OJ's Midtown Restaurant in Gillett do. Bonnie prepares her best-selling chocolate peanut butter pie by combining the filling ingredients in a microwave-proof bowl, zapping it three times for three minutes each time, stirring gently after every interval. Joan uses shorter intervals and more stirring in making the Sour Cream Raisin Pie on page 174. An added benefit to using the microwave is freeing your hands to do other tasks. Says Joan, "If you cook [filling] on the stove, you have to stir it constantly or else it scorches easily. The microwave is handy, too, especially if it's near to where you're cooking other things."

I tried the microwave method, and it worked like a charm. Then Joanne, exhausted from her stovetop catastrophes, tried it, too. Success at last!—T. A.

# *Peanut Butter Pie*

## BRENDA'S VILLAGE CAFE, EXELAND
### *Brenda Beise*

People drive for miles for a piece of Brenda's peanut butter pie, a creamy vanilla custard pie zipped up with peanut butter–powdered sugar nuggets layered in the bottom and sprinkled over the meringue top. In March 2005, Brenda took over Exeland's tiny cafe, a fixture on Main Street for over sixty years.

*Pie*
- ½  cup peanut butter
- 1  cup powdered sugar
  9¾- or 10-inch deep-dish pie shell, baked
  scant 2 cups whole milk
- 2  heaping tablespoons cornstarch
- 1  cup sugar
- 3  large egg yolks
- 1  tablespoon butter, at room temperature

*Meringue*
- 6  egg whites, at room temperature
- ½  cup sugar
- 1  teaspoon vanilla extract

Mix peanut butter and powdered sugar until mixture forms into crumbles. Place about two-thirds of the crumbles into the bottom of the pie shell.

Heat oven to 375 degrees.

To make custard, combine milk, cornstarch, 1 cup sugar, and egg yolks in a heavy saucepan. Heat over medium flame, stirring almost constantly, until mixture comes to a boil and thickens, about 10–15 minutes. Do not let the mixture boil for more than a minute or so. Stir in butter. Spread hot custard over the crumbles.

To make meringue, place egg whites, ½ cup sugar, and vanilla in a large, clean mixing bowl and whip with electric beaters at high

## AMIABLE SEPARATION

Eggs separate more easily when they are cold, but they whip to a greater volume after they've warmed to room temperature. To separate an egg, crack it open into a small bowl. Hold one hand out, palm side up, and raise your fingers slightly to form a scoop. Use this "soft-edged scoop" (not your finger nails!) to gently scoop the yolk out, letting the egg white drain out through slightly loosened fingers.—T. A.

speed until stiff. Carefully spread whipped egg whites over custard, sealing the meringue against the edges of the crust. If you'd like, use a knife to create attractive peaks with the meringue. Sprinkle remaining peanut butter crumbles over the meringue. Bake until golden brown, 10–15 minutes. Cool completely before serving. Serve at room temperature or chilled. Makes 8–10 servings.

# Butterscotch Pie

## CLINTON KITCHEN, CLINTON
*Connie and Jim Farrell*

Connie inherited the recipe for this soothing, sweet, and tongue-pleasing cream pie from her grandmother, who used the phrase "cat's eyes" to describe how the bubbles look when they burst open wide on the surface of the pudding as it cooks. When the cat was wide awake, she knew it was done. Be sure to use whole milk and large eggs for this recipe.

*Pie*
- ¾ **cup brown sugar**
- 2 **tablespoons cornstarch**
- 1 **tablespoon flour**
  **pinch of salt**
- 3 **egg yolks**
- 2¼ **cups whole milk, divided**
- 2 **tablespoons butter**
  **9-inch baked pie crust**

*Meringue*
- 3 **egg whites, at room temperature**
  **pinch of cream of tartar**
- ⅓ **cup sugar**

Heat oven to 350 degrees. To make filling, mix brown sugar, cornstarch, flour, and salt in saucepan. Add egg yolks and ¼ cup of the milk; whisk until well blended. Stir in remaining milk. Heat over medium flame, stirring very often. When mixture begins to get hot, stir it constantly until bubbles or "cat's eyes" form and pop on the surface. Turn off the heat and stir in the butter.

To make meringue, beat egg whites and cream of tartar with electric beaters at medium speed in a clean, dry bowl until foamy throughout. Raise speed to high and continue beating while gradually adding the sugar, until mixture is stiff. Pour hot pie filling into baked pie shell. Spread meringue over filling, creating a seal where the meringue meets the crust. If you'd like, use a knife to create attractive peaks with the meringue. Bake until meringue is light brown, about 15 minutes. Cool pie completely. Serve at room temperature or chilled. Makes 6–8 servings.

## MANAGING MERINGUE

A baked or browned meringue pie topping made of egg whites and sugar invariably produces liquid on its underside as it cools off. That's because the underside of the meringue—the part touching the filling—is seldom fully cooked by the time the top is browned. The uncooked portion then "weeps" as the pie stands.

One thing that helps is to have the filling piping hot when you spread the meringue over it, which allows the bottom of the meringue to cook more quickly. Hint: place the pie in the hot oven while you're whipping the meringue.

There are other remedies. Some cooks prepare a cooked cornstarch paste and beat it into the egg whites. This helps stabilize the structure and makes the meringue less prone to weep both inside and on top. The downside: this adds a time-consuming extra step that most cooks avoid.

"You can try all sorts of things—make a sugar syrup and cool it, use cream of tartar, cornstarch, etc.," says Joan Farrell of OJ's Midtown Restaurant in Gillett. But she has her own secret for dealing with the excess moisture: she inserts a knife between the filling and the meringue, slides it in an inch or two, then tilts the pan over a sink to pour out the liquid. "But be careful," Joan adds. "Once I wasn't paying attention and the meringue slid right off!"

For more meringue tips, see page 162.—T. A.

## Meringue Tips

🥄 Separate the eggs while they're cold (see sidebar on page 159), but bring the whites to room temperature before beating them. You'll get more volume that way.

🥄 Whipped egg whites are fragile and will easily lose their "mojo," so don't start beating them until just before you need them in a recipe.

🥄 Use a clean, dry, deep bowl. Avoid plastic bowls, which can have a slight film on the surface even when they appear clean. Likewise, be sure your beaters are absolutely clean.

🥄 Take care not to allow any egg yolk in the whites. Even a small amount of yolk fat can prevent the whites from frothing.

🥄 Work the beaters up and down and through the egg whites as you beat them. This incorporates air and creates maximum volume.

*(continued on facing page)*

# Lemon Meringue Pie (Number One)

### CJ's Cafe, Blair
*Sherry and John Rawson*

The base for the foolproof filling in this pie is an easy, dependable Jell-O pudding mix. It's just the thing for people who like their lemon pie to go down smooth and sweet. "Customers say this is the best lemon pie they've had," says Sherry. "People will order them whole to buy and take home. Some people tell me I'll make headlines with my pies because they're so good!"

Sherry uses an unusually generous eight egg whites to make her meringue soar. "Remember," she advises, "it takes a while beating to make an excellent meringue."

For additional meringue tips, see sidebar. Sherry's pie crust recipe can be found on page 189.

*Pie*
- ¾ **cup sugar**
- 3 **egg yolks**
- 1 **box (4.3 ounces) Jell-O Lemon Flavor Cook & Serve Pudding & Pie Filling**
- **powdered sugar**
- **9-inch pie crust, baked**

*Meringue*
- 8 **egg whites, at room temperature**
- 1 **cup sugar**

Heat oven to 350 degrees. To make filling, mix sugar, egg yolks, pudding mix, and ½ cup water in a medium saucepan. Stir in another 2½ cups water. Cook over medium flame, stirring constantly until mixture comes to a full boil. Turn off heat. Stir the filling once or twice while you're making the meringue.

Beat eggs whites with electric beaters at medium speed in a large, clean bowl until foamy. Raise speed to high and continue beating while gradually adding the sugar, until stiff peaks form.

Pour the hot pie filling into baked crust. Spread meringue over filling, creating a seal where the meringue meets the crust. Use a knife to create attractive peaks with the meringue. Bake until meringue is light brown, 15–20 minutes. Cool pie completely. Serve at room temperature or chilled. Makes 6–8 servings.

# Lemon Meringue Pie (Number Two)

## BRENDA'S VILLAGE CAFE, EXELAND
### *Brenda Beise*

This recipe was tested with fresh lemon juice, but Brenda gives permission to substitute bottled juice, introducing yet another dimension to the never-ending debate about just what makes the "best" lemon meringue pie.

*Pie*
- 1 **cup sugar**
- 3 **heaping tablespoons cornstarch**
- 1 **scant cup fresh lemon juice**
- 4 **egg yolks**
- 1 **tablespoon softened butter**
  **9-inch pie crust, baked**

*Meringue*
- 6 **egg whites**
- ½ **cup sugar**
- 1 **teaspoon vanilla extract**

Heat oven to 375 degrees. To make the custard, combine sugar and cornstarch in heavy saucepan. Gradually add lemon juice and egg yolks until well combined. Heat mixture over medium flame, stirring very often (almost constantly) until mixture comes to a boil and thickens considerably, about 10–15 minutes. Do not let the mixture boil for more than a minute or so. Turn off the heat and stir in the butter. Cover with plastic to keep mixture hot while you make the meringue.

To make the meringue, place egg whites, sugar, and vanilla in a large, clean mixing bowl and whip with electric beaters at high speed until stiff. Pour hot custard into pie shell. Carefully spread whipped egg whites over custard, sealing the meringue against the crust. Use a knife to create attractive peaks in the meringue. Bake pie until meringue peaks are golden brown, 10–15 minutes. Cool completely before serving. Serve at room temperature or chilled. Makes 8–10 servings.

*(continued from facing page)*

- Stop beating when the whites are stiff enough to form firm, high peaks. Overbeating makes them even more fragile than they already are.
- When spreading meringue over a pie filling, take care to bring it to the edge all the way around the crust. Meringue that isn't "sealed" to a crust will shrink back as it cooks.

—T. A.

### Sweet Showdown

Why have we included two recipes for lemon meringue pie in this cookbook? Whenever we received more than one recipe for the same dish, our idea was to publish the best of the lot. But in the case of lemon meringue pie, best, as we learned, is relative.

Faced with two recipes lauded at their respective cafes, I decided to have a panel of food professional friends blind-taste one against the other. One friend is a career waitress who has probably served thousands of slices of lemon meringue pie, one the former manager of a gourmet bed-and-breakfast, and one a restaurateur and respected pastry baker. If any group could help decide which pie was the more cookbook-worthy, this had to be the one.

Pie Number One was made from a recipe contributed by Sherry Rawson, owner of CJ's Cafe in Blair. It featured a custard filling based on tried-and-true Jell-O lemon pudding mix and a gloriously ample, bronzed meringue made the typical way—by gradually beating sugar into egg whites. The pie crust was made with Crisco shortening.

Pie Number Two, made from a recipe submitted by Brenda Beise, owner of Brenda's Village Cafe in Exeland, was a classic from-scratch version using freshly squeezed lemon juice. Its vanilla-scented meringue was a little out of the ordinary, however, in that the egg whites and sugar are combined before beating. Since Brenda didn't send along a recipe for pie crust, I figured I should make one that "fit" the filling. So I made one the old-fashioned way, with lard.

Any scientific analysis needs a hypothesis, and this was mine: Pie Number One would be easier and quicker to make, but Pie Number Two, being "the real thing," would win in looks and flavor.

My first surprise? The two pies took about the same amount of time and effort to make. The use of the Jell-O pudding mix in Pie Number One did save time over squeezing lemons, but this was offset by Pie Number Two's faster method for making meringue.

The next twist was appearance. Despite some liquid that formed in the bottom of the pan in Pie Number One, the judges were wowed by its thick, nicely firm, deep yellow filling under a towering range of meringue peaks. Pie Number Two, by contrast, had a less impressive cap and a paler, looser filling.

But the big shock was about taste. My judges could reach no agreement on which pie had better flavor. In fact, their opinions were all over the map.

"Tart!" said one judge about the filling made with real lemons. "I think it needs a bit more sugar."

"No way!" said another. "I like it tangy. The other one isn't lemony enough."

"I love the high meringue," offered one.

"It might be too much meringue," challenged another.

"This filling tastes creamier."

"That one tastes more authentic."

"This crust is flakier."

"That crust is tastier."

On it went as Pie Number One and Pie Number Two began to disappear. And by the end of the evening, I was no closer to knowing which lemon meringue pie was the "best" than when I started out.

If food "authorities" like these can't agree on which lemon meringue pie to publish and which to let perish, who could? And this is why there are two recipes in this cookbook.—T. A.

## ODE TO THE "REAL" THING

On a frosty March day, I am joined at the counter of Brenda Beise's Village Cafe in downtown Exeland by Art Sampson, who as a boy back in the 1930s relocated with his parents from Chicago to a small Sawyer County farm. Though Art has just dropped off his wife at the senior center in the former Exeland school, the cafe is far more to his liking. "I don't want to sit with people who talk about the pills they're taking," he explains.

As steam struggles to convert itself into ice on the front windows, Art and I exchange talk over burgers and thick wedges of lemon meringue pie. Although people come miles for Brenda's peanut butter pie, it's her lemon meringue pie that is Art's favorite. Brenda used to call him whenever she made it, but he no longer comes in so often. That's all the more reason I am glad to have him for company at the counter.

Lemon meringue pie is one of my favorites, too. My mom made a wicked good lemon meringue pie when I was a kid, but made it so infrequently that friends dubbed it her "State Fair Pie." It was something great that happened only once a year.

A lemon meringue pie like Mom's is all about truth and balance.

Truth: Give me a pie made from the juice of puckery real lemons, a pat or two of pale yellow Wisconsin butter melted into the sour-sweet filling, and a meringue of fresh egg whites whipped into an Easter bonnet froth. I'll reject every time the fakery of bottled juice, artificial lemon flavor, food dye (better a pale filling than one the color of Crayolas), and foamy, everlasting meringue.

Partial Truth: Yet I, admitted pie snob that I am, positively swooned over Sherry Rawson's Jell-O pudding pie—so much so, in fact, that I personally requested the recipe for this book. My conviction wavers slightly.

Balance: Give me a pie—I concede, even Jell-O pie as good as Sherry's— with filling more thick than stiff, more sour than sweet, and tempered with the subtle, silky, salty richness of butter. Crown it with a thick egg white confection spooned into soft waves with crests lightly browned in a hot oven. Serve it to me very fresh and still warm, or day old with beads of sugar sweat like liquid sugar pearls.

I'll be devoted for life.—J. S.

# *Schaum Torte*

## OAK STREET CAFE, JUNEAU
### *Diane Moulai and Santo Pulvino*

A twist on traditional schaum torte, this luscious dessert includes a cream cheese layer between sweet meringue and strawberries. You might like to experiment with other seasonal fresh fruits such as pitted cherries, blueberries, and raspberries. Be sure to let the egg whites warm to room temperature for meringue with maximum volume.

The Oak Street Cafe closed its doors in April 2005, which makes us even happier to share the recipe for Diane's schaum torte. It is much too good to be forgotten.

*Meringue*
- 6  **egg whites**
- 1/2  **teaspoon cream of tartar**
- 1  **teaspoon vinegar**
- 2  **cups sugar**

*Filling*
- 1  **package (8 ounces) cream cheese, softened**
- 1  **teaspoon vanilla extract**
- 1  **cup sugar**
- 2  **cups mini marshmallows**
- 2  **cups heavy or whipping cream**

*Topping*
- 4  **cups fresh or frozen, thawed strawberries, or other fruit additional sugar, if desired**

Heat oven to 325 degrees. To make meringue layer, beat egg whites and cream of tartar with electric beaters at medium speed in large, clean, dry bowl until they are foamy. Beat in the vinegar. Raise speed to high and gradually beat in the sugar and continue beating until mixture is thick and smooth, 5–6 minutes total. Spread meringue evenly over the bottom of a 9-by-13-inch baking dish. Bake until meringue is high and golden brown, 50–60 minutes. Turn off oven, open door, and allow meringue to cool in the oven. The sides will stay high but the center will fall. Let it cool completely before topping it.

To make filling, beat softened cream cheese, vanilla, and sugar in bowl until smooth. Fold in marshmallows. Whip the cream in a clean, deep bowl until stiff peaks form when you touch the surface. Fold whipped cream into cream cheese mixture. Spread over cooled meringue layer.

Toss fresh strawberries with a little sugar, if desired. Allow the mixture to stand 15–30 minutes, to bring out the juices. If you're using frozen, thawed strawberries, you probably won't need to add additional sugar. The strawberry topping may be added after the meringue has cooled—its juices will soften the texture of the meringue—but for a classic, crunchy meringue, add the fruit topping just before you serve the torte. Makes 12–18 servings.

### STRAWBERRIES ON A CLOUD

Of all the decadent desserts Diane Moulai made at the Oak Street Cafe in Juneau, the strawberry schaum torte was her customer's favorite. "The sheriff's department says I'm the schaum torte queen," she told me when I dropped in for a visit a few years ago. "I have people who will call up, and if we don't have schaum torte, they won't have anything."

She served me a piece on a plate and asked, "What do you think?"

I poked my fork through the fresh strawberries on top, down through the middle layer of cream cheese, miniature marshmallows, and whipped cream, and into the baked meringue base. What did I think? It was divine, heavenly. It was so good, I couldn't stop eating. It was strawberries on a cloud.

I had been hunting cafes for two weeks when I found the Oak Street Cafe. It was the first truly exceptional cafe of my journey, and my spirits were buoyed at last. Many owners had justified their shortcuts in the kitchen, claiming no one was making real mashed potatoes anymore or baking their own bread or rolling out their own pie crusts, until I was nearly convinced that William Least Heat-Moon's legendary seven-calendar cafes might no longer be found in Wisconsin. But Diane and her partner, Santo Pulvino, restored my faith. Diane's strawberry schaum torte was my Eucharistic wafer.
—from *Cafe Wisconsin*

# *Chocolate Almond Torte*

## TERI'S RESTAURANT, BARABOO
*Teri Scott*

Although Teri retired and sold her cafe in 2003, her dessert-making legacy lives on. A specialty of Teri's Restaurant was this torte, served in pieces large enough to split with a friend but too sinfully good to split honestly.

2 **cups crushed vanilla wafers**
3 **tablespoons melted butter**
2 **Hershey's Milk Chocolate with Almond bars (each 6 ounces)**
16 **large marshmallows**
⅓ **cup milk**
1 **cup heavy cream or 2 cups nondairy whipped topping, thawed**

For the crust, combine crushed vanilla wafers and melted butter. Press evenly into a 9-by-9-inch pan. Chill.

For the filling, break up the chocolate bars into pieces. Combine chocolate, marshmallows, and milk in double boiler or heavy pan and place over medium-low heat. Melt the mixture slowly, stirring often and without letting it boil. Cool.

Meanwhile, if you're using real whipped cream, whip the heavy cream until stiff, and keep it chilled. When chocolate mixture is completely cool, fold in the whipped cream or whipped nondairy topping. Pour into prepared crust and chill thoroughly. Makes 6–8 servings.

## TOTALLY TORTE

Pie may well be the iconic diner dessert, but in your rush to get to the à la mode, don't overlook torte. I don't mean linzer torte, sacher torte, or other fussy layered cakes with Germanic pedigree. Here in Wisconsin, torte is a blue-ribbon designer dairy dessert, a three-, four-, or five-tiered refrigerator confection made by spreading layers of ooey-gooey goodness on a buttery bottom crust. Torte "looks a little fancy and is oh, so good," exclaims Helen Myhre in her Norske Nook cookbook.

Made in a humble cake or jelly roll pan, tortes have been concocted, perfected, and passed on from one generation of church ladies and extension homemakers to the next. As proof I offer my copy of the semicentennial *Wisconsin Extension Homemakers Cookbook* (1990), a collection of recipes from women throughout the state. Fifty-four of the 182 recipes in the desserts chapter are for torte, incorporating ingredients as innovative as sliced Twinkies. Imagine that! I'm further compelled to point out that recipes for desserts, bars and cookies, candy and snacks, cakes and frostings, and pies and pastry make up well over half of the entire cookbook.

Patted or pressed into the pan, crusts are made by mixing melted real butter—this is the Dairy State after all—with flour and nuts, crushed Ritz crackers, saltines, zwieback, graham crackers, pretzels, and cookies (including Oreos, vanilla wafers, chocolate wafers, and pastel-colored, frosting-filled sugar wafers), as well as dry cake mix and brownie mix. Ten or fifteen minutes in a refrigerator or hot oven and the crust becomes the bedrock for a pairing of creamy fillings. Generally a cream cheese–based layer comes first, followed by a gelatin, pudding, fruit, or ice cream mixture. Last but far from least comes a final frosting of snowy white real whipped cream or Cool Whip, either unadulterated or sprinkled with chopped nuts, crushed candy bars, or crumbs reserved from the crust layer.

The components of the layers, and the layers themselves, are building blocks that can be mixed and matched, stacked and restacked, fused and fused again into countless dreamy possibilities. Chocolate and peanut butter, rhubarb and custard, meringue and marshmallows, candy bars and pudding, ice cream and caramel sauce, strawberries and whipped cream, gelatin and poppy seeds, apples and sour cream, even Twinkies and chocolate pudding. The possibilities, the varieties, the eating are positively endless.—J. S.

## A RAW DEAL

In older days, families would rarely have worried about the raw eggs used in desserts like Banana Split Torte or French Silk Pie. Sad to say, we do have to think about that these days, when few cooks know the source of their eggs or how the chickens that laid them were raised. To avoid the increased risk of salmonella that is largely the result of our industrialized food system, I recommend that you avoid the "factory-farmed" eggs shipped from afar and sold at corporate chain stores. Go for eggs from chickens raised nearby, organic if possible, and purchased at your local farmers' market, food cooperative, or grocery store. —T. A.

# Banana Split Torte

## JOAN'S COUNTRY COOKIN', HUSTISFORD
### *Joan Nehls*

The recipe for this popular torte comes "from the St. John's Catholic Church cookbook," says Joan. "It is truly famous in our restaurant. We have it ready at six in the morning. By ten a.m. it is gone already!" If you're making this during berry season, by all means substitute three to four cups sliced fresh strawberries for the frozen ones.

*Layer One*
2 **cups graham cracker crumbs**
½ **cup (1 stick) butter, melted**

*Layer Two*
1 **cup (2 sticks) butter, melted**
2 **eggs**
2 **cups powdered sugar**
1 **teaspoon vanilla extract**

*Layer Three*
1 **can (20 ounces) pineapple tidbits, drained**
2 **packages (each 10 ounces) frozen strawberries, thawed and drained**
4 **bananas**

*Layer Four*
1½–2 **cups heavy or whipping cream**
    **sugar (optional)**

*Layer Five*
¼–⅓ **cup finely chopped walnuts**
¼ **cup finely chopped maraschino cherries**
    **chocolate syrup**

To make the first layer (crust), mix graham cracker crumbs and melted butter. Press mixture evenly over bottom of a 9-by-13-inch baking dish. Refrigerate the crust while you make the second layer. Place melted butter, eggs, powdered sugar, and vanilla in mixing bowl and beat on medium speed until creamy, thick, and light-colored, 8–10 minutes. Spread over crust and chill 1½ hours or longer.

To make the third layer, spread pineapple and strawberries over torte. Cut the bananas lengthwise into three long pieces each and lay these over the other fruit.

For layer four, whip the cream with electric beaters on high speed until soft peaks form. Sprinkle in a few tablespoons of sugar, if desired, and continue beating until firm peaks form when you touch the surface of the cream. Spread whipped cream over fruit.

For the final layer, sprinkle walnuts and maraschino cherries over top of torte. Drizzle with chocolate syrup. Chill until ready to serve. Makes 16–24 servings.

# French Silk Pie

## LITTLE BABE'S CAFE, MUKWONAGO
*Lin McConnell and Missy Ramsdell*

This is *the* pie for chocolate lovers. The secret to its melt-in-your-mouth silkiness is in the beating. "The more you beat it, the better it is," explains Missy, who got the recipe from her ninety-six-year-old grandmother. Missy uses the good, reliable prepared crusts from Pillsbury but admits, "My grandma would never have used store-bought!" For an extra special touch, decorate this pie with dollops of whipped cream and grate some chocolate over the top.

1½  **ounces unsweetened baking chocolate**
 1  **cup butter, softened**
 1  **cup sugar**
 1  **teaspoon vanilla extract**
 4  **eggs**
 1  **baked pie crust (9-inch deep-dish or 10-inch), cooled**

Break chocolate up into small pieces and place in small bowl. Microwave for 10–20 seconds at a time, stirring after each heating, until melted. (Alternatively, you may melt the chocolate in a double boiler over simmering water.) Set aside to let it cool. Place butter, sugar, and vanilla in a large mixing bowl and whip with electric beaters, 2 minutes. Add melted chocolate and beat until well blended. Beat in eggs one a time, beating 2 minutes and scraping the sides of the bowl after each addition. After you add the last egg, beat it 3 minutes. Spread it into the cooled pie crust. Chill the pie at least one hour before serving. Makes 7–8 servings.

# Poppy Seed Pie

## RUDY'S DINER, BRILLION
### *Kevin and Rosemary Clarke*

Poppy seed pie has been served at Rudy's, a Wisconsin institution, for over sixty-five years. This is a family recipe passed on to Kevin and Rosemary from Rudy Seljan, the cafe's founder and namesake. Says Rosemary, "This is one of the most popular pies we serve. Customers stop in just for a piece—old and young, salesmen and families." The recipe appeared in an issue of *Bon Appétit* magazine as a result of a reader's request.

| | |
|---|---|
| 3 | **cups whole milk** |
| ½ | **cup sugar** |
| 1 | **teaspoon vanilla extract** |
| 3 | **egg yolks** |
| 3 | **tablespoons cornstarch** |
| 1½ | **tablespoons poppy seeds, divided** |
| | **9-inch baked pie crust** |
| 2–4 | **cups whipped cream** |

Combine milk, sugar, and vanilla in saucepan. Bring to simmer, stirring often. Beat the egg yolks and cornstarch with ¼ cup water. Whisk the egg mixture into the simmering milk; stir until thickened, 1–2 minutes. Remove from heat and stir in 1 tablespoon of the poppy seeds. Pour filling into pie crust. Cool pie completely and then chill it. Top pie with whipped cream and sprinkle with remaining ½ tablespoon of poppy seeds. Makes 8 servings.

### A "CAFE WISCONSIN" BIKE RIDE

The inspiration for *Cafe Wisconsin* comes from Sunday morning bike rides with friends in Eau Claire. As the sun rose above the wooded hills, we'd roll out of town. Some thirty or forty miles later, we'd lean our bikes against the front of the Downing Cafe in Downing, the former Cardinal Cafe in Eleva, the Red Dot Cafe in Augusta, or the Sand Creek Cafe in Sand Creek, where we'd refuel on daily breakfast specials, pie, cinnamon rolls, toast, and coffee for the return trip home.

We call these excursions pie rides. I have since learned that we are not unique in our pursuit of home cooking worth riding for, and that bicyclists all over the country go on pie rides. Even knowing this, I was thrilled to receive out of the blue an e-mail from Don Piele of Racine, who embarked on a five-day pie ride and then wrote about it. You may have seen his article in the

August 2005 issue of *Silent Sports*. He shares a second helping below.

In May 2005, I took off on a five-day, 250-mile bike ride from my home in Racine to Ellison Bay, at the top of Door County. I purposely planned my route to pass through small towns and to stop at as many cafes as possible that are featured in *Cafe Wisconsin*. My reward for traveling fifty miles by bike every day was often a homemade piece of freshly baked pie—à la mode, of course.

My route took me from the Coffee Pot Cafe in Cedarburg, where I ordered Greek lemon soup, to Perry's Cherry Diner in Sturgeon Bay, where I ate the one-of-a-kind Andyjacks Cherry Wrap, and ended at the Viking Grill in Ellison Bay, where I had a bowl of whitefish chowder. Along the way, I stopped at several other small town cafes where I always sat at the counter, ordered any specialty, asked to meet the owner, and took their picture holding *Cafe Wisconsin*. They always obliged.

One of my most pleasant Cafe Wisconsin dining experiences began when I rode into Brillion, parked my bike in front of Rudy's Diner, walked in, sat down at the counter, and ordered meatloaf, the special of the day. The meatloaf dinner at Rudy's was a trip back to the 1950s. It was made from scratch and served with real mashed potatoes and gravy, corn on the side, and homemade bread. The last time I had anything like it was at Mom's table back home.

Rudy's interior was strikingly well designed and uncluttered, with a bank of green and white booths behind me and a long row of chrome-plated counter stools beside me. In 1993, the new owners, Kevin and Rosemary Clarke, began a remodeling project to expand the small original cafe to twice its size. They paid a lot of attention to style and design and built the best looking diner I've ever seen. They preserved a piece of the past, too. On the walls are historical pictures of Brillion, the original diner, and, of course, Rudy Seljan himself.

I returned the next morning to have a piece of Rosemary's freshly baked and still warm rhubarb pie. It was hard leaving town, but I was thankful that *Cafe Wisconsin* had led me to Rudy's, and other small town dining treasures.

I felt perfectly safe riding alone every day of my five-day bike ride. I was never run after by a dog, harassed by bad boys, or threatened by a hot rod. In fact, I passed more cows than cars by a factor of one hundred. There are wonderful, hardworking, friendly people in the small town cafes and mom-and-pop motels in Wisconsin. Take your own Cafe Wisconsin ride. Just remember, always sit at the counter, be on the lookout for fresh pie, and be sure to show them "the book." Now, you're on your own. Enjoy!

—J. S.

# Sour Cream Raisin Pie

## OJ's Midtown Restaurant, Gillett
*Owen and Joan Farrell*

Joan serves this heavy custard pie chilled, but a lot of customers like it warm. "It doesn't look as good then because it's still kind of loose, but they want it anyway!" she says. The filling is made in the microwave so Joan can to tend to other tasks at the same time. For more on this see, page 158.

*Pie*
- 1½ cups sugar
- 3 tablespoons cornstarch
- ¾ teaspoon ground cinnamon
- 2 cups sour cream
- 5 egg yolks
- 1¼ cups raisins
- 9- to 9¾-inch baked pie shell

*Meringue*
- 5 egg whites, at room temperature
- scant ½ cup sugar

Heat oven to 375 degrees. Mix sugar, cornstarch, and cinnamon in a bowl. Mix sour cream and egg yolks in a separate, microwave-proof bowl. Add sugar mixture and stir until smooth. Microwave 2 minutes and stir well. Heat 2 minutes again and stir. Continue heating for 1 minute at a time, stirring after each time, until mixture bubbles, turns translucent, and gets thick and glossy. Fold in the raisins. Spread in prepared crust.

To make the meringue, place egg whites in a large, clean mixing bowl and whip with electric beaters at medium speed until foamy. Raise speed to high and continue beating, gradually adding the sugar, until stiff peaks form. Carefully spread meringue over filling, sealing meringue against the edges of the crust. If you'd like, use a knife to create attractive peaks with the meringue. Bake until golden brown, 10–15 minutes. Cool completely. Chill before serving. Makes 8–10 servings. (Note: Learn more about making meringue pie topping on pages 161–163.)

## SOUR CREAM RAISIN PIE FOR
## OFFICIAL WISCONSIN STATE PIE

In May 2005, a Florida lawmaker unsuccessfully petitioned to make key lime the official Florida state pie. It was a repeat of an attempt seventeen years earlier that was killed by a bitter debate over key lime and pecan that squared off southern and northern legislators. I have to side with the southern Floridians who argued that pecan pie was the culinary property of the state of Georgia.

Yankees just may be more sensible when it comes to pie politics. Massachusetts snatched up Boston cream pie—is it a pie or a cake?—as its official dessert in 1996, with Vermont claiming apple in 1999. The Vermont State Pie Act reads in part, "When serving apple pie in Vermont, a 'good faith' effort shall be made to meet one or more of the following conditions: a) with a glass of cold milk, b) with a slice of cheddar cheese weighing a minimum of one-half ounce, c) with a large scoop of vanilla ice cream."

Those Green Mountain legislators sound a lot like dairy-loving Wisconsinites.

All this got me to thinking about an official state pie for Wisconsin. Door County cherry came immediately to mind, but we'd no doubt have a battle on our hands with our neighbors in Michigan's Upper Peninsula defending our right to claim cherry.

Terese suggested apple, but Vermont's already claimed that.

"How about lemon meringue?" she offered. "That's one of the pies Helen Myhre's holding on the cover of the Norske Nook cookbook."

Lemon meringue is a diner favorite with a supporting role in the Oscar-winning film *Million Dollar Baby,* but completely lacking in dairy products as it is, it doesn't say anything about Wisconsin.

"Maybe cream pies in general deserve icon status," Terese suggested. "You know, the whole dairy thing."

The Midwest is without a doubt America's Cream Pie Belt, but my intent is to narrow the field and eliminate Indiana, Nebraska, the Dakotas, and other heartland contenders to the cream pie crown. Banana cream? Chocolate cream? Coconut cream? They're all as common as pie. I'm looking for something a little more obscure, a little more unique, and a lot more Wisconsin.

I submit to you my nomination for Wisconsin's official state pie: sour cream raisin.

Terese is inclined to disagree on the grounds that it is "somewhat obscure . . . maybe not in old-timey cafes, but I can't think of anyone who would name it as a top Wisconsin-wide specialty. I wasn't fully aware of it, except as a lovely old-fashioned specialty, until you came into my life."

Obscure. Lovely old-fashioned specialty. Precisely.

Sour cream raisin, a "specialty of bakers in Minnesota, Wisconsin, and Iowa," is rarely seen outside Midwest dairy country, according to *Roadfood* authors Jane and Michael Stern. (By declaring it Wisconsin's official pie now, we'll beat Iowa and Minnesota to the punch, the way Vermont beat out every other state for apple.) In 1976, the Sterns swooned over the sour cream raisin pie made by Helen Myhre at the Norske Nook. Sixteen years later, the heavy, sweet tanginess lingered in their gastronomic memory. In the 1992 edition of *Roadfood,* the Sterns rhapsodized, "Sour cream raisin . . . is the flavor you must try if you are passing this way only once. Cut into titanic slices, its quivering, cream-sweet ivory custard is clotted with swollen raisins, heaped high with ethereal meringue, and piled into a wafer-thin crust."

Sour cream raisin quickly became the top-selling pie in the Nook's extensive repertoire, with pie lovers driving across the country for a taste of the farm belt favorite. With every bite, Helen's reputation as a pie queen increased. "If folks had told me years ago that I'd own a restaurant and then that *Esquire* magazine would call it 'one of the USA's ten best,' that it'd be featured on *NBC Nightly News* and in the *New York Times,* and that I'd have to teach that crazy David Letterman how to make a pie, I'd have done nothing but run around in circles wondering how I'd ever make that one come about!"

As the gospel of sour cream raisin pie spread, so did Helen's recipe. Since appearing in her cookbook, *Farm Recipes and Food Secrets from the Norske Nook,* it has spread to countless recipe websites and personal blogs. It also appears in the pie maker's tome *Pie,* by Ken Haedrich, who describes the Nook's specialty as "classic dairy country sour cream custard."

Despite the amazing notoriety, Helen has remained farmwife humble and true to her dairyland roots. Her success is all due to Wisconsin's "big, beautiful milk cows [seen] in every direction. They'll be just standin' there, lazily chompin' grass. They're the ones to thank for making this pie, and every other dessert I make, good."

And that pie she made on *Late Night with David Letterman?* None other than sour cream raisin. My vote for Wisconsin's official state pie. Join me at the ballot box, won't you?—J. S.

# Sour Cream Raspberry Pie

## NORSKE NOOK RESTAURANT AND BAKERY, OSSEO
### *Jerry Bechard*

Ask any number of pie lovers to describe what heaven would taste like. The response may very well be, "It tastes like the Norske Nook." The Nook in downtown Osseo became Wisconsin's most celebrated cafe after being featured in the first edition of Jane and Michael Stern's *Roadfood* (1977). Seekers come by the busload for its famous pie, crowding out year-round Wisconsin residents like the host of the popular public radio show *Michael Feldman's Whad'Ya Know?* Quips Feldman, "The only trouble I have with the Norske Nook . . . is getting to it. The crowds are so large they show up in satellite photographs."

It may help Michael to know that the mother lode of pies is now also available at Nook restaurants in Rice Lake and Hayward.

This sour cream raspberry pie is a happy accident. Jerry was cooking two different pies on the stove when the raspberry boiled over into the sour cream and voilà! A huge seller! Served every day, all year long, it is a favorite pie of the Nook's many, many customers.

>     2  cups sour cream
>     2  large egg yolks
>     1  cup sugar
>     2  tablespoons flour
>     1  small box (3 ounces) raspberry gelatin
>     3  cups fresh raspberries or 12 ounces frozen raspberries,
>            thawed
>        9-inch deep-dish or 10-inch regular pie crust, baked
>     2  cups sweetened whipped cream

Mix sour cream and egg yolks in large saucepan until smooth. Stir in sugar and flour until smooth. Cook over medium heat, stirring, until mixture is thick and pudding pulls away from the sides of the pan when tilted. Take care not to let it scorch; stir constantly after it begins to heat up. Remove from heat and stir in dry raspberry gelatin, mix until smooth. Let cool 10 minutes. Gently fold in raspberries. Spread filling in crust. Chill it thoroughly. Dollop each piece with whipped cream before serving, or decorate whole pie before cutting. Makes 8 servings.

# Sour Cream Peach Pie

## STACKER CAFE, CORNELL
*Paula and Ed Jenneman*

For a taste of summer any time of the year, use fresh or frozen, thawed peaches in this deceptively simple single crust pie, baked hot but served cold at the Stacker Cafe. To peel a peach without sacrificing a scrap of sweet flesh, dip it into boiling water for ten to twenty seconds. The skin will slip off easily with a sharp knife.

> 1 cup sugar
> ¼ cup flour
> 1 teaspoon lemon juice
> ⅛ teaspoon salt
> 2 eggs
> 1 teaspoon vanilla extract
> 1 cup sour cream
> 3½ cups peeled, sliced peaches
> ⅛ teaspoon cinnamon
> ⅛ teaspoon nutmeg
> ⅛ teaspoon almond extract
>   10-inch deep-dish pie crust, unbaked

Heat oven to 350 degrees. Mix sugar, flour, lemon juice, and salt. Beat in eggs and vanilla. Stir in sour cream, peaches, cinnamon, nutmeg, and almond extract. Place pie crust on a foil-lined baking sheet. Add filling. The crust will be very full, so carefully transfer to oven and bake until custard is set, 60–70 minutes. Cool completely. You'll get the best flavor when the pie is served at room temperature, but if you want it firmer, chill before cutting. Makes 8 servings.

### PIE IN THE SKY

Need I admit it? I am a pie snob. Only the very best satisfies me. My friends are equally amused and disgusted by the way I approach a piece of pie because I can never just insert the fork and pull away an entire cross section. I first have to study it, pick at it, dissect it, and decipher it before actually deciding whether I'll eat it. To wit:

Starting at the tip, hold a fork in a straight up-and-down position and cut away a small piece. Examine it closely before placing it on the tongue. Swirl it in the mouth, as you would wine in a glass. Savor the heady flavor. If it is fruit pie, try to determine whether the fruit is fresh or frozen. (Don't even bother with pies made from canned filling.) If it is cream pie, search for irregularities in texture, such as clumps of corn starch, hard bits of cooked egg, shards of egg shells, or kernels of unsoftened tapioca. Sometimes more than one bite is required to get a thorough and adequate evaluation.

Next, move on to the crust. Note the texture of the bottom crust where the filling and crust meet. Is it soggy or mushy? This may indicate a pie that has not baked quite long enough, or it may indicate one that has been sitting on the counter past its prime—a day old, perhaps. Let's continue. Is it grainy or sugary? The pie may not have baked at a hot enough temperature, or for too little time, so that the sugar did not melt. Is it pasty or gluey or milky in color? The temperature or length of baking time did not allow the cornstarch, flour, tapioca, or other thickening agent to work properly. The top crust can be affected in the same way, so scrutinize it as well. If the top crust is latticed, the pie maker has gone above and beyond the call of duty. A rhubarb custard pie that is not latticed is improperly dressed.

Next, turn the plate around and examine the back crust and fluted edge. Break off a piece and taste it, paying attention to its flavor. Having grown up in suburbia, I never developed a taste for lard, but I appreciate that it is a preferred ingredient for pie makers because it makes a beautifully flaky crust. (It's all about how the fat molecules adhere to the gluten molecules.) I much prefer the taste of butter-flavored Crisco. A good crust should be flaky and crisp, almost layered like sheets of phyllo dough. The fluted edge should be pretty and even, not so thin as to be delicate but not so thick as to be cord-like. Since this is the part of the crust that can easily be overhandled, there's a danger that it will be tough. It shouldn't be. The fluted edge should be as flaky as the rest of the crust.

If I am satisfied with the pie so far, I eat the entire rest of the piece, crust and all, even the fluted edge. If I am not pleased with the crust but approve of the filling, I will eat only it. I remove the top crust and carefully eat the filling, scraping it off the bottom crust and pushing all of the pastry "skins" into a mound on the back rim of the plate. (After all, a calorie saved is a calorie earned for another piece of pie.) Likewise, if I reject the topping, especially stiff and waxy nondairy whipped topping—I'm all for billowy Cool Whip—I scrape it from the filling and add it to my little rubbish heap.

A few more things. If the fruit in a cream pie is yucky—such as brown bananas or flavorless canned peaches—but the cream is worth eating, I will pick out the fruit. Sometimes the cream isn't worth eating either, and then the entire piece gets rejected unless, of course, the crust and/or meringue is satisfactory, in which case I may eat only that. Sometimes, the egg white meringue topping is the only decent thing on a piece of cream pie or lemon meringue. It should be firm but not sticky or rubbery, a sure sign of day old. It should be high, made with no fewer than three egg whites, with four being ideal. Meringue should accessorize a pie, not overwhelm it; for this reason,

I am not overly endeared to the pompous pompadour known as mile-high meringue made with a veritable henhouse of egg whites. A meringue worth eating should be smooth, with no small chunks of hardened sugar, and shouldn't taste too much of cream of tartar. It should also be lightly browned in a hot oven. And I like the little sugary sweat beads although I can't say exactly why.

Now you understand why my friends are either amused or disgusted, and frequently both.—J. S.

# Raspberry Cherry Streusel Pie

## OJ's Midtown Restaurant, Gillett
### *Owen and Joan Farrell*

There may be pie-makers more famous than Joan, but we doubt there are many more creative. She's a pie inventor, a pie artist.

Part of the daily dozen or so desserts at OJ's are the seasonal pies she schedules every month. "In October, I'll do blueberry and cranberry. We call it Booberry pie. In November, it's maple nut. We call it Maple Fallnut. For January, it's Blueberry Blizzard—a combination of condensed milk, whipped cream, and lemon juice swirled with blueberry pie filling. In summer, there's Triple Berry pie made with cherries, raspberries, and strawberries."

You may get frustrated trying to decide which of her masterpieces to try. But at least one question will be easy to answer. "Would you like that à la mode?" But of course.

> 1/3  **cup sugar**
> 1  **heaping tablespoon flour**
> 2  **cups fresh or frozen and partially thawed raspberries**
> 1  **can (21 ounces) cherry pie filling**
>    **10-inch pie crust, unbaked**
> 1½–2  **cups Brown Sugar Pecan Streusel (recipe below)**

Heat oven to 350 degrees. Mix sugar and flour in large bowl. Gently toss in raspberries until they're coated with the mixture. Gently mix in cherry pie filling. Spread the mixture in the unbaked pie crust. Sprinkle streusel evenly over pie, making sure it reaches to edges of pie so filling won't bubble over the edges as it bakes. Place pie on lined baking sheet. Bake until pie bubbles near the edges and is lightly browned on top, 45–50 minutes. Makes 8–10 servings.

# Brown Sugar Pecan Streusel

## OJ's Midtown Restaurant, Gillett
*Owen and Joan Farrell*

This makes enough streusel for about five or six pies. It freezes beautifully and can be used right from the freezer to top pies. Or make an easy fruit crisp: Toss sugar, honey, or maple syrup with berries, apples, pears, or other fruit (chopped if necessary). Place in a buttered baking dish, cover with a layer of streusel, and bake until bubbly. Serve this for breakfast or dessert, with or without ice cream.

 2 **cups flour**
 2 **cups quick oats**
 2 **cups brown sugar**
 1½ **cups (3 sticks) butter, at room temperature**
 1–2 **cups chopped pecans**

Mix all ingredients together with pastry blender or fork until crumbly. Makes about 9 cups streusel.

# Rhubarb Custard Pie

## LAKEWOOD CAFE, WINTER
*Jill and Larry Petit*

When Jill's customers start bringing in armloads of fresh rhubarb, she knows it's their way of saying they're hungry for this sweet, eggy rhubarb pie. It's been a Lakewood specialty for some forty years, going back to when her two aunts made the first pie using a family recipe. Customers "ask for it if too much time goes by without our having it," Jill says.

Certainly use fresh fruit if you have access to it from a backyard patch or a generous friend. If you're using frozen fruit, Jill advises, "Thaw it out in microwave until it's soft, five minutes at the most—be careful that it doesn't get to the cooked stage." Then drain the juice off before adding it to the filling ingredients. And note, while fruit pies generally bake for 45–60 minutes, a little extra time as needed for this one to prevent the filling from turning out soupy. If the crust starts to brown too much before the filling is done, cover the pie loosely with aluminum foil and finish baking.

Jill makes a hefty 10-inch pie and cuts it into seven ample pieces. We've reduced her recipe to fit a standard 9-inch pie pan used by most home cooks.

> **dough for a double 9-inch pie**
> 2 **eggs**
> 1⅓ **cups sugar**
> 2 **tablespoons milk**
> ¼ **cup flour**
> ¼ **teaspoon nutmeg**
> 3½–4 **cups chopped rhubarb**
> 1½ **tablespoons butter, cut up**
> **additional milk and sugar**

Heat oven to 350 degrees. Roll out two pie crusts and line pie pan with one of them. Whisk eggs, sugar, milk, flour, and nutmeg in large bowl until smooth. Fold in rhubarb. Pour into pie crust and dot with butter pieces. Top with second crust, fold the edges together and crimp to form a decorative edge. Poke holes with a fork in the top crust to allow steam to release while pie is baking. Brush crust with a little milk and sprinkle with sugar. Bake 60–70 minutes. Cool. Serve plain or with ice cream. Makes 8–10 servings.

# Cottage Cheese Raisin Pie

## DIXIE LUNCH, ANTIGO
*Gary "Gus" Ourada and Sue Ourada Stanton*

From Gary and Sue's mother, Georgian, comes this cheesy, subtly sweet pie suitable for breakfast as well as dessert. "My mother makes this pie every Tuesday and has been doing so since 1945 when my parents bought this restaurant. It's her own recipe," Gary proudly tells us.

Gary is known to friends and family as "Gus." When we asked which name he prefers, he answered, "No preference—and I've been called worse!"

> 3 **eggs**
> ¾ **cup sugar**
> 1 **container (24 ounces) cottage cheese (about 2½ cups)**
> ⅓–½ **cup raisins**
> ¼ **teaspoon vanilla extract**
> ⅛ **teaspoon salt**
> **9¾-inch pie crust, unbaked**
> **ground nutmeg**

Heat oven to 375 degrees. Beat eggs and sugar together. Stir in cottage cheese, raisins, vanilla, and salt. Pour into pie crust. Sprinkle surface with nutmeg. Bake until filling is barely set in the middle, 1 to 1½ hours. Cool. Serve at room temperature. Makes 8 servings.

## WE ARE WHAT WE DO

The Ourada family—first Ed and Georgian, then their sons Larry and Gary ("Gus"), and daughter, Sue—has operated the Dixie Lunch in Antigo for more than sixty years, the longest period of family ownership of any cafe in Wisconsin. Long ago, before World War II, before the space race, before the Cold War, before computers, Ed Ourada was working at a local bakery and thought it just might become his lifelong career. But military service intervened, and when he returned to Antigo, he wound up buying a little lunch counter. Two years later, he tore it down and replaced it with the new and improved Dixie Lunch, pausing during the June 13, 1947, grand opening celebration long enough for photos with his brothers and partners, Rudy and George.

The years passed, with the sturdy Formica and chrome furnishings withstanding continuous use and the changing fads in interior decorating. Ed married Georgian and together they raised Larry, who jokes, "I'm sure I was born in the back booth," and Gary and Sue. In 1996, Larry took over the family business and, feeling it was overdue for a remodel, got rid of the 1940s look. When the doors opened after ten days of round-the-clock updating, "the customers loved it, and the business almost doubled." In 2003, Larry sold out to Gary and Sue.

Why has the Ouradas' ownership been so enduring, especially when the average length of cafe ownership rarely exceeds five years? There are many reasons—excellent food, commitment to community, good business sense, family tradition—but foremost, I think, is that the Ouradas regard their business as synonymous with themselves. Running the Dixie Lunch is not what they do. The Dixie Lunch is who they are.

Some cafe owners enter the business on a lark because they have always loved to cook, or because they think it would be fun, or because they want to work for themselves. A few months or a year into it, they are disappointed to discover that the work is harder than they thought, that people are difficult to deal with, or that their idea of good cooking isn't shared by their customers. So the For Sale sign goes up in the window, and one owner's disillusionment is traded in for a new owner's optimism. And the cycle repeats.

But not in Antigo. The photos of Ed, Rudy, and George hanging on the wall attest to that. No less confirmation are Georgian's baked goods, especially her cottage cheese and raisin pie. Served at the Dixie Lunch "since day one," it has an interesting mixture of flavors and textures that reminds me of a slightly chewy cross between buttermilk pie and cheesecake. It is the taste of history, tradition, and the staying power of the Ourada family. It is the taste of the Dixie Lunch.—J. S.

# *Sweet Potato Pie*

## RUSTY ROOSTER CAFE (FORMERLY O'BRIEN'S RESTAURANT), PARDEEVILLE
*Nancy Zarn*

Don't scrimp by using canned yams in this recipe or you'll find yourself wondering just how this pie could be so addictive. Instead, buy fresh yams or sweet potatoes and boil them, or better yet, bake them for a sweeter, more caramel-like flavor.

- 2  **cups mashed sweet potatoes**
- 1  **cup sugar**
- ¼  **cup butter (4 tablespoons), melted**
- 3  **eggs, beaten**
- ¾  **cup evaporated milk**

¼  **teaspoon nutmeg**
   ¼  **teaspoon salt**
      **9- to 9¾-inch pie crust, unbaked**

Heat oven to 425 degrees. Combine mashed sweet potatoes, sugar, and butter. Beat in eggs one at a time. Stir in evaporated milk, nutmeg, and salt until mixture is smooth. Spread in unbaked pie crust. Bake 20 minutes. Reduce heat to 325 degrees and continue baking until pie is barely set (it will jiggle a bit in the very middle), 30–40 minutes longer. If pie crust edges begin to brown too much during the baking, use a pie shield to prevent burning. Cool completely before serving. Makes 8 servings.

## HONEY OF A PIE

At her namesake Pardeeville restaurant, Lisa O'Brien specialized in real, slow-cooked foods that teased customers into coming back again and again. She was always on the lookout for something new to make—and in many cases, her something new was something old. She experimented with old-time midwestern recipes from a yellowed farm cookbook and even dipped into the culinary traditions of other parts of the country.

Luckily, Lisa passed on many of her recipes to Nancy Zarn, who bought the cafe in June 2004 and renamed it Rusty Rooster Cafe. This recipe for sweet potato pie was missed, however. When Nancy learned we'd collected it for the *Cafe Wisconsin Cookbook,* she happily accepted a copy. "It will be a great pie for fall," she said.

Sweet potato pie was featured on the daily specials board the day in 2002 that I dropped in for a visit with Lisa O'Brien. I was surprised to find soul food this far north. "There's a story," Lisa told me. "I had a lady who worked for me from Texas, and she said, 'Honey, there's nothin' better than a sweet potato pie.' So I tried it, and it was good, but nothing is better than a good apple pie."

Apple pie might be all-American, but sweet potato pie is all southern. A Thanksgiving favorite—think of it as a variant of the northerner's pumpkin pie—sweet potato pie is easy and inexpensive to make. Spiff it up the way generations of southerners have done with add-ins such as brandy, bourbon, orange juice, and lemon juice. (Dyed-in-the-wool northerners might try honey or real maple syrup.) Then crown the custard delight with toppings such as Joan Farrell's Brown Sugar Pecan Streusel (see page 181), marsh-mallows puffed in a hot oven, or whipped meringue. À la mode anyone? Try real Wisconsin cream, whipped cream, or ice cream on pie still warm from the oven. Like Lisa's Texas lady, you'll be saying "Honey" and "Y'all" in no time.
—J. S.

# Possum Pie

KNOTTY PINE RESTAURANT, OOSTBURG

*Debbie and Jeff Saueressig*

"We have a lot of possums in this area and this pie is black and white, hence the name," says Debbie. "I always get a laugh out of our customers when they ask me, 'What is possum pie?' I always start by telling them, 'Well, on my way to work this morning . . .'"

Don't use low-fat milk in this pies, as the pudding will fail to firm up properly. For an extra special touch, use a piping bag to pipe the whipped cream onto the chocolate layer in a pretty design or in decorative mounds. Top off your masterpiece with shavings of chocolate.

> 1   package (8 ounces) cream cheese, softened
> ¾   cup powdered sugar
>     8-inch graham cracker pie crust, store-bought or use recipe below
> ¼   cup chopped pecans
>     heaping ⅓ cup instant chocolate pudding (half of a 3.9-ounce box)
>     heaping ¼ cup instant vanilla pudding (half of a 3.4-ounce box)
> 2   cups whole milk
> ¾   teaspoon vanilla extract
> 1–2   cups whipped cream

Mix cream cheese and powdered sugar until smooth. Spread evenly into the bottom of the pie crust. Sprinkle with the pecans. Combine instant puddings, milk, and vanilla extract in a bowl; whisk until smooth and let stand until thickened, about 5 minutes. Spread this over the cream cheese layer in the crust. Spread whipped cream over pudding layer. Chill thoroughly before serving. Makes 6–8 servings.

# Graham Cracker Pie Crust

Graham cracker crust is as easy as pie . . . way easier, actually. Mix 1¼ cups graham cracker crumbs, 3 tablespoons sugar, and 4 tablespoons melted butter, and press the mixture into an 8-inch pie pan. That's it. For a larger size pie pan, use 1½ cups crumbs and an additional tablespoon each of sugar and melted butter. The crust can be chilled, frozen, or baked for 10–15 minutes at 350 degrees.—T. A.

## POSSUM PIE

Debbie Saueressig grew up in Port Washington and moved to Oostburg in the mid-1990s. She began working at the Knotty Pine for its previous owner and then stepped into the ownership role. The transition between owners was nearly seamless, and the loyal regulars didn't miss a beat in their daily rituals. They continue to line up before the official daily opening time of six thirty. The men still gather at the corner table every day between three and three thirty for coffee (which Debbie has waiting for them in full pots). Local artist Edwin Wynveen doesn't miss any of his six to eight visits a day. He comes in for talk and coffee, talk and cherry Coke, talk and pie, including his pie of choice, possum pie.

"Possum pie?" I ask.

Edwin launches into a long discussion about possums, how they're hunted and cooked and eaten in the southern United States. Debbie stands by smiling. Her possum pie includes no primordial marsupials, but is instead a sweet concoction of cream cheese, pecans, and vanilla and chocolate pudding in a graham cracker crust. To be on the safe side (my southern friends have told me about eating "greezy" old possums), I choose banana cream, with a sweet custardy filling made in the microwave and poured into a parchmentlike crust. It was delicious. But next time, I'll try the possum pie.

Edwin wears spotless black pants and a black vest over a crisp white shirt. At first I thought he was an undertaker, but he represents one of Wisconsin's largest nurseries. He speaks quickly and rather haltingly, and I miss about half of what he says. But there is no mistaking his praise for Deborah's cooking. "It's perfect. It's tops."—from *Cafe Wisconsin*

## How to Roll Out and Shape a Pie Crust

Place dough for a 9- to 9³/₄-inch pan on a floured surface. Using a floured rolling pin, roll it out to an 11-inch circle. Use a thin, flat utensil like a spatula to loosen the dough circle from the work surface. Fold the circle in half, transfer it to a pie pan, and carefully unfold it. Gently fit the dough into the pan, folding the overhanging edges to make a top edge. Crimp the edges attractively. One way to do this is to hold a small portion of the top edge between two fingers of one hand, then gently push the dough into a "V" with one finger from the opposite hand. Continue doing this all around the top edge of the pie crust. You can use the crust right away, or, if possible, refrigerate it 30 minutes or longer to let it relax again before filling and/or baking. If you are rolling out—but not immediately using—more than one crust, the additional crust may be wrapped and frozen for future use.

—T. A.

# Hot Water Pie Crust Dough

## Ideal Cafe, Iron River
### *Mary and James "Mac" McBrair*

Mary McBrair's renegade method for making pie dough bucks tradition by using hot water instead of ice water. You won't get the full flakiness of a classic crust here, but you will get an easy-to-mix, easy-to-roll-out dough that bakes into a crumbly textured crust with fine flavor.

Mary says, "This recipe came from the *St. John's Guild Cookbook* published in 1956 that my mother gave me in the early 1970s when I got my first apartment. It wasn't until 2002 that I noticed she had written 'good' near the recipe. Since I've always hated making pie crusts, I thought I'd try it. It's wonderful—easy to make and easy to roll out. This is the only recipe I use for pie crusts now." She also uses it for pasties, chicken pot pies, and other main dish selections.

This makes two crusts, each for a pie pan 9 to 9¾ inches in diameter. (For instructions about rolling out pie dough and prebaking an unfilled crust, see sidebar.) If you don't need to use both crusts, roll out and shape the second one into a pan, wrap it, and freeze it for a future use.

    1   cup lard, cut into small pieces, brought to room
          temperature
    ½   cup boiling water
    3   cups flour
    ½   teaspoon salt
    ½   teaspoon baking powder

Place lard in mixing bowl. Pour boiling water over it. Let stand until lard is mostly melted, 5–10 minutes. Beat until thick and creamy. Whisk flour, salt, and baking powder in a separate bowl. Stir flour mixture into lard just until dough forms; avoid overmixing. Divide the dough into 2 equal portions and shape each into a thick disk. To allow the dough to relax, cover disks or wrap them in plastic wrap, and refrigerate 1 or more hours. Remove dough from the refrigerator and let it soften to room temperature before rolling it out. Makes enough for two 9¾-inch crusts.

## TALK ABOUT CRUST

There are as many ways to prepare pie crusts as there are fillings to put in them. Debates rage about what type of fat is best (lard, butter, shortening, or oil), what to use to cut it into the flour (pastry cutter, two knives, food processor, or your fingers), and how to crimp the edges (plain, fancy, and everything in between). The truth is, no single recipe can relay the way to a perfect crust. You'll need some good advice from experts and the hands-on experience of personal practice. Here are a few tips from seasoned bakers around the state. The practice part is up to you.

**Joan Farrell, OJ's Midtown Restaurant**, Gillett: "The best pie crust is made with lard, but the problem I've had is with its consistency. Really hot summer days, humid days, dry, cold—it all plays out with the pie crust. I make my crust with flour, salt, ice water, and a high-quality shortening similar to Crisco. We wear disposable gloves because the oils from your hands make the crust real tough. The less you play with the dough, the better it is."

**Sherry Rawson, CJ's Cafe**, Blair, no-fail pie crust: "Blend together with a fork one cup flour, $1/2$ cup Crisco, $1/4$ cup ice water, dash of salt. [When they're in the pan,] sprinkle pie crusts with powdered sugar. Bake at 350 degrees 8 to 10 minutes. This is from *Our Savior's Lutheran Church Cookbook* from Whitehall, Wisconsin."

**Mary Davis, M & M Cafe**, Monticello: "I cut shortening and salt into flour with a food processor. I fill a large tub with this pie crust mix and add ice water to about two cups to make one crust. Keep the dough cold and don't overhandle it. Keep a light hand on the rolling pin."

**Jerry Bechard, Norske Nook**, Osseo: "We bake in quantity and use a large mixer to make the dough. We use butter-flavor Crisco because it has the most consistency; lard tends to be inconsistent in fat content. We mix together the Crisco, water, and salt, and always add the flour last—and we always short it, then add more slowly until it's moist to the point of being tacky and has just the right feel. Feel comes from experience. Don't overmix or overwork the dough or it will get tough. Don't be afraid. Making pie crust is fun. Make enough to play and experiment for a couple of days."

**Rosemary Clarke, Rudy's Diner**, Brillion: "Rendered lard makes such a flaky crust, and, of course, it's what grandmas have been using for years. We get our lard from Roehrborn's Meat Market here in Brillion. We mix the lard, vinegar, salt, and water, then add the flour. We get right in the bowl with our hands and mix it literally with our fingers. (We wear gloves.) People tell us, 'This pie tastes just like Grandma's'—even Great-Grandma's now. You have to go back just about that far to find crust made from rendered lard anymore."

## HOW TO BLIND-BAKE AN UNFILLED PIE CRUST

Heat oven to 400 degrees. Gently line the pie crust with aluminum foil, leaving the top edges exposed. Fill the pan with uncooked dried beans or metal pie weights. Bake until edges are light to golden brown, 15–20 minutes. Remove foil and beans. Prick bottom and sides of crust lightly with a fork all over. Continue baking 5–10 minutes. (If crust puffs during this time, prick the puffed portions and gently push the crust back into place.) Cool to room temperature or use immediately, depending on what kind of pie you're making.—T. A.

**Jill Petit, Lakewood Cafe**, Winter: Jill's pie crust recipe is a closely guarded secret, but she did give one part of it away. Asked if she uses lard, she said yes.

**Missy Ramsdell, Little Babe's Cafe**, Mukwonago: "Pillsbury makes a good one."

—T. A.

# Chocolate Cherry Cake Bars

## IDEAL CAFE, IRON RIVER
### *Mary and James "Mac" McBrair*

Cafe cooks find some of their best recipes in newspaper food sections. That's where Mary found this one many years ago. Besides being quick and easy to make, these bars stay moist a long time. Not that they need to, she admits, since it's rare to have leftovers when she bakes them.

*Bars*
1  **box (about 1 pound, 2¼ ounces) devil's food cake mix**
1  **can (21 ounces) cherry pie filling**
1  **teaspoon almond extract**
2  **eggs, beaten**

*Frosting*
1  **cup sugar**
5  **tablespoons butter**
⅓  **cup milk**
1  **cup chocolate chips**

To make bars, heat oven to 350 degrees. Oil or butter a 10-by-15-inch or similarly sized baking pan. Mix dry cake mix, pie filling, almond extract, and eggs by hand until well blended. Spread mixture into prepared pan. Bake until toothpick inserted near center of pan comes out clean, 20–30 minutes.

Meanwhile, prepare frosting. Combine sugar, butter, and milk in saucepan. Bring to boiling, stirring constantly. Remove from heat, add chocolate chips, and stir until frosting is smooth. Spread over baked bars while they are still warm. Cool completely before cutting. Makes 20–30 bars.

## MEXICAN FRIED ICE CREAM

I dropped in at the Greenwood Family Restaurant in Greenwood (sadly, now closed) late on a quiet Wednesday afternoon. When I learned that authentic Mexican food was prepared by owner Ernesto Rodriguez every Saturday, I found myself back for dinner a few days later. My enchilada was immense, so I ate what I could and saved the rest for lunch the next day. Eating frugally always allows room for dessert, so I moved on to Ernesto's deep-fried ice cream, the top-selling dessert on the menu.

Ernesto grew up in Mexico, in the state of Puebla, where he ate fried ice cream as a boy. It's a traditional Mexican treat that he learned to make by watching his mother. There isn't really a recipe, but he was willing to write one down in order to share it. We are very glad he did!

Ernesto takes slightly softened vanilla ice cream and folds in raisins and shredded coconut, shapes it into a tennis-sized ball, and freezes it solid. When the balls are rock hard, he moistens them in beaten eggs, then rolls them in a mixture of crushed cornflakes and cinnamon. Back into the freezer they go, to be pulled out when they're solid again, for a second dipping in the cornflake mixture. Then it's the cold treatment once more, which readies them for the deep-fat fryer. When an order comes in, Ernesto pops a frozen-solid ball into 375-degree fat for 15 seconds. Served with a couple mounds of nondairy whipped topping and a maraschino cherry, the ice cream is crunchy-crusted on the outside and frozen on the inside. The taste, texture, and weirdness of the whole are beguiling.—J.S.

# Ice Cream Drinks
## Koffee Kup, Stoughton
### *Kendall and Trish Gulseth*

Postdinner ice cream drinks are a classic adult dessert at supper clubs around the state. At the Koffee Kup—the only Wisconsin cafe that serves them—the malt machine does double-duty whenever someone orders a Brandy Alexander or a Grasshopper.

For an inexpensive home version of a commercial malt machine, get yourself an immersion blender, a feisty little handheld pureeing contraption perfect for blending ice cream concoctions, soups, and sauces. By moving the whirring blade up and down and throughout the ingredients, you'll achieve the same creamy-thick texture as a malt machine. Home-size stationary blenders and food processors don't do the job quite as well, but if that's all you've got, go for it.

*Brandy Alexander*
**3–4 large scoops vanilla ice cream**
**1 jigger brandy**
**1 jigger crème de cacao**
**chocolate syrup**

Blend the ice cream, brandy, and crème de cacao until smooth with an immersion blender or in a stationary blender or food processor. Transfer mixture to fancy glasses. Drizzle with chocolate syrup. Makes 1 large, 2 medium, or 3 small servings.

*Grasshopper*
**3–4 large scoops vanilla ice cream**
**1 jigger crème de menthe**
**1 jigger crème de cacao**
**whipped cream**

Blend the ice cream, crème de menthe, and crème de cacao until smooth with an immersion blender or in a stationary blender or food processor. Transfer mixture to fancy glasses. Drizzle with chocolate syrup. Makes 1 large, 2 medium, or 3 small servings.

## DESSERT DRINKS IN STOUGHTON

It is becoming increasingly common to find small town cafes with a beer license that allows them to serve Wisconsin's favorite brew along with the ritual Friday night fish fry, but very few cafes have a license for anything stronger than that. Some owners just don't want one. Others can't get one.

The State regulates just how many liquor licenses are available in a given community, so unless a business owner has ten thousand dollars squirreled away to buy a brand new one, he has to be quick on the draw when one is being given up. When Kendall Gulseth, owner of the Koffee Kup in Stoughton, learned that the local Pizza Hut was surrendering its liquor license, he marched right down to city hall and applied for it. "I didn't want some competing restaurant moving into town," he explains.

Kendall started out slowly by adding a few common brands of canned and bottled beer. But once his regular customers got used to that, they began making requests for their favorite wine and mixed drinks. Lined up behind the counter near the mouth-watering Koffee Kup Treats board, you'll find the award-winning Prairie Fumé from Wisconsin's own Wollersheim Winery alongside brandy, gin, whiskey, and Bailey's Irish Cream.

One winter night, a well-fed and contented gent sighed, "I'd sure like a Brandy Alexander." He instructed the staff on how to make one using vanilla ice cream and the nearby malt machine, and a new Koffee Kup treat was born. The Grasshopper wasn't far behind. Think of them as specialty milkshakes for the over-twenty-one crowd.—J. S.

# *Further Reading*

Adams, Marcia. *Cooking from Quilt Country: Hearty Recipes from Amish and Mennonite Kitchens.* New York: Clarkson N. Potter, 1989.

Allen, Terese. *Bountiful Wisconsin: 110 Favorite Recipes.* Black Earth, WI: Trails Books, 2000.

———. *Fresh Market Wisconsin: Recipes, Resources and Stories Celebrating Farm Markets and Roadside Stands.* Amherst, WI: Amherst Press, 1993.

———. *Wisconsin Food Festivals: Good Food, Good Folks, and Good Fun at Community Celebrations.* Amherst, WI: Amherst Press, 1995.

———. *Wisconsin's Hometown Flavors: A Cook's Tour of Butcher Shops, Bakeries, Cheese Factories and Other Specialty Markets.* 2nd ed. Black Earth, WI: Trails Books, 2003.

Apple, R. W., Jr. "The Smoky Trail to a Great Bacon." In *Best Food Writing 2000.* Edited by Holly Hughes. New York: Marlowe, 2000.

Bauer, Joan. *Hope Was Here.* New York: Scholastic, 2000.

Baumann, Richard J. *Foods That Made Wisconsin Famous: 150 Great Recipes.* Madison, WI: Wisconsin Trails, 1999.

Colwin, Laurie. *More Home Cooking: A Writer Returns to the Kitchen.* New York: Harper Perennial, 2000.

Cook, Marshall. *Murder Over Easy.* Madison, WI: Bleak House Books, 2003.

Edge, John T. *Apple Pie: An American Story.* New York: Putnam, 2004.

———. *Donuts: An American Passion.* New York: Putnam, 2006.

———. *Fried Chicken: An American Story.* New York: Putnam, 2004.

———. *Hamburgers and Fries: An American Story.* New York: Putnam, 2005.

Fertig, Judith M. *Prairie Home Cooking: 400 Recipes That Celebrate the Bountiful Harvests, Creative Cooks, and Comforting Foods of the American Heartland.* Boston: Harvard Common Press, 1999.

Fussell, Betty. *I Hear America Cooking.* New York: Viking, 1986.

Gisslen, Wayne. *Professional Cooking.* 5th ed. New York: John Wiley, 2003.

Hachten, Harva. *The Flavor of Wisconsin: An Informal History of Food and Eating in the Badger State, Together with 400 Recipes.* Madison: State Historical Society of Wisconsin, 1981.

Hagen, Jeff. *Fry Me to the Moon.* Madison, WI: Prairie Oak Press, 1999.

Heat-Moon, William Least. *Blue Highways: A Journey into America.* Boston: Atlantic/Little Brown, 1982.

Hubbell, Sue. "The Great American Pie Expedition." In *Far-Flung Hubbell,* 3–30. New York: Random House, 1995.

Kaplan, Anne R., Marjorie A. Hoover, and Willard B. Moore. *The Minnesota Ethnic Food Book.* St. Paul: Minnesota Historical Society Press, 1986.

LeDraoulec, Pascale. *American Pie: Slices of Life (and Pie) from America's Back Roads.* New York: Harper Collins, 2002.

Lockwood, William G., and Yvonne R. Lockwood. "Pasties in Michigan's Upper Peninsula." In *The Taste of American Place,* 21–36. Edited by Barbara G. Shortridge and James R. Shortridge. Lanham, MD: Rowman and Littlefield, 1998.

Mariani, John. *America Eats Out: An Illustrated History of Restaurants, Taverns, Coffee Shops, Speakeasies, and Other Establishments That Have Fed Us for 350 Years.* New York: William Morrow, 1991.

McGee, Harold. *On Food and Cooking: The Science and Lore of the Kitchen.* New York: Scribner, 1984 and 2004.

*Michael Feldman's Whad'Ya Know?* http://www.notmuch.com.

Myhre, Helen, and Mona Vold. *Farm Recipes and Food Secrets from the Norske Nook.* Madison: University of Wisconsin Press, 2001.

Parsons, Russ. *How to Read a French Fry: And Other Stories of Intriguing Kitchen Science.* New York: Houghton Mifflin, 2000.

Rombauer, Irma S., Marion Rombauer Becker, and Ethan Becker. *The All New, All Purpose Joy of Cooking.* New York: Scribner's, 1997.

Stern, Jane, and Michael Stern. *Blue Plate Specials and Blue Ribbon Chefs.* New York: Liebhar-Friedman Books, 2001.

———. *Chili Nation.* New York: Broadway Books, 1999.

———. *Roadfood.* 6th ed. New York: Broadway Books, 2005. First published 1977 by Random House.

———. *A Taste of America.* Kansas City and New York: Andrews and McMeel, 1988.

Stuttgen, Joanne Raetz. *Cafe Wisconsin: A Guide to Wisconsin's Down-Home Cafes.* 2nd ed. Madison: University of Wisconsin Press, 2004. First published 1993 by NorthWord Press.

Thorne, John, and Matt Lewis Thorne. *Serious Pig: An American Cook in Search of His Roots.* New York: North Point Press, 1996.

Villas, James. *American Taste: A Celebration of Gastronomy Coast-to-Coast.* New York: Lyons and Burford, 1982.

*Wisconsin Extension Homemakers Cookbook, 1940–1990.* Printed by Arcadia News-Leader, 1990.

# Index